Rona Shapiro

P9-DEE-367

MEMOIRS

MEMOIRS

by

Ben Gold

WILLIAM HOWARD PUBLISHERS
New York

Library of Congress Catalog Card No: 84-25300

ISBN 0-9614288-0-5

Contents

Sadie and Ben Gold, photographed after the latter's release from jail following his arrest and beating during the 1932 Hunger March to Washington.

A Clarification

It is not my intent to write the history of the Fur and Leather Workers' Union. More than thirty years ago, Dr. Philip S. Foner wrote that history, and his book will, without any doubt, occupy a most important place in the history of the American labor movement.

Dr. Foner evidently knew and understood the need for a history of the Fur and Leather Workers' Union. That is why he did so much research and gathered such clear and incontrovertible evidence to prove that all that he wrote in his book and everything he told about the history of the Union was factual. The documents and the proofs are all there in his book.

In my memoirs, I intend to briefly jot down my connections with the historic struggle of the heroic fur workers who, in spite of terrible difficulties, persecutions and indescribable suffering, refused to give up their righteous battle until their victory over their conscienceless enemies was assured.

I do not intend to write about my personal problems such as, for example, how many times I was arrested, or about my "vacation" in jail, or about the policemen's clubs and the gangsters' blackjacks that made a "deep impression" on me. I will note only my connections with the history of the struggle of the courageous workers, and, of course, my deep joy over their wonderful achievements.

I want to express my gratitude to another member of the Foner family, Henry, who guided my manuscript from the original Yiddish into English, with the help of the skillful translation of Mrs. Shulamith Friedman, into the form in which you now read it.

Ben Gold

Prologue

My First Love

I was already a big fellow entering my sixteenth year and already a fur operator. But I could not find a job. It was a bad year, and many fur workers were unemployed, Many of them also had to work in an additional trade in order to make a living. So did I.

A skilled straw-hat operator who lived in a four-room apartment taught me the trade. In his bedroom was a machine, and there I worked two hours every day. After two weeks, Louis told me that I already knew the trade and should look for a job. I paid him ten dollars, thanked him for teaching me the trade, and went to look for a job.

The straw-hat season was in full swing. After a few days of job hunting, I noticed a cardboard sign on the wall of a building on Bond Street: "Straw-hat operator wanted." I ran to the elevator, got off at the fourth floor and found myself standing in the shop. I didn't move. I was a little confused and a little frightened. The shop was very long, narrow and dark. The windows facing the front and the windows facing the back yard were not able to supply sufficient light; in the center of the shop, large cartons were piled one on top of the other. Two long rows of machines, facing each other, filled the shop with their deafening buzzing. The air smelled dank and musty.

I wanted to run out of that prison, but I needed a job. Everyone in my family was unemployed. So I knocked on the little office window not far from the elevator door. A young girl opened the window, and I mumbled: "An operator; you need an operator?" She replied that she would talk to Carmela, the forelady, who was at the first machine, and she closed the window. Like a condemned person, I walked slowly to the first machine where a well-rounded female body occupied the chair, her head bent down to the machine which kept running and buzzing without a stop; a coal-black braid hung over her shoulder. "Carmela," I whispered, but the buzz of the machine swallowed my voice. "Carmela," I called again with a stronger voice. Carmela's machine died; her round, full face turned to me, her large, black eyes looked at me, and a soft, friendly voice quietly asked: "Yes?" I answered: "I am the operator." Her soft, warm eyes measured me from head to toe, and she asked me how old I was. I replied, "Sixteen years."

"Follow me," she said. "Here," she pointed with her hand, "hang up your jacket," and then we walked to the last unoccupied machine near the window facing the yard. On the stand of the machine was a bundle of hemp (fancy straw) and a cement hat form. "Here," Carmela said, and walked back to her machine.

I sat down on the chair to work, but what happened to my hands? Time and again, my hands tried to make the "tip," but they were not successful. The tip came out crippled and couldn't serve the purpose. I couldn't understand what had happened. In Louis' bedroom on Norfolk Street, my hands had created dozens of perfect "tips," and here, my hands couldn't produce even one good "tip." In desperation, I decided to walk out of the shop and to return to my school on Norfolk Street.

But suddenly, Carmela stopped near my machine and asked me whether anything was wrong with the machine. I did not answer. I got off the chair; she sat down and — one — two — the tip was born, the machine was humming and the hat was growing. She asked me if this was my first job.

"Yes," I answered.

"Have you a family?"

"Yes," I said.

"Are you the oldest?"

"No. I am one of nine children."

"Are they working?"

"No, they are all unemployed."

"Carmela, Carmela," a voice filled the shop. A tall, well-dressed, handsome young man approached us and in a loud voice said, "Carmela, I am looking for you all over the shop. Why are you losing time with him?" There are plenty of good operators looking for jobs! Send him away!"

"Bob! A family of nine children, all unemployed! I will not send him away!" Carmela cried out in a resentful, determined, ringing voice.

The man, obviously the boss, said in a soft voice: "Well, then give him cheaper straw," and like a beaten man, he marched back to his office.

Carmela brought a bundle of broad, white straw, put it on the stand of the machine, told me to try this straw, and walked back to her machine.

A miracle! My hands did exactly as my mind ordered them to do, and without any effort, created a perfect "tip." My machine was galloping and singing, the crown was done, the brim was done and the hat was done, and a charming pillar of hats, one on top of the other, was growing.

Six o'clock. All the machines stopped. A deafening silence filled the shop. The operators rushed to the elevator; some, too impatient to wait for the elevator, ran down the stairs. Carmela told me to come to work the next day. I ran down the stairs.

In the street, I stopped for a while near the building. How vast the outside is! And how light! Slowly, I walk on the sidewalk on my way home. The sidewalk is crowded with workers on their way home from work. I know that they talk loud, and that their laughter is ringing. I have heard them many times, but that day I don't see their faces. I don't hear the voices. Neither do I hear the usual noise of the automobiles and trucks in the street. I only see Carmela's full, round face and her beautiful, big, black eyes. I only hear Carmels's ringing outcry: "B-o-b! Nine children in the family! All unemployed!" And I wonder, "Why is she concerned about my family? She does not know my family — she never met them." And I hear Carmela's challenging, resentful, deter-mined voice: "I will not send him away!"

Why? Why was she fighting for me and my family, risking her position as forelady, and maybe even losing her job, too? I decided there is only one answer. Carmela is one of the great people who are blessed with exceptionally deep fellings that overwhelm them with irresistible desires to help needy people, even at the expense of their own well-being. Yes, yes, indeed, this is the only correct and true explanation of Carmela's attitude toward me, and her daring to contra-dict her boss. I felt proud and fortunate, not only because I had gotten a job that I so badly needed, but because I was privileged to meet such a beautiful personality as Carmela and to work in the same shop with her tomorrow and other tomorrows.

I decided not to tell anybody what happened to me. No one would believe me; my friends would laugh at me. They would say that such people don't exist and that I had invented the whole story. No, I would not tell anyone about Carmela.

Every day I went to work as if I were going to a party. Carmela's attitude toward the workers was like the attitude of a devoted sister toward her brothers. She never raised her voice to a worker. She settled any dispute among workers. My respect for her grew daily. I loved her.

For five weeks I worked in that straw-hat shop. Every week I earned more that I had earned in a month as a fur operator. When Carmela told me that there was no more work, that the season had ended, I told her that I would never forget her and what she had done for me. Her beautiful black eyes opened wide and sparkled; a broad smile spread over her face, and she almost sang out that that was her great pleasure.

Years, stormy years gathered. Complicated problems hailed on me. Enemies surrounded me and fired their poisonous arrows at me. But also pleasure and joy warmed and encouraged me. My shrunken youth was swallowed by a sudden adolescence which saddled me with serious responsibilities that kept me busy. But Carmela never moved out of my memory. The thought that I was indebted to her and that I would never be able to repay my debt to her did not let me rest. Where could I find her. Where was she?

It is no secret that in the course of a man's life, it sometimes happens that an unexpected, unbelievable, thrilling event suddenly surprises him. Because it is impossible to explain such a sudden occurrence, we say that a "miracle" happened, even though we don't believe in miracles. Yet what happened to me sounds like a miracle, which was the result of a series of coincidences created by some unknown power according to a well worked-out, detailed plan.

In 1936, the left leaders of the Furriers Union were faced with difficult and highly responsible organizational activities. In 1935, both unions, the right and the left, had finally united into one union under left leadership. We mobilized all our forces to correct the damage that the ten-year desperate struggle had caused. The fight to organize the open shops, the sweatshops, the contracting shops, was the contest of decisive importance and kept everyone in the union busy from early morning to late in the evening. I was the manager of the union.

One beautiful day, Jack Schneider, one of the beloved union leaders, came into my office. With him also came a medium-built but quite heavy woman. Her thick, shining gray hair added charm to her round face. Suddenly, what an astonishment! It was Carmela! Jack and Carmela sat down in the chairs near my desk, facing me. I quickly lit a cigarette to pacify my nerves, but just as quickly, I had to put it out because my hand was suddenly shaking.

Jack spoke: "This lady, Mrs. Carmela Biacci, is Freddie's mother." I took a quick look at Carmela and met her big, black, penetrating eyes. Jack continued: "She wants to talk to the union chief. Ben, you know what it's all about. We declared a strike against the shop of Binder and Company, and within two weeks, the firm was out of business. With the exception of Freddie, all the other workers were placed in shops where they receive union wages. It is difficult to find a job for him because he is not a good operator yet. For $18 a week, he was a shipping clerk, a shop cleaner, and a few hours a day, he was learning to become an operator, but as you know, it takes time to become a mink operator."

"I had to come to you," Carmela said quietly in a voice that expressed deep concern. "My husband is very ill with a stroke. I have to take care of him and of my other two children, who are still in school. When my husband was well and worked in the shop, we saved a few dollars, but very little remains. Freddie's weekly earnings were a great help. My son, Freddie is very modest. He has great respect for Jack. But he needs a job! I had to come to you...." The shining light of her beautiful eyes was extinguished, her voice became low and sad.

I knew that it was almost impossible for the union to find a job for Freddie because he was not yet a mechanic. I asked Jack where Freddie's last job was. He informed me that Moishe, the foreman at "Blank & Co.," who was my friend, had agreed to employ Freddie, but not at this time because they had a large order of high-priced mink coats, and Freddie would have to wait a few weeks when the firm would be producing the cheaper mink coats.

I asked Jack to call Moishe and tell him that I wanted to talk to him; it did not take long to get the foreman on the phone, and I spoke to my old union friend, Moishe, who was a most devoted, progressive union member.

I talked to him loudly so that Jack and Carmela could hear the conversation. "Moishe, have you time to talk to me?" Moishe answered that he could talk to me until the shop closed.

"Moishe," I said, "I want to ask a favor of you about something that concerns me very much. Last week, Jack brought up to you a young worker who is only a half-mechanic and you employed him only one day. Moishe, I ask you to please take him into your shop, put him to work and teach him to become a mechanic."

Moishe replied: "Ben, send him up to work tomorrow morning." "How much will you pay him?" I asked, and Moishe answered that he would pay him $40 a week the first two weeks, and after that I should leave it to him. I thanked Moishe and the conversation ended.

I then said to Carmela and Jack: "You heard my conversation with the foreman of that shop. Freddie will go to work tomorrow. He will get $40 a week, and after two weeks, I am sure he will get an increase."

Carmela's big, black eyes grew bigger and sparkled. Her face was shining and she suddenly looked younger.

"And now, Carmela," I said, "If you want, the union will give you a small loan which you can repay when you are able to."

"No, no," Carmela replied. "I will never forget what you did for my family. I never knew such nice people exist in our world." I jumped up from my chair as she stretched out her arm to shake my hand. I wanted to say something, but she embraced me and shut my lips with a hearty kiss.

This was no surprise to Jack. Very often, workers embraced and kissed him, too, to express their admiration and love for him. But Jack did not know of my deep joy that I had finally paid my great debt to her.

Jack was always full of joy when I used my influence and succeeded in helping a worker and his needy family. He did not know that when Carmela helped me when my family was in need, she was not a leader of workers. She was an ordinary worker, a human being blessed with deep human feelings, overwhelmed with a determined desire to do her duty as a human being to help the needy.

And Jack did not know that somewhere in my very minute storage-memory, Carmela's name was engraved in golden letters and that my admiration and love for her was never exstinguished. Her kiss was my joy. My Carmela!

Meyer London

Meyer London was one of the outstanding leaders of the American Socialist Party. He was also the attorney for many trade unions. I attended a number of mass meetings at which he was the main speaker, but I never met him personally until the year 1919.

Under the incompetent and corrupt so-called "Socialist" leadership of the Furriers' Union, the union became constantly weaker; the workers distrusted and resented these union leaders, but they could do nothing about it. In 1919, I was elected to the Joint Board of the union, which consisted of about twenty elected workers who were the authoritative leaders of the union. The majority of the delegates, who were devoted supporters of the paid union officers, were elected and re-elected to the Joint Board year after year.

The Joint Board meetings were held every Tuesday evening. I was astonished, and at times actually shocked, by the attitude of the Joint Board toward the workers and by the unjust decisions made by the Board with respect to workers' problems. There were a few delegates who voted against these incorrect decisions of the Board, but they were a small minority and were always outvoted in their efforts to correct decisions that were not in favor of the workers. It did not take long before I was involved in sharp battles with the union leaders over the manner in which they handled workers' problems. Every time a worker came to the Board to appeal the decision of a business agent and submitted facts to support his appeal, the majority of the Board would, as usual reject his appeal, and a battle would be on between me and the majority of delegates of the Board, lasting for hours. Not all the battles were lost. If I relate here briefly one example, the reader will have a clear idea of the value of my stubborn battles.

One Tuesday evening, a worker came to the Joint Board and stated his complaint: He was in need of a job and was lucky to get one that paid $65 a week, but the boss kept back $15 each week as a guarantee that he would not leave his job. After ten weeks, he found a better job with higher wages. He asked his boss to return the $15 that he had held back from his wages. The boss refused. The worker complained to the business agent, but he lost his case and he wanted the Board to help him.

The business agent who had handled this worker's complaint reported to the Board that the firm's books showed that the worker had received his full wages of $65 each week for all the ten weeks he had worked there. A motion was immediately made to reject the worker's complaint, and the battle started. I demanded that a committee of the Joint Board investigate this case, because it was impossible for a worker to invent such a story. A half-dozen of the administration's supporters attacked me in their speeches. I replied, and finally, when the debate reached a point of wild accusations, I was threatened with expulsion from the Joint Board. I replied that I would bring the case to an impartial committee and would submit the unimpeachable facts which I knew.

At this point, the business agent who handled his case spoke. My threat to bring the matter to an impartial committee must have frightened him. He admitted that he had not seen the firm's books, that there was a standing, honorable agreement between him and the representative of the bosses' association, with whom he had worked for a long time, that if one examined the books of a firm, the other would accept his findings. This time, the representative of the bosses' association had examined the books, and the business agent believed him when he told him that the boss had paid the worker his full wages for all the ten weeks.

This explanation by the business agent petrified all the delegates of the Joint Board. The chairman adjourned the meeting.

Several days later, I sat in a small hall in the "Forward" building, where I was to answer charges preferred against me by Morris Kaufman, the manager of the union. The judges invited by Mr. Kaufman, without my consent, were Feinberg, the manager of the Cloakmakers' Union, and Meyer London. Thus, I met London personally for the first time.

In his speech, Kaufman claimed that I, as an elected delegate to the Joint Board, disrupted the Board meetings with my provocative speeches and deprived the delegates of time for the constructive problems of the union. The procedure, Kaufman said, was that workers who were dissatisfied with the settlements of their complaints against their bosses by their business agents would bring their cases to the Joint Board. "To delegate Gold," said Kaufman, "every worker is right, and the business agents are wrong and incapable of defending the interest of the workers. Before the Board expels him, it is possible that he might correct his conduct if you — Feinberg and Meyer London — use your influence and correct his manners."

Feinberg, who acted as chairman, did not notice my raised hand indicating that I wanted to say something in my defense. He began to deliver a lecture — that I was too young and didn't have enough experience to judge experienced and tested leaders who used all their abilities to defend the interests of the workers and to solve the most complicated union problems. And he wanted me to know that in the labor movement, one didn't have to pray in two pairs of phylacteries ("tfillen")! He also wanted me to know that not all workers were saints. In every union, he said, there were many who sinned against God and against the union; these workers considered the union their enemy and had to be dealt with in a manner they deserved. "Ben Gold," he raised his voice, "to criticize is easier than to build! If you want to be holier than the Pope, lock yourself up in a monastery!"

Suddenly, Meyer London, without waiting for the chairman to introduce him, jumped up on the low platform. His voice rang through the hall. He said: "Well, Ben, you heard what Feinberg told you. Now listen to what I tell you. In the labor movement, it *is* necessary to pray in two pairs of phylacteries! Unfortunately, some union leaders pray very often with their friends at card tables! And I tell you the workers *are* saints! In the shops, under the whips of the foremen, they strain all their strength and energy to produce more and more. They are exploited and robbed by the bosses. They live in filthy old apartments. Their lean wages are not enough to feed their wives and children, and they become ill with fear and worry over the next day. Yes, they are saints because they carry such a heavy and painful yoke! Our friend certainly knows that the wicked live in luxury, and the saints live in need. Even the old sages long ago recognized this terrible truth. Of course, not all workers are perfect union members, but that is not their fault. They are not class-conscious. We have to teach them with patience and friendship, and not condemn them!"

He stretched out his arm and pointed his finger at me as he said: "I tell you, Ben Gold, defend and protect workers! Always be on the side of the wronged. Avoid quarrels with the Joint Board members, but differences of opinion — honest, principled differences — are no danger for trade unions. Often, they are a necessity. And remember, Ben, that the most sacred principle is to fight for the well-being of the workers.

I was elated when I left the hall. I was enthused and inspired by London's speech. A wave of respect for and confidence in Meyer London engulfed me. I liked the way he whipped the two union leaders and separated himself from them. With principles and as a human being — a true Socialist!

1920

In 1920, I met Meyer London again. That year, the war prosperity ended and economic conditions in the country became critical. Unemployment increased daily. Thousands of fur workers were unemployed. The union called a conference with the bosses' representatives and appealed to them to employ the needy, jobless workers for two or three days a week. The bosses replied that they worried about their business, and the union should worry about its needy, unemployed workers. The manager of the union asked the bosses what the union could do for the unemployed workers, and Mr. Samuels, the president of the bosses' association, answered: "Drown them!" Workers in the shops demanded equal division of work; the bosses refused and shop strikes broke out. The bosses declared a lock-out. The union was forced to call a general strike.

It is impossible to describe briefly the incompetence, the dishonesty, and the meanness of the strike leaders, or the suffering of the helpless, desperate strikers.

The cruel, brutal bosses hired gangsters to deliver and protect their scabs and to drive the pickets away from the buildings where their shops were located. The General Picketing Committee, which was composed of the strong-arm boys of the union's Organization Committee, did not have the courage to protect the strikers from the bosses' gangsters, and the union leaders hired an outside gang to stop the bosses' gangsters from beating up the strikers. Within one week, both gangs — the union's gang and the bosses' gang — became partners, and together, they protected the scabs.

In the course of three months, about three hundred independent employers settled with the union, but many of them worked for the firms whose workers were on strike. When strikers interfered with the shipping clerks who delivered the merchandise from the settled shops to the shops on strike, they were beaten up by the union gangsters. When strikers came to the union in the evening to complain to the General Strike Committee — the leaders of the strike — they, too, were beaten up.

Hungry, angry, desperate, helpless and hopeless, many strikers returned to work. The strikers appealed to the leaders of the left-wing opposition for help, but the left-wing leaders were helpless. We finally decided that I should go to Meyer London and ask for his help. I called London, and he told me to come to his office. He sat at his desk and I sat facing him. I talked for almost an hour. The telephone didn't ring, no one knocked at the door, and he did not interrupt me — not even once.

When I had finished describing the tragic situation of the strike, he asked me what I was doing about the strike. I told him that Kaufman had appointed me hall chairman of a small hall and that I had chosen six of my friends for the Hall Committee; that I had nothing to do with the General Picketing Committee; that instead I had chosen fifteen young, energetic, intelligent reliable strikers, and they were doing an excellent job in keeping scabs out of the shops in the hall where I was chairman; and that every week, two or three hundred strikers from my hall marched in front of the large shops. Meyer London thanked me and I left his office without knowing whether he would do anything to help.

But suddenly, unexpectedly, London appeared the following Tuesday evening at the meeting of the General Strike Committee and stayed until the meeting was adjourned. And he came to the next meeting of the committee. Then he called a conference of the leaders of the needle trades unions and appealed to them to assist the strike, but those union leaders knew that the strike could not be won. They argued that the seven-month strike, with an army of scabs and demoralization of the strikers, could not be saved.

The strike fell apart. The workers of the largest shops returned to work. The gangsters who worked for the union disappeared; they were no longer needed. The workers in the settled shops stopped paying their weekly strike tax. The union was impoverished. The outside gangsters were fired. Only the union's Organization Committee — the strong-arm boys — were still useful.

Meyer London met with the lawyer of the bosses' association about settling the strike. The lawyer told him that the association leaders considered it below their dignity to deal with a degenerate, underworld union.

London contacted the well-known, respected and influential Dr. Judah L. Magnes, who was the Impartial Chairman of the Conference Committee of the union and the bosses' representatives. Dr. Paul Abelson was the secretary. At the call of Dr. Magnes, the association leaders agreed to come to a conference with the union, on the condition that none of the leaders of the union would be on the union committee. At the conference, Dr. Magnes appealed to the bosses' representatives to settle with the union in the name of justice and the sacred ideals of mankind. But the bosses were not impressed; they continued their determined arguments that the union had nearly ruined the industry, and that they wanted nothing to do with the union.

In a polite manner, Dr. Magnes opened up an offensive against the stubborn leaders of the bosses. "Gentlemen," he said, "the union is very weak, but it will not disappear! Workers need a union! They must have a union! I assure you that soon the ranks of the workers will be united, under more capable leadership. You suffered losses because of the depression. You suffered still more losses because of the strike. The economic situation in the country is beginning to improve, and just when you will begin to make up your losses, it is not excluded that new, capable and experienced union leaders will call shop strikes, just when the season will be in full swing. Do you want to ruin another season? As practical businessmen, you must realize that it is in your interest to settle with the union now and prevent shop strikes, and maybe even a general strike. Settle the strike! It is in the interest of the workers, but much more in your interest because you've got much more to lose."

The strike was settled! Meyer London was elated. We knew that he had contributed a great deal to settling the strike and saving the union. My respect for London rose still higher.

1922

The biennial convention of the International Fur Workers' Union was held in May, 1922 in Philadelphia. Kaufman, who was the manager of the New York union and also president of the International, had been driven out of his manager's position in the 1921 elections, after the disastrous strike. He had then moved into the office of the International Union as its president and had taken with him his co-workers who served him loyally when he was manager of the union and led the tragic 1920 strike. President Kaufman's paid organizers represented, as delegates, a number of local unions which existed only on paper.

Meyer London came to the convention. Sharp disagreements developed between the left-wing and the Kaufman right-wing delegates about the problems of the union. A very heated and sharp debate developed over a resolution introduced by President Kaufman's supporters, to condemn the Bolshevik dictators of Soviet Russia and demanding that the jailed Socialists, who, they claimed, had been falsely accused of counter-revolutionary activities, be freed.

Meyer London was the last speaker on that resolution. With a voice full of protest and resentment, he fired questions at the delegates: "What do you know about the Russian revolution? What do you understand about the Russian revolution?" And he continued: "I want you to know that the greatest general strike in the history of civilized mankind broke out in Russia, and those who fight against this general strike are scabs! Scabs! Why do you make such a hullabaloo about the mistakes committed by the leaders of the Russian revolution? Don't you make any mistakes when you have a general strike? God Almighty!

"There in Russia, they are surrounded by internal enemies who are supplied with weapons by the outside enemies. In addition to the counter-revolutionary gangs of murderers and pogrom-makers, the awakened Russian people are suffering hunger and sickness, and you sit here, well-fed and happy with your fortunate positions, and you are judging the leaders of the Russian revolution. With all their strength, they battle for the sacred ideals to free the millions of peasants from slavery, from the land owners and the rich rulers! They fight to free the workers from exploitation and oppression! They fight for liberty, for Socialism!

"Are you really so naive as to believe that Lenin will be frightened by your resolution and will submit to your demands? Your job at the convention is to unite your split ranks and to strengthen your union in order to be able to defend the interests of the workers, instead of wasting time and energy condemning the leaders of the Russian revolution. They have enough enemies without you! And I tell you that their enemies are also your enemies!"

The majority of the delegates applauded him, but the resolution was approved.

I was almost certain that London would withdraw from the Socialist Party, would disassociate himself from the corrupt Socialist leaders, and would raise his powerful voice against the corrupt and degenerate union leaders and become the respected and beloved leader of the vast masses of workers. But I was wrong....He did not leave the Socialist Party. He continued his close comradeship with the leaders of the Party, whom he rightly considered hypocrites, and he remained indifferent about the corrupt union leaders. Why? Who knows? Didn't his conscience trouble him that he had betrayed his sacred ideals? Or did he lose his conscience? Who can tell?

Zuckerman Under Charges

When the 1925 agreement between the union and the bosses' association was about to expire, and a strike was inevitable because the bosses had rejected the demands of the union, I was occupied, in addition to my daily activities, with preparations for the strike apparatus. I had a list of names of devoted union members from which I had to choose, according to their qualifications, the various committees. Each committee was responsible for its assigned task.

To begin with, I had to choose the tested, experienced and able active union members for the General Strike Committee — the leaders of the strike; then the law committee, the settlement and control committee, the Hall chairmen and the Hall committees, a Women's Committee, and a General Picketing Committee of several hundred of the most class-conscious union members. In addition, I had to work out the strike budget.

One morning, someone knocked on the little window of my office. It was a Mr. B. J. Zuckerman, the labor editor of the daily Jewish newspaper, *The Day*, who wished to speak to me. *The Day* was known as the *Tammany Day*. I explained that I was too busy to talk to him. Besides, *The Day* did not represent the workers. Our newspapers — the papers that represented the workers — were the *Morning Freiheit* and the *Daily Worker*.

At about ten o'clock the next morning, Mr. Zuckerman came again, for the same purpose, and he received the same answer. That same afternoon, someone gave me a copy of *The Day* and called my attention to an article written by Zuckerman, in which he wrote that he had had a conversation with Mr. Samuels, the president of the employers' association, about the conflict between the bosses and the union, and that he, Zuckerman, was convinced that the union demands were just, that the bosses' profits increased every year, and that it was fair and just that the workers' working and living conditions should be improved. When Mr. Zuckerman again knocked on the little window of my office, I opened the door and invited him in. It was about ten o'clock in the morning when we started our conversation. Eleven o'clock, twelve o'clock, and I was still talking to the very pleasant Mr. Zuckerman.

As usual, at about fifteen or twenty minutes after twelve, workers crowded into my office with their various complaints against their employers. Mr. Zuckerman moved into a corner of the office, listened attentively and observed what was going on. At about one o'clock, when the workers left to rush back to their shops, the business agents came in with their various complicated problems.

When I got through with the business agents, I invited Mr. Zuckerman to have lunch with me. Our conversation in the restaurant became even more interesting.

When the strike broke out, Mr. Zuckerman came to the picket line every day, and from the picket line, he came to the union. He never missed a mass meeting or a shop chairmen's meeting. His daily reports about the strike, which he wrote in *The Day*, were true and correct. He never expressed his own opinion or feelings about the strike in his articles — he only reported what happened on the picket line, in the union, at the mass meetings and at the shop chairmen's meetings.

Mr. Zuckerman was well known to the strikers. They considered him a friend. They respected him, and when he came into the hall where the chairmen were gathered for their meeting, they greeted him with warm applause. At every mass demonstration, Mr. Zuckerman would march in the front row. Small wonder that a warm friendship developed between Zuckerman and the leaders of the strike, particularly since the Socialist *Forward* hurled daily attacks upon the "Communist" strike leaders, and Mr. Zuckerman, the labor editor of the *Tammany Day*, wrote about the devoted, warm friendship that existed between the strikers and their leaders.

President Sigman's Charges

Suddenly, Morris Sigman, the president of the cloak and dressmakers' union, got in touch with Mr. Shapiro, the owner of *The Day* and preferred charges against Zuckerman, his labor editor. The charges were of such a serious nature that Mr. Shapiro could not ignore them, and he called upon Zuckerman to answer them before an impartial person. Mr. Barondess, who was a well-known and respected leader of the Jewish community, was to act as the impartial judge in this serious matter.

President Sigman told the judge that Mr. Zuckerman was Ben Gold's brother-in-law, and that, because of that relationship, Zuckerman was a devoted servant of Ben Gold. Also that in the sharp struggle between Ben Gold and the president of the International Fur Workers' Union and the president of the AFL, Zuckerman defended his brother-in-law, Ben Gold. And in his reports on the furriers' strike, Zuckerman wrote that when Ben Gold addressed a mass meeting of the strikers, there was a thunder of applause by the strikers, and Zuckerman praised Ben Gold to high heaven as one of the greatest labor leaders.

Zuckerman replied that the strike of the thousands of fur workers concerned him very much; that he came to the picket line every day, and he visited the halls where the strikers gathered, and that never before had he seen such unity, such enthusiasm and determination of strikers as he witnessed in the furrier strikers, and that the friendship and devotion between the strikers and their leaders were amazing.

And, said Zuckerman, the strikers were actually enraged against President Oizer Shachtman and against AFL President Bill Green because they were convinced that they had been betrayed by these two presidents with their secret agreement with the bosses. And further that he, Zuckerman, believed that the furrier strikers would win their just demands, and that this would indeed be a blessing for the cloak and dressmakers.

And finally, Zuckerman said that Ben Gold was *not* his brother-in-law, that Ben Gold had never met Mrs. Zuckerman and was never in his home, and he, Zuckerman, had never met Gold's wife because Gold was not married. The first time he met Gold was one week before the strike broke out. Before he met him, he had never even known of Gold's existence.

As for his reports in *The Day* about the strike, Zuckerman said that he had brought with him several issues of the paper, and he read five of the news reports he had written about the strike. When he finished reading the fifth article he had written, Mr. Barondess, the impartial judge, announced that it was not necessary for Mr. Zuckerman to read any more, that in his opinion, Zuckerman served the strikers conscientiously, and that he, Barondess, was inclined to believe that President Sigman, in the name of justice, would withdraw his charges against Mr. Zuckerman.

And that was the end of the trial.

CHAPTER I

Victory of the Rank-and-File

In 1924, a group of shop workers who had been loyal supporters of the Kaufman administration split away from Kaufman's leadership and gave themselves the name the "Progressive Group."

The members of the Progressive Group were Joint Board delegates. Together with the few left-wing Board delegates, they constituted a majority on the Board and became the legal rank-and-file leaders of the New York Furriers Union. They assured the workers that their objective was to unite and strengthen the union so that it could fight for the interests of the workers.

But the fur workers did not rush to support the Progressive Group. They were convinced that the Progressive Group lacked either the ability or the courage to wrest the union from Kaufman's corrupt gang which dominated the union, and that they would soon rejoin their old friends. After all, hadn't they supported them for a long time?

The leaders of the Progressive Group were very much upset over the fact that the workers did not trust them. They called a conference of the workers with whom they worked in the shops — their friends — in order to explain to them why it was important for them to join the Progressive Group and to help them gain the confidence of the workers.

However, the conference did not help the Progressive Group. Their friends told them, in a friendly way: "You, the leaders of the Progressives, knew that the Kaufman administration is rotten and corrupt, and remains in power in the union with the help of gangsters, and still for years you supported the Kaufman administration. Now, all of a sudden, you have become saints and you think that the workers will trust you. You helped the Kaufman administration to frame up and terrorize the left-wingers and now, suddenly, you say that your objective is to unite the union so it can serve the workers. Overnight, you became left-wingers and you think that the workers will believe you. If you are really serious and you really want to serve the workers, you must unite with the left-wingers." On this note, the conference ended.

The Left Wing and the Furriers Union

None of the despicable methods that International President Kaufman and his lieutenants used to attempt to destroy the left wing in the Union — or at least to stop their activities and reduce their influence among the workers — were able to produce the desired results. No more effective were the wild attacks of the "Socialists" on the left wing in the Furriers Union — that they were Communists and carried out the orders of the Communist Party, that Communists were the enemies of the democratic workers' movement, and that the left-wingers were poisoning the minds of the workers with their Communist propaganda and doing harm to the Union. Even the gangsters of the Union's "Organization Committee" didn't dare use their "strong arguments" against the left-wingers.

The left-wing opposition in the Union grew and flourished. Young, class-conscious workers, who were being exploited by the bosses and appealed that their bosses paid "protection money" to assure that the Union would not "mix in their business," became active, energetic and devoted fighters for the left-wing program for a union that would fight for the interests of the workers. The influence of the left wing spread and grew among the workers.

The Conference with the Progressives

The "Progressive Group," which had failed to win the confidence of the workers and had begun to feel its lack of power, decided to turn to the left-wingers for help. I agreed to hold a short conference with two of the top leaders of the Progressive Group, Oizer Shachtman and Isidor Winnick. My friend Aaron Gross and I would represent the left-wingers.

Shachtman opened the conference with a long, substantive speech. He said: "Ben Gold, you know that each member of the Progressive Group is an honest worker and feeds his family by honest labor; and that none of them have ever received one cent from the Union for their union activity. You yourself worked with a few of our Group in the very same shop. Despite the fact that they were loyal supporters of the Kaufman administration for many years and fought against the left-wingers, they still maintained friendly relations with you. Isn't that true?

"But now, Ben we're no longer fighting against the left-wingers and the Communists. We have permanently divorced ourselves from Kaufman and his adjutants. We joined into one group in order to save the Union from the swamp into which Kaufman has dragged us. We are fighting for an honest, democratic union. We were sure that the left-wingers would help us attain this objective. But you left-wingers ridicule us. You ignore us. Ben! That means you are actually helping Kaufman to defeat the Progressive Group! You are helping the corrupt Kaufman administration to continue its gangster power in the Union! Isn't that right, Ben?"

My Answer

I said: "Shachtman, you made a fine speech. you broke with the traitorous Kaufman administration, and you organized a group and crowned it with the high-sounding name, the 'Progressive Group.' You speak fine words to the workers about a democratic union which will faithfully serve them, but you are doing nothing for the workers which would support your words.

"You know that the bosses laugh at the agreement with the Union and rob the workers, and you do nothing to help the workers. You know about the 'protected' shops. The bosses pay weekly graft to the gangsters of the Organization Committee so that the Union should not get in their way of robbing the workers, and you are silent. You know about the stealing within the Union, and you are silent. You know that the business agents betray the workers, and you are silent. Now, you cackle like hens and keep saying that you want to build an honest union. What do you want, you leaders of the Progressive Group? Are you asking the left-wingers to help you remain silent about the tragic conditions in the Union?"

Winnick Speaks

Winnick, who was one of the highest-paid workers, had been a loyal supporter of the Kaufman administration but was never active in the Union and never had any connection with the fight against the left-wingers. He answered me this way: "Ben, let us speak openly. We are surrounded by enemies. Kaufman has his people in the Joint Board and on the executive boards, and the Union manager and the business agents are Kaufman's loyal hand-maidens, and the 'boys' from the Organization Committee are Kaufman's 'boys.' They are all waiting for us to dig ourselves into a hole so they can bury us. Do you understand that, Ben? We know what we have to do! We have to start with the top men, not with the underlings. Do you understand? But first, we must be assured that the left-wingers will be our partners. Is that clear, Ben?"

I assured him that the left-wingers would help to the best of their abilities in all the struggles that the Progressive Group would undertake to further the interests of the workers. The conference was over.

The 1925 Storm

We waited, and it finally happened. At the beginning of 1925, the Joint Board, with a majority over the minority of Kaufman's delegates, decided to hire an accountant to investigate the Union's finances. After a thorough investigation, the accountant reported that a large sum of money — a thousand dollars — was missing. He pointed out that the person responsible for this loss was the manager of the Union.

The manager was also a vice-president of the International Union, and President Kaufman said that the International Executive Board would judge him. But there was no trial because at the first hearing, the Union leader confessed that for the past several years he had been stealing from the Union — how many thousands of dollars, he couldn't remember.

That was the last pre-trial hearing, because this fine, reliable union leader disappeared from the Union. The secretary-treasurer, who knew about the thievery and kept silent about it, also left his job.

The Joint Board decided that Shachtman and Winnick should manage the Union until elections for paid officers would be held in the month of May.

An Important Conference

A few weeks later, in the month of March, when the storm among the workers over the theft in the Union had quieted down a bit, Gross and I had a conference with Shachtman and Winnick in the latter's home.

Shachtman opened the conference with the explanation that he had called it in order to save the Union.

"The situation in the Union is critical," he said. "Kaufman's organization is paralyzing the Union. Since I have been manager, the 'boys' are no longer on the Union's payroll, but they haven't dropped out of the Union. Every day, until late in the evening, they are at the Union headquarters. They still control two executive boards and the business agents.

"Workers don't want to come to the Union headquarters. At shop meetings, the workers sit like mutes. They don't say a single word. They are afraid to open their mouths. They know the 'strong-arm boys' are here in the Union."

"In my opinion," Shachtman said, "There are a hundred shops that are being 'protected' by Kaufman's Organization Committee. The business agents tell me that they avoid these shops because they don't want to risk their lives.

"I can't and I don't want to be the manager of the Union," he moaned.

Gross answered Shachtman: "And if you should resign as Union manager, will the gangsters move out of the Union?"

"I'm not resigning. I am not running away from the battlefield!" Shachtman retorted. "To rescue the Union from the terrible swamp is my goal, my ideal, and I will fight until we are victorious. Is that clear, Mr. Gross?"

"And now to the major issue," Shachtman continued. "The Progressive Group has worked out an excellent, practical plan. We propose that the left wing and the Progressive Group unite! A united front! The united front will put fear into Kaufman's crowd. And you, Ben Gold, will be the manager of the Union.

"I know that Kaufman and his vice-presidents of the International Union have excluded you from the Union, but when the workers will elect you as Union manager, President Kaufman will choke on this exclusion.

"I know that Kaufman and the *Daily Forward* will create a big stir that the Communists, the agents of Moscow, have gathered power in the Union. Let them carry on and scream! We won't even owe them an answer.

"Well, Ben Gold," Shachtman addressed his remarks directly to me. "You have lectured us that we aren't doing anything for the workers, that we aren't doing anything about the gangsters and the grafters in the Union. Now you have an opportunity! Take over the leadership of the Union and of the united front and get to work!" Shachtman had finished his speech.

I answered: "The left-wingers will not agree to join a united front with the Progressive Group as long as Hyman Sorkin remains one of the leaders of the group. The workers know that Sorkin was Kaufman's right hand, that he has very strong ties with the 'boys' of Kaufman's Organization Committee, and the workers haven't got the slightest confidence in him, and..."

"We know, we know all about that," Shachtman broke in. "We have spoken with Sorkin about this matter. Winnick, you tell him what Sorkin said. I have spoken enough already. Now, Winnick, you talk."

Winnick then told us that they had had a long conversation with Sorkin about the fact that because of him, the left-wingers wouldn't unite with the Progressive Group, and Sorkin had told them that when Gold became the Union manager in a united front, he, Sorkin, would have nothing more to do with the workers. Gold would have complete charge over issues concerning the workers. Sorkin wouldn't even walk into Gold's office, unless Gold should call for him.

My answer was that we would discuss this with the left-wingers and would let them know what we decided.

Shachtman then spoke again: "Before we finish this meeting, I want you to know that I will not remain as manager of the Union. If the left wing doesn't accept our plan for a united front, and I won't be Union manager, and you, Ben, don't want to be manager either, perhaps Sorkin will become the manager. Ben, do you understand what the situation is? And Ben, tell your friends," Shachtman said to me in a voice that sounded like a command. "Tell them that the Progressive Group is ready to accept the left-wing program. Don't let them start throwing 'rocks in the garden.' We agree to:

"A democratic union and the right of Union members to express their opinions about union problems freely and without restrictions.

"The organizing of the open shops. To use the power and know-how of the Union in the best interests of the workers and the right of the workers to belong to whatever political parties they choose.

"I have nothing more to say," Shachtman, tired out from his long speech, concluded. "I hope that the left-wingers will accept our plan. There is no other alternative."

The Left Wing and the Union Leadership

During the meeting of the left-wing fur workers, where it was unanimously decided to accept Shachtman's proposal to create a united front of the left-wingers and the so-called Progressive Group (the right-wing group), I fought as hard as I could against the point that I would have to become the manager of the Union.

I argued that the responsibilities of a union manager, especially in the Furriers Union, were exceptionally serious, complicated, and loaded with difficulties, and that I did not possess the necessary qualifications to undertake such a responsible position in the Union. I had never been a business agent in the Union, had never negotiated with bosses about workers' problems, and had never conducted any conferences with the Conference Committee of the bosses, which was made up of experienced and clever bosses.

But I pleaded in vain. My best friends and colleagues simply laughed at my arguments. Seventeen of the colleagues voted for me to accept the nomination for manager. Only one voted against — myself.

I was very unhappy about the vote, but what choice did I have? So I accepted the nomination, ran, and was elected.

The morning after the election, when I arrived at the Union and entered my "office" — the manager's office — I suddenly felt a strange uneasiness, a feeling of not belonging engulfed me. The office suddenly seemed to shrink in size. The desk which had been used by the corrupt previous managers and the bench on which the traitorous union leaders had sat disgusted me.

Strange thoughts entered my mind. I recalled that years ago, we left-wingers had been opposed in principle to accepting any paid office in the Union, because the hatred for the paid officers in the Union was so widespread among the workers, and that the cynical remarks by workers about paid officers was an expression of their hatred for the corrupt Union leaders. Whenever a worker had accepted the nomination to run for business agent in the Union, the other workers would say, "He doesn't want to earn a living through honest work; he wants to live a life of shame."

Of course, I knew that the attitude of the workers toward the left-wingers was friendlier, that they trusted the left-wingers, and that they were convinced that they were responsible fighters for the interests of the working class. But still, I was a paid officer.

My first day as elected manager of the Union was a very difficult one for me. The elected business agents of the Progressive Group and from the left-wingers, as well as Shachtman, who was elected secretary-treasurer of the Union, and even Sorkin, were all happy with the victory of the United Front. Only I got no pleasure from the victory celebration.

All of a sudden, however, my spirits revived. Even before the work day was over, workers packed into my office. They came to congratulate me. The large hall on the first floor, which was empty all day, was now packed with workers. The hall resounded with laughter and shouts of "Mazel-tov! Congratulations! Finally, finally, the Union is our own!"

Every evening after work, workers packed my office to tell their complaints about their bosses. Every evening, I heard fifty or more complaints: One boss was paying the workers less than the minimum wage scale that had been written into the agreement with the bosses; another boss was only paying half-pay for a holiday; a complaint from workers that during the month of February, the boss had cut their wages with an agreed upon promise that in April he would give them a raise, but he didn't honor the agreement, and so on.

But the bitterest complaints came from the workers in the "protected" shops, in which there were no union conditions. The bosses there had no fear at all of the workers. The gangsters were no longer in the Union. Their office was locked. So the workers now came to the Union to ask for help, and the faster the better.

But Kaufman's loyal co-workers who had been elected in July, 1924 were on the Joint Board and on the executive boards that were supposed to handle the important union problems of the locals they represented. The next elections for Joint Board delegates and executive board members were scheduled to be held in July, 1925. Should I wait until the elections? Should I remain quiet about the graft and other corruption? No! the local executive boards met every week. One of the main duties of the executive boards was to decide whether an apprentice, learning his trade in a shop, was skilled enough and therefore entitled to receive a Union book, which meant that the boss must start paying him wages up to the minimum set down in the agreement between the Union and the bosses.

Each week, on the appointed evening, when the executive boards held their meetings, tens of workers waited at the office doors to be called in about their Union books, but only a few applicants actually received them. Those that were rejected came again the next week, and so, week after week, they kept coming back until they gave up all hope of becoming Union members and kept working in the shops for starvation wages. They didn't know that in order to get a Union book, they first had to pay a hundred dollars in graft to the top man of the executive board.

During the first week after I became manager of the Union, I gathered plenty of facts about the graft system as it applied to Union books. Twenty workers told me that after working for a long time without Union books, they had found out about the "system." They then paid the "collector" the required hundred dollars, and at the very next meeting of the board, they only had to wait at the door for a few minutes before they were called in and issued their Union books.

Each one of the twenty workers told me almost exactly the same story about the "system." As soon as these men got their Union books, the bosses raised their wages.

To my question as to why they didn't tell the previous Union manager about the graft system, they all replied that the "collector" had warned them that if they should "sing," they would lose their tongues. But now, they were no longer afraid and would talk.

A Meeting with the Union Leaders

I called a meeting of all the paid officers of the Union. At this meeting, I told them that I had heard many complaints from workers and had indisputable evidence that a graft system was in operation regarding the issuance if Union books by the executive boards.

I declared that I was determined to put an end to the graft system and to clean out the grafters, and that I was also determined to open the locked doors of the "prisons" — the "protected" shops. Nor was I going to wait long. The battle to heal the wounds of the Union would start soon — in fact, now!

Then a discussion began. Brother Sorkin was the first to speak. He said that as soon as I would start a battle to get rid of the grafters on the executive boards, they would proceed to shout "frame-up" and would appeal to the president of the International Union, and that President Morris Kaufman would be more than happy to step into the fight to save his "boys." We would then be drawn into a long battle. It was his opinion, Sorkin said, that in the July elections, the United Front would elect honest workers as executive board members, and we would thus get rid of the grafters without a big fight. It was only a few weeks until the July elections, and we could afford to wait those few weeks.

As to my decision to start a fight against the "protected" shops, Sorkin explained to me that the big shops among them were connected with underworld racketeers, from whom the bosses bought stolen goods, and that their deals involved hundreds of thousands of dollars. A fight against the "protected" shops meant a war, not only with "our boys," but also with the underworld racketeers, and he, Sorkin, doubted whether we had enough strength to undertake such a bloody war.

The left-wing business agents answered that Sorkin's opinion meant that out of fear of President Kaufman, the present Union leaders would have to sanction graft in the Union. No — the United Front Union leaders could not be guilty of such a crime.

As for the "protected" shops, it was clear from Mr. Sorkin's words that because of fear of the underworld racketeers, the Union leaders should refuse to help the workers suffering in these "protected" shops. No — that would mean betraying the workers, and...

Sorkin interrupted with the explanation that a war with the underworld would mean risking the lives of workers and business agents, and was not a practical way to help workers, but a terribly risky gamble.

I answered that the business agents would not be involved in any way with the fight against the "protected" shops. Committees of workers, under the leadership, would wage the fight with the bosses of the "protected" shops and with their "protectors."

Shachtman said: "When the United Front was established, it was agreed that Gold would be the leader of the Union and that he would be in charge of all worker issues and worker problems. We know that the workers trust Ben Gold. The Union offices are packed with workers every evening. The 'strong-arm boys' have run away from the Union. There are shop meetings every day. The Union has revived. Gold says that workers will wage the battles with the 'protected' shops. It is clear that he doesn't expect any miracles." He ended his speech with these few words: "Ben, I am certain of the success of your enormous undertaking." On this note, the meeting ended.

"The Day of Reckoning"

That evening, before the workers packed into my office and filled the entire first floor where my office was located, I had a short conversation with the clerk of the Complaint Department. I told him that I did not doubt his honesty, but I wanted him to know that many workers had told me that when they brought their complaints to him, their bosses knew about it. How did he explain this?

He answered that for a long time now, every evening, a member of the Organization Committee had come into his office, had sat down close to his desk, and had taken a great deal of interest in the complaints of the workers.

I asked him why he had allowed these fine gentlemen to sit in his office. He certainly must have understood that they were spies for the bosses.

He answered that if he had tried to chase out his "guests," he would have paid dearly for it. He assured me that he was ready to resign from his job.

I returned to my office and tried to calm myself after this latest discovery. When workers began coming into my office, I took a short walk on the first floor where my office was located. When I saw a large number of workers already filling the entire first floor, and saw that my left-wing friends were among them and were having discussions with the workers, I did not return to my office, but instead, I went into the office of the Complaint Department and there I saw what I expected to see. The complaint clerk was sitting at his desk and writing down the complaints given to him by a worker in his book. Not far from the desk, on a bench, the bully L---- was sitting, listening to all the conversations between the workers and the complaint clerk.

"Hello, L----," I greeted him. "Be so kind as to step out of this office," I said in a friendly tone.

He said, "This is not your office. I am a Union member and I sit where I want to, and I don't take orders from you."

I opened the office door wide and shouted, "I know what you are doing, L----! Get out of here!" My shouts resounded over the whole floor and the workers rushed toward the open door where I stood. A few workers pushed me into the office.

Deathly pale and frightened, the famous "strong man" got up from the bench and walked toward the door, but when he noticed the mass of workers blocking his way, he hid behind my back. I told the workers to move aside and make a path all the way to the steps of the entrance, and to the "heroic gentleman," I said, "Don't be afraid, L----. Come with me." And through the narrow path between two thick rows of workers, I led him to the exit, and he ran down the steps as though he was running from a fire. The workers applauded and shouted, "The day of reckoning! Congratulations! Mazel-tov!"

After I had accompanied this gentleman out of the Union building, I went back into the office where the executive board of the operators' local was meeting to consider applications for Union books. I took the books and the applications that were lying on the table near the chairman of the executive board and said in a strong, loud voice, so that the workers would hear me through the open door: "The executive board members are accused of dishonest deals with Union books. Until this matter is cleared up, the executive board will not handle applications for Union books."

I marched out of the office and went back to my own office. Two gentlemen, the leaders of the board, both active members of the Organization Committee and pillars of the Kaufman administration, came into my office and demanded that I return the applications and Union books which I had grabbed from "their" executive board meeting.

I answered them that the executive board was suspended and that the next day, the Joint Board would hold its weekly meeting and they could come to the Board with their complaints about me.

They said they would come to the Joint Board, but in the meantime, they loudly demanded that I return "their books." "We were elected by the workers and you have to respect our rights," they shouted belligerently. And one of the gentlemen confronted me with, "Do you think you are the dictator of the Union? Well, dictators don't last long!"

I opened the door of my office and yelled, "Good-bye, gentlemen!" And the workers camped outside my office also yelled, "Good-bye, good-bye, gentlemen!"

The numbers of workers filling the area in front of my office and their shouts of "Good-bye" filled these audacious heroes, who for years had helped their friends to terrorize the workers, with fear. They remained standing stock still as if turned to stone. They didn't make a move. The workers moved aside, making a narrow path, and shouted, "The road is open for you!" Then the gentlemen disappeared. Again the workers shouted, "The day of reckoning! The day of reckoning!"

About My Daring

In one evening, I had dared to force the intruder out of the Complaint Department, and only a few minutes later, had cut down the might and the limitless opportunities of the grafters to carry on their graft system in the executive board. I didn't do this because I felt that the gangsters would suddenly hold me in great esteem. I was convinced that the gangsters and grafters of Kaufman's Organization Committee knew that the left-wingers were their worst enemies, and that at the first opportunity, they would use their fists and their knives against the left-wingers and their leaders.

I dared to do what I did because I knew that my left-wing friends, the class-conscious, principled, courageous fighters for the interests of the workers, were watching me carefully. I also knew that the Union offices, which had always been empty halls, with no workers around, had, since I became manager of the Union, been packed with workers every evening, and that my left-wing friends, who were well loved by the workers, were always present among them. This friendship between the left-wingers and the workers grew stronger, and every day, the army of loyal Union members who were ready to fight for a democratic, militant union grew bigger and more powerful.

The "heroic" leaders of the strong-arm Organization Committee were well aware that their might was crushed. They felt their loss of power particularly that evening, as they moved slowly through the narrow paths that the workers had cleared to let them pass through. They felt the hatred of the workers. They heard the shouts of "The day of reckoning! The day of reckoning!" The situation had become reversed. The workers were no longer afraid of these scoundrels — now *they* were afraid of the workers. That is why I dared to confront them, and they didn't dare to oppose me.

A Lucky Coincidence

Now that I had succeeded, with the help of the workers, in ousting the bosses' spy from the Complaint Department, I decided that that intelligent, principled "Socialist" — the clerk of the Complaint Department — had to be removed from that department. The excuse that he had given me — that he tolerated the gangsters in his office because he was afraid of them — was unpalatable to me. What disturbed me even more was the fact that he hadn't told me about his "guests" who would park themselves in his office every evening.

But where could I found a class-conscious, principled and able person to take over this responsible office? This problem worried me.

On morning, a young man walked into my office and told me that he was a student at City College and that during the summer months, when the college was not in session, he needed a job because he was short of money. He had worked once in a fur shop, so he came to me to see if the Union could help him get a job in a fur shop. His name was Irving Potash.

In the course of my brief conversation with Potash, I found out a great deal about his background and even who his friends were. I told him to return in two or three days and I might find a good job for him.

Potash made a very good impression on me, and I felt that he would be able to help me out in the Complaint Department. I got in touch with his friends, who were also acquaintances of mine, and all of them expressed a high opinion of him.

When Potash came to me two days later, we had a really long conversation. The situation in the American trade unions was not foreign to him, and he even knew a little about the happenings in the Furriers Union. When I told him that I had a job for him in the Complaint Department of the Union, his face lit up with joy.

Potash served the Union more than those three summer months. He served the Union for thirty years. In a short time, he became one of the best-loved leaders of the Furriers Union.

The "Protected" Shops

The problem of the protected shops did not let me rest. I was afraid that if I waited too long, there was the possibility that the fighting spirit

31

of the workers would wane. I knew that a successful fight to smash the fortress of the racketeers and gangster-controlled protected shops would lead to freeing the workers from slavery in these shops and put an end to the curse of gangsterism in the fur industry. Waiting too long would be interpreted as a sign that the union was weak and did not dare to undertake such a gigantic fight.

Therefore, I decided not to wait and got down to the business of preparing the battle apparatus of the Union — to set up the various workers' committees and to make certain that each committee was headed by a competent chairman.

I called in two or three workers from those shops and told them to inform the rest of the workers in their shops to be ready. I chose several shops from among the protected shops to be the first to be involved in our fight. I also made other necessary preparations to insure the success of my first contest with the bosses and their powerful protectors.

Friends in the Enemy Camp

I was not aware that I had so many friends in the camp of my enemies who were concerned for my welfare. As soon as I had taken over the union leadership as manager, Dr. Paul Abelson, the impartial chairman chosen by the Union and the employers' association, paid me a visit. He congratulated me on my victory at the polls and wished me success. Then he explained that there was a custom that the elected Union manager and the president of the employers' association have lunch together and discuss the problems of the fur industry.

I replied that I had not forgotten that Mr. Samuel N. Samuels, the president of the employers' association, had explained his attitude toward the workers in 1920 during the conference between the representatives of the Union and those of the bosses. That conference was concerned about the thousands of jobless furriers. The Union committee had appealed to the bosses to help out the neediest unemployed workers by giving them one or two days of work in their shops, Mr. Samuels had answered that the bosses worried about their businesses and the Union should worry about the unemployed workers. Mr. Kaufman, who was then Union manager, asked what the Union could do with the jobless workers, and Mr. Samuels had retorted, "Drown them!"

Dr. Abelson had been present at the conference. He had heard President Samuels' suggestion about what the Union should do with the unemployed workers. I declined the honor and pleasure of enjoying the company of such a noble person at lunch.

A few days later, I had another important visitor — Mr. Comrade Abe, a wealthy manufacturer. He had been one of the founders of the

Furriers Union and one of the leaders of the 1912 strike which had forced the employers' association to sign an agreement with the Union. In 1914, he became a manufacturer and thanks to the war, he prospered, enlarged his shop and became a member of both the employers' association and its Board of Directors.

However, he had remained a member of the Socialist Party and often helped the Union in its early conflicts with the bosses. During our conversation, he stated that he felt it was his duty to the Union to ask me to have lunch with Association President Samuels. He assured me that if I showed a little respect for President Samuels, it would be good for the Union. It was true, he explained, that Samuels was a reactionary and didn't like any unions, but that was why he was the leader of the bosses. And, he continued, in the interest of the Union, I must try to establish a friendly relationship with Samuels, and he, Comrade Abe, would help me in this.

I answered that I did not want any relationship at all with the "Drown the unemployed workers" gentleman. I knew that Mr. Samuels used his power and all his capabilities to fight the Union, and I would use the power of the Union to protect it from such mortal enemies of the workers and of the Union.

Comrade Abe spoke seriously: "Well, there's no point talking any more about Samuels. But, Ben, I want you to know that Herman Scheidlinger is the chairman of the Conference Committee of the bosses and the Union, so you will be meeting him often at conferences. Scheidlinger is a leader in the employers' association, but he is no union-hater. The workers in his shop respect him. He is a lawyer, an intelligent man. He is a boss, but he is also a 'mentsch' [person of character]. Scheidlinger asked me to arrange a lunch meeting with you. He wants to chat with you and get to know you."

I answered, "Well, that's different. I will let you know." Our conversation ended on a friendly note.

My Socialist Friends

Four men who were members of the Socialist Party and loyal supporters of the Kaufman administration came into my office. All had fought against the left-wingers, but had done so in a friendly and respectful way. They did not howl that the left-wingers were Communists and "agents of Moscow, enemies of the Union and a threat to the American labor movement," as Kaufman and the Socialist *Daily Forward* did. They were almost friends of the leaders of the left wing.

"Ben, we have come to you as friends and comrades," the leader of the group began. "We haven't always agreed with you, but we never fought against you. Politically, we are divided, but concerning the Union, we are united. We want to tell you truthfully that in the Union elections, we voted for you, even though it wasn't easy for us to vote for a Communist." He entrusted me with this secret with a smile. "Ben Gold, we have come to talk with you about a serious Union issue, and you must be patient with me because it is impossible to tell you what has brought us here to you in only a few words."

I answered that I knew that he never expressed himself briefly, and that even when he would say that he simply wanted to make a remark, it became a whole speech, and I assured him that he could say what he wanted, speak as long as he wished, and that he needn't worry about my patience.

"Then listen carefully to what I have to tell you," his speech began. "First, you have embroiled the Union in a fight with the Organization Committee and chased them out of the Union because you have talked yourself into believing that the committee is made up of gangsters. I'm telling you that you are wrong. It is true that there are a few within the committee that use the power of their fists, and we have long suspected that they aren't honest, but all the other people on the committee are devoted fighters for the Union.

"Ben, the Union cannot exist without a good Organization Committee. Drive out the suspected ones, but don't throw out the loyal and devoted members who work for the Union night and day and earn their wages honestly. Without the Committee, the Union will be weakened. The bosses will become even more brazen toward the workers. Ben, you have to make use of the Organization Committee.

"Secondly, there is talk that you will soon plan an attack on the so-called 'protected' shops. I am telling you that means dragging the Union into a long and bloody war. Those shops are protected by the same underworld gang that protects many of the cloak and dressmaker shops. The big, strong and rich Cloak and Dressmakers Union, which has a very large and powerful Organization Committee, doesn't dare to start a fight with that gang in the protected shops. And you, Ben, want to drag our small, weak and poor union into a war with the underworld gangsters.

"I want to tell you something else: the bosses of the Association will use this opportunity to worsen the conditions in their shops because the Union will be involved and busy with its war against the gangsters.

"Ben, we have come to you as friends and we are appealing to you. Don't drag the Union into such a disaster. The workers have confidence in you. They trust you. They are exciting you to use the power of the Union to improve the working conditions in the shops. It is almost July, and they are expecting the Union, under your leadership, to negotiate good July raises. They are not looking forward to bloody wars which will ruin our Union." With these words, he finished his speech.

One of the other of my four friends wanted to say something, but I

34

asked him to wait because I first wanted to answer the first speaker: "My answer will be short and to the point. First, about your Organization Committee. Kaufman and the business agents needed their Organization Committee very badly because the 'boys' of the committee terrorized those workers who had the nerve to protest against the Union leaders who had neglected their duties and responsibilities to the workers. The left-wing Union condemns these gangster methods and the workers hate the gangsters who have terrorized them. You, my Socialist friends, are not ashamed to appeal to me that I should utilize this band of terrorists in the Union!

"And another thing: it is widely known both among the workers and among the bosses that the chief gangsters in your Organization Committee are on the payrolls of many manufacturers, and you're telling me a cute story that only a few gentlemen on the Organization Committee are suspected of dishonesty! The Union will belong to the workers.

"Secondly, you are appealing to me not to drag the Union into a bloody war with gangsters who are protectors of the 'protected' shops. This means that I should allow the bosses of these shops to exploit and rob the workers! And you really thought that I would agree with you and that I would become afraid of this bloody war, as you call it? I well know that the possibility exists of their using bloody gangster methods. The gangsters don't want to lose the source from which they get many thousands of dollars with very little difficulty. Regretfully, you do not believe that united and well-organized workers have the ability to defeat the gangster bunch. Well, we are not in agreement." And this concluded our talk.

A Successful Beginning

There were seventy protected shops on the Union's list. We decided to call a strike of the workers in thirty of these shops as a beginning. These shops were all located on 27th Street between 7th and 8th Avenues.

For two days, the pickets marched happily along the sidewalk and watched their shops to make sure that no worker "strayed" into a shop that was on strike.

On the third morning, six passengers got out of a car and hammered at the heads and bodies of the pickets with their fists. The gangsters, however, were not aware of the fact that the strikers were prepared for this attack. Nor did they know that twenty selected workers had taken their vacation time and were marching with the pickets. Now they found out, but it was too late and they had no stregth left to save themselves. It took the police to save them. The police led the poor, beaten and bloody gangsters into one of the protected shops. The news of the battle brought joy to thousands of fur workers. It was their first victory over the gangsters!

The strike lasted one week. The bosses signed an agreement with the Union and put up money as security that they would uphold the agreement. The raises that the workers got were higher than they had expected.

The other protected shops realized that their "protectors" had lost their power, and they also settled with the Union, in order to avoid strikes in their shops. June was a stormy month: shop strikes, a struggle to clean the grafters out of the Union, a bloody fight with the gangsters, and the breaking down of the fortress of the protected shops. These, plus the shop meetings, shop chairmen's meetings, and meetings of the locals, together with other energetic activities of the Union, brought new life to the thousands of fur workers.

The July Raises

The season in the fur trade started in June-July and ended in December. During the first few months of the year, thousands of workers were unemployed. Little by little, the shops came back to life. When the workers gradually returned, their season-wages were cut, and only in July did the bosses raise the workers' wages. These were the July raises.

For the past few years, the bosses had taken advantage of the incompetence and dishonesty of the Union leaders and the hopelessness of the workers. At the beginning of each year, they cut wages mercilessly. The July raises that they gave the workers did not even cover the cuts that had been made at the beginning of the year. The protests of the workers were to no avail.

But in 1925, under the left-wing Union leadership, the newly-awakened and revitalized workers demanded higher July raises. They didn't request them — they demanded them. In a few of the shops, the rich, arrogant bosses insisted that they would decide the amount of the July raises, not the workers. The business agents tried to reach a compromise with these bosses without success. I also tried, but likewise without success. Shop strikes broke out.

A Distinguished Visitor

Suddenly — a guest in my office. Andrew Wenneis, the secretary-treasurer of the International Union, came into my office. Wenneis was a decent, honest and friendly man. He had divorced himself from the ugly swamp that the Kaufman administration had created in the Union. He had never uttered a derisive word against the left-wingers or the Communists in the Union.

We greeted each other warmly, and he told me that Mr. Samuels, the president of the employers' association, had telephoned him and told him that the Union had called strikes in dozens of shops that were owned by bosses who belonged to the association, and that the workers were demanding unheard-of July raises. Samuels warned that if the Union didn't send the workers back to their shops within 24 hours, the association would break the agreement, and that this would lead to a lock-out. It was to avoid such an undesirable situation that Wenneis had come to see me.

I calmed him down and explained to him that the bosses were not likely to cause a lock-out at the height of the season. A lost season would mean bankruptcy for a large number of manufacturers. I informed Wenneis that Dr. Abelson had called a conference of the Union and the employers' association for 10 o'clock on the very next morning to discuss precisely this matter.

"Oh, very good!" Wenneis said, obviously pleased. He continued, in a friendly manner, to explain to me that this would be my first conference with the bosses, and that I should be aware that the Conference Committee of the bosses was made up of able, but sly and arrogant men, and that I should be ready for them. I invited him to come to the conference.

The Conference

The conference opened with a sharp attack on the Union, developed into a hot discussion, and then gradually cooled down. Mr. Scheidlinger the chairman of the bosses' Conference Committee, opened the attack on the Union:

"In the agreement with the Union, the major point was clearly stated that conflicts which the Union and the association could not settle were to be referred to the impartial chairman, whose decision must be respected by both sides. The Union has ignored the impartial chairman, broken the agreement, and taken the law into its own hands.

"Secondly, the second major point of the agreement is that shop strikes are strictly forbidden. The Union has called strikes in dozens of shops and again broken the agreement.

"Thirdly, the Union is demanding fantastic July raises which the bosses cannot possibly pay. The strikes have already caused losses for the employers. The Union has no right to dictate to the bosses how much they should pay the workers. And...."

He went on to demand that the Union should call off the strikes immediately, that the impartial chairman should condemn the irresponsible behavior of the Union and that the Union should now state in writing that from that day on, it would adhere strictly to all the points in the agreement.

As soon as Scheidlinger had finished his speech, all of the bosses on the Conference Committee literally jumped out of their seats, demanding to speak next. But the impartial chairman ruled that, in all fairness, Manager Gold was entitled to answer these serious charges that Mr. Scheidlinger had made against the Union.

I glanced over at Andrew Wenneis. His round, fat face showed deep worry. A strange calm came over me. I was glad that Scheidlinger's accusations against the Union had given me the opportunity to become a plaintiff. And quietly and politely, I stated that I was compelled to believe that Mr. Scheidlinger would not have made his accusations against the Union if he were aware of all the ugly facts involved in this entire controversy.

"Mr. Scheidlinger has argued," I continued, "that the Union has ignored the impartial chairman and taken the law into its own hands. Not true! I had asked the impartial chairman to resolve the controversy over the July raises, and he explained that according to the agreement, he had no right to get involved in this matter.

"Mr. Scheidlinger's accusation that the Union is dictating how much the bosses should pay their workers is also not true. The truth is that the business agents of the Union and the representatives of the association appealed to each boss individually to settle this matter. But they had no success. The bosses refused even to discuss the issue. The fact that we asked Dr. Abelson's help is further evidence that the Union is not trying to dictate how much the bosses should pay their workers.

"As for the accusation that the Union is demanding 'fantastic' July raises, let me tell you that I have a list of dozens of manufacturers who cut wages last year in March and April by 20%, and where the subsequent July raises amounted to only 10% to 12%. This year, the bosses again cut the wages by almost 20%. This deep cut in the workers' wages the bosses consider 'kosher' and just, not 'fantastic,' but, God forbid, the demands of the workers for a fair and just July raise — that you condemn as 'fantastic.'

"And moreover, Mr. Scheidlinger told you that the Union called the workers out of the shops on strike. Let us examine that. There were no pickets at the shops. The Union did not put out a circular declaring that these shops were on strike. The truth is that the workers walked out of those few shops because they were dissatisfied with their cut wages. No one can force workers to work in shops against their will. It seems to me that slavery was abolished a long time ago.

"No, we did not break any provision of the agreement. If you so desire, the Union will issue a circular announcing that the workers in those shops are not on strike. They simply don't want to work in those shops for cut wages."

I ended by stating that there and then, face to face with witnesses and confronted with incontrovertible evidence, Mr. Scheidlinger should, by all that was just, retract his charges against the Union.

Now the bosses began to shoot their arrows. One after another, these gentlemen hammered at the Union:

"Is that so? The workers are not on strike — they merely don't want to work? Now the Union says it will distribute leaflets stating that the workers don't want to work because the bosses are cutting wages. This means that they are inciting the workers against the bosses!" This was the line of the bosses' argument.

"There are no strikes; there are no pickets. Is that what you're saying, Mr. Gold? But 20 manufacturers are left without workers in mid-season and their businesses are being ruined."

"Mr. Gold, you're telling us that the workers don't want to work for small July raises. The workers indeed! And you, Mr. Gold, the leader of the workers never spoke to the workers about this matter! What do you take us for — school boys? Don't you think we know who is responsible for these strikes?"

I didn't even have to reply. Mr. Scheidlinger halted the debate. He called his Conference Committee for a caucus and he assured the Union representatives that it wouldn't last long.

The bosses went out into another office. Dr. Abelson and the Union Committee remained in the large hall where the conference was being held. Wenneis called me over to a corner of the room and said to me: "I have lived to derive proud pleasure from the New York Union. The victory over the gangster-protected shops is a wonderful achievement. And now the fight of the Union for more just July raises is a big one indeed, but the victory of the workers is assured, because underneath all the bad-mouthing by the bosses, I can hear their loud cry: 'Send the workers back to the shops!' Now I can return to my work in the International feeling satisfied and pleased." And he walked out of the conference room.

When the bosses returned from their caucus, Scheidlinger invited me into the separate little office to confer with him. He started with an appeal to me. He told me that the workers would be suffering significant losses from the strikes, and that therefore it was my duty to settle the strikes as quickly as possible. He thought that the best settlement would be that the July raises should cover the cuts in wages that the bosses had made at the beginning of the year: "If you agree with my proposal, you have to send all the workers back to work tomorrow."

"And what if a few of the bosses remain obstinate and don't agree to give the workers such a raise?" I asked him.

"We'll call in the impartial chairman; his name is Dr. Abelson," he said in a joking manner, "and we'll tell him the agreement we reached for a settlement, but that for practical reasons, he should announce the verdict about the July raises."

I understood at once that Mr. Scheidlinger had presented me with such a good settlement because he was afraid of the possibility that the shop strikes could spread and that many manufacturers would suffer severe losses. This was very clear to me. I wanted to avoid a wave of shop strikes, because the Union was not yet ready for such a serious confrontation with the employers' association. Therefore, I accepted Scheidlinger's proposal, and the issue was settled.

The strikers unanimously accepted the settlement, not only because they received higher raises, but also because they had finally succeeded in putting an end to the system that the bosses had established whereby wages were cut each year. A large number of workers managed to get even higher raises from their bosses. The fear of strikes broke down the arrogant attitude of many of the bosses.

"Greekland"

When the fight for the July raises was over, with substantial gains for the thousands of fur workers, and when it had become clear to even the enemies of the United Front leadership that the thousands of fur workers had come to life again during the past three months, and were enthusiastically supporting the activities and struggles of the Union, I decided to undertake the crusade of organizing the Greek fur workers.

Fifteen hundred Greek-schooled workers were slaving in the shops of the Greek bosses, working long hours for very low wages, and their bosses ruled over them like anointed kings. The Union shops were closed to the Greek workers; no Union books had been issued to them. Isolated and helpless, with no outlet through which to protest, they had had to accept the dictates of their bosses with bowed heads. The corrupt Kaufman administration didn't even attempt to organize the Greek workers. The Kaufman bunch had nicknamed their shops "Greekland."

I called a meeting of all the paid Union officials and told them that there were still four months left before the season ended. and that I had decided to mobilize all the energies of the Union to organize the enslaved Greek fur workers. A dreadful fear seized our partners in the United Front—the Progressives. They sat there, astounded. It was as if they had lost their power of speech. The room became very quiet. Not one of the officers who was a member of the Progressive Group uttered a single word.

Finally, Brother Sorkin opened the discussion. He could not control his agitation, and for the first time since I had been elected manager, he delivered a lecture to me. He attacked me with sharp and critical words:

"Friend Gold, are you serious or are you joking?" With this question, he began his lecture.

"You seem to have a nice dreams, lovely fantasies. Do you honestly believe that you are completely finished with the right-wingers and the Organization Committee? Have you forgotten that Morris Kaufman is the president of the International Union, and that he is sitting not far from here in his office on Long Island, and that he and his army are waiting for you to make a blunder? It seems to me that you are a little drunk from the few big successes you have had.

"Do you know what's doing in 'Greekland?' There are two thousand Greek workers working in a hundred Greek-owned shops. The Greek bosses brought these first-class workers over from Greece. The workers live in houses that belong to the bosses. They are mortgaged to the bosses from their heads to their toes. Their souls belong to their priest and their bodies belong to their bosses. They don't understand a single word of English. They have absolutely no concept of what kind of a creature a union is. I, friend Gold, don't gamble when I am sure to lose."

I knew that it was the fear of such an enormous undertaking that had driven him to deliver his lecture to me, to speak like an experienced union leader instructing a young, inexperienced union officer. For understandable reasons, I had not told them that I had been holding meetings with a group of Greek comrades, members of the Communist Party and with their left-wing friends, all of whom were intelligent workers and all of whom spoke English. Their influence on the workers in the shops was growing daily, and they didn't have the slightest doubt that the Greek workers would answer the call of the Union with joy. I had to keep any knowledge of these meetings secret.

However, in my answer to Sorkin's speech, in order to dispel the fears that his words had instilled in all those present, I had to give a short explanation that first of all, the Greek workers were not at all happy with their working conditions and with their meager wages; and secondly, that I was sure that a large number of Greek workers would answer the call of the Union. And...

"You are sure? And how do you know that the Greek workers are dissatisfied?" Sorkin interrupted me with his questions.

I resented being interrupted in the middle of my statement, so I answered him a bit sarcastically that I would tell him how I knew that the workers were dissatisfied after he was "bar-mitzvahed," and that my certainty than many workers would respond to the call of the Union came from my belief in God and in the workers.

Shachtman closed the discussion. He said that the undertaking was extremely difficult and daring. He said that he agreed with Sorkin that we were surrounded by enemies who were waiting for our defeat. "But if Gold is telling us that he knows what is doing in the Greek shops, and that he is certain that we will not fail, he surely knows what he is saying, and my opinion is that even if we should succeed in organizing a few of the Greek shops, it would be the biggest triumph in the history of the Union. I propose that we approve Gold's recommendation to try to organize the Greek shops." His proposal was approved.

Everything Goes Smoothly

I did not anticipate that it would be so easy. True, the first meeting of the Greek furriers called by the Union was poorly attended, but all the other meetings were encouragingly successful. The Greeks packed the hall. Some of the Greek workers made stormy, rousing speeches. I was the last speaker at these meetings. When the chairman wanted to translate my English speech into Greek, the workers shouted that it was not necessary. They had understood everything I had said.

At one of the meetings, a worker asked a very important question in very clear English. He asked his question after he had made a bitter attack on the Union. He said: "Mr. Gold, this is my first meeting. I did not want to come to any of the previous meetings because neither I nor my friends have any faith in you. You union is not a union. You union is a Jewish organization. Greek workers are not taken into your Jewish organization, and the Jewish shops are not open to Greek workers. So we remain prisoners in the Greek shops. You never showed any concern before for our suffering and our helplessness. All of a sudden, you have discovered that the Greek workers are also people. So I want to know if there is going to be one union of Jewish and Greek workers, or will there be two separate unions — a Jewish union and a Greek union — and will we remain prisoners of our Greek bosses?"

A terrible hush hung over the hall. I shouted out my answer: "Brothers and sisters, I am giving you my word of honor that when the strike of the Greek workers for better living and working conditions will be over, all the strikers will receive Union books from one united union of Jewish and Greek fur workers!" A storm of hearty applause broke out in the hall.

My Greek comrades informed me that the report of that meeting was the major topic of conversation among the workers, and that the masses of workers were asking them why the Union wasn't calling a strike. They argued that this was the best time because the season was in full swing and the bosses were loaded down with orders. We decided not to wait any longer.

A Week of Struggle and Victory

One beautiful, clear morning, fifty Jewish and Greek workers distributed contributed circulars among the Greek workers — the call of the Union for a strike! And sixteen hundred Greek workers packed the Union hall. The shops of the Greek manufacturers were empty and paralyzed.

Neither the priests nor the bosses — not even the threats that the Communist trouble-makers would be deported to Greece — were able to weaken the solidarity and fighting spirit of the strikers, who were determined to win their justified demands. There was a real family unity among the strikers. The bosses organized themselves into an association and proposed that they would come to an agreement with a union of Greek workers. The strikers answered that they had one union and the bosses had to settle the strike with their Union.

The bosses felt they were powerless. Only one week of strike had convinced them that their workers had suddenly become an unbeatable force. And the association of the Greek fur manufacturers signed an agreement with the Union that guaranteed their workers all the conditions that workers in the other Union shops had: a 44-hour week, instead of a 48-hour week; time-and-a-half for overtime; six paid holidays, and all other union conditions. And raises! Many of the workers, especially the women working on the cheap furs, had slaved for very low wages. According to the agreement, the bosses now had to pay no less than the minimum wage scale. That is why the raises were even higher than the workers had expected — ten and twenty dollars a week. Those workers who worked on the better furs received even higher raises.

When I completed my report on the agreement with the bosses, there was a storm of applause. The strikers were gripped by a festive joyousness. They hugged and kissed each other and shouted. Shouts of "Long live the Union!" filled the hall.

I sat on the platform and sopped up the joy of the workers. My fatigue from a very tense week of very hard work disappeared. The joy of the victorious strikers renewed my strength. I was thinking that I would never forget this wonderful week.

Wearing their national costumes, the Greek strikers closed ranks on the street where the Union was located. Then at 12 noon, the lunch hour, they marched through the streets of the fur market and the masses of workers who were out on Seventh Avenue at that hour greeted them with open arms.

Sorkin's "Brainstorm"

After the victorious strike of the Greek workers, Sorkin asked me to call a meeting of the union officials. He wanted to propose a plan which he said would be a blessing for the Union.

I called this special meeting, and in an exalted mood, Sorkin unfurled his plan. He started the meeting with a well-prepared speech. He explained: "The unceasing activities and the gigantic accomplishments of the Union during these last few months, way beyond what anyone could have imagined would be possible, has raised our Union to the highest level in its history.

"At the same time that the Union has been embroiled in daring and risky struggles against the brutal enemies of the Union, President

Morris Kaufman of the International Union and his helpers have carried on daily attacks against the New York Union. The tens of thousands of dollars that the New York Union pays into the International are not being used by him to help weak locals through the country. Instead, he is using these dollars for his 'boys' that interfere with our holy work for the benefit of the workers.

"It is essential that we cut out this cancer! We must call for a special convention of the International Union and chase Morris Kaufman and his machine out of the Union. According to our constitution, a special convention can be held when one-third of the International locals demands it. The prestige of the New York Union is a guarantee that the necessary number of the locals will support our demand for a special convention. Let's not lose any time. Let's get to work."

I didn't want to express my opinion about Sorkin's plan. Shachtman, the spokesman of the Progressive Group, was also silent. But the business agents, the members of the group, were enthusiastic about the plan. They called it a "brainstorm."

They argued that what the United Front had accomplished for the workers in New York in these few months was more than Kaufman had even dreamed of doing in his ten years as Union president for the furriers of the entire country. The weak locals all over the country were in need of capable, creative leadership. "Morris is already a smoked-out pipe," one of them said. "His machine is all rusted." The International Union needed intelligent, energetic leadership. Sorkin's plan for calling a special convention was a "stroke of genius."

Shachtman then spoke and said that he doubted that we would have enough delegates at such a convention to oust Kaufman. Kaufman and his organizers were agitating among furriers all over the country against the Communists who had seized power in the New York Union, and in some locals, the leadership was corrupt — they were a part of Kaufman's gang. But he agreed with Sorkin's plan because there was nothing to lose and everything to gain.

I remarked briefly that if we didn't win, we would lose a great deal. But Sorkin answered that he convinced that we would not lose. He said he knew of several locals which would like to get rid of Morris Kaufman and his organizers. With the delegates from these locals, we would have a majority. Sorkin's proposal was accepted.

On the Eve of the Convention

The locals supported the call by the New York Union for a special convention, and the International leaders were obliged to call a convention. President Kaufman suddenly became energetic and active. He ran from local to local to fortify his position and make sure that the delegates they sent to the convention would be actively opposed to those whom he called the enemies of the American labor movement, particularly in those locals that were controlled by his "strong men" — devoted, paid characters.

When I received the letter from the leader of the Chicago Furriers Union in which he let me know that Kaufman had challenged me to come to Chicago for a debate, Shachtman was struck with fear. "No! Absolutely not! It's out of the question! You must not go to Chicago," he said with determination.

Why? Because a few years earlier, while he was the leader of the Chicago Furriers Union, he had had to leave Chicago to come to New York because he refused to be a partner to the gangsters who controlled the Chicago Union. He felt that in Chicago, my life would be in danger. There, I would not be protected by workers, as I was in New York. The left-wing groups had only a few people, and they were deathly afraid of the gangsters. "No," he said, "You must not go to Chicago." He was sure that they were already getting things ready for me there in Kaufman's stronghold.

Sorkin did not agree with his friend Shachtman: "You, Shachtman, were a business agent in Chicago for two or three years," he argued, "and I was business agent in New York for a few years in Kaufman's administration. I was also a vice-president in the International Union. So I am also well aware of what's doing in the Chicago Union. First of all, by this time, there are many more than a few left-wingers in the Chicago area, not a few as when you were there. On the second point, it is true that the 'strong boys' control the Union and that Kaufman carouses with them at their banquets when he comes to Chicago, but I have some close, old friends in the Chicago Union. I will go to Chicago with Gold and I will bring him home alive."

I thanked my friend, Sorkin, for his loyalty to me, and a day later, I left for Chicago with my guardian, Sorkin.

The Debate

In Chicago, Sorkin and I both moved into my hotel room. We had our breakfast, and Sorkin, my protector, went off to meet his friends in the Union office. I went off to meet my friends in the office of the Communist Party, and there I had a very interesting conversation with Bill Foster. When I told Foster why I had come to Chicago, he asked me where and when the debate would take place and when it would end. I did not understand why Foster was asking me these questions, but when the debate was over, I understood it very well.

At eight o'clock in the evening, the dramatic debate began. My guardian, Sorkin and I had come to the meeting at twenty minutes to eight. The elevator brought us up to the hall where the debate would take place. It was already filled with fur workers.

In the large entry hall which led to the meeting halls, and not far from the elevator, Kaufman was sitting on a bench, chatting with a friend. Sorkin and I waited for Kaufman to go into the meeting first. When he finally entered the hall, we heard the loud applause with which the assembled workers greeted him.

A few minutes later, when Sorkin and I marched into the meeting, we got a very cool reception. The enthusiastic applause of the small left-wing group was swallowed up by the icy stillness in the rest of the hall. The several hundred assembled workers sat in their seats as if they were sunk in a deep sleep. Sorkin and I were led to two empty seats which the left-wing group had reserved for us, right beside them.

Suddenly, before I had even sat down, a powerful woman's voice called out: "Mister Ben Gold, what did you come her for? Who needs you here? Did you come to split and break our union? Get out of here! Go back where you came from!"

There was dead silence in the hall. I remained standing, staring at the woman who was giving me such a friendly greeting. I marvelled at her tall, broad, heavy figure and her pretty, round, fat, flaming face, and smiled at her. After she finished her greeting and sat down, I also sat down. Again there was dead silence among the assembled workers.

The manager of the Chicago Union, who was the chairman of the meeting, broke the silence. He opened the meeting with a short explanation, that even though Brother Kaufman was the president of the International Union, he would not have any more time to speak than Ben Gold. "This is democracy," he said. "In our Chicago Union, the principles of democracy are strictly adhered to! President Kaufman will speak for one hour. Then Ben Gold will also speak for one hour. Then both speakers will close the debate — twenty minutes for the president and twenty minutes for Ben Gold."

President Kaufman spoke, pouring fire and brimstone on the Communists, the Moscow agents who had grabbed power in the New York Union. He explained that they carried on daily propaganda that was full of lies — outrageous, false accusations against the honest, devoted leaders of the International Union. He read a letter from a member of the New York Union that said that the Communist union leaders forced their workers to donate money to the Communist Party, and that the manager of the New York Union, Ben Gold, was the dictator in the Union and he had established Communist discipline in the Union; workers were afraid to express any opinions which were not in agreement with the orders of the Communist dictator.

"They, the Communists, have seized the New York Union," Kaufman shouted, "and now they are demanding a special convention in order to seize the International Union for the Communist epidemic."

When he had finished speaking, the chairman of the meeting pressed his hand and assembled workers rewarded him for his enlightening speech with thunderous applause.

"And now," the chairman shouted, "Ben Gold is next!" I walked up to the platform and was greeted by the assembly with friendly silence. No one cursed or heckled me.

I said: "Friends, President Kaufman did not tell you that a group of workers, members of the Joint Board of the New York union, who were active in the union for many years and were devoted friends of Kaufman and loyal to his administration, suddenly broke with him and his administration and told the workers that they could no longer keep quiet about the tragic situation of the union, which was the result of the degenerate, corrupt and treacherous Kaufman union administration.

"President Kaufman did not tell you that a well-known accountant who was hired by the Joint Board, found that a large sum of union money was missing. Kaufman did not tell you that the manager of the union, who was also a vice-president of the International Union, confessed that for several years, he had been stealing union money. And, yes, the secretary of the union knew about it, but did nothing about it.

"And Kaufman knew that fourteen hundred workers were working without union books, for very low wages. Union books were sold to the workers if they paid graft to the leaders of the Executive Board."

I told them about the fight the present union leaders had conducted to free the Union of grafters. I told them that I had brought with me twenty affidavits from workers who had to pay a hundred dollars in graft in order to receive their union books.

I then told them about the seventy "protected" shops, where the workers were forced to work for low wages without any union conditions — that the present union leadership was duly elected by a large number of votes, by the workers, and the election had been supervised by the Civil Liberties Union, and that meant that the elections were carried out honestly.

I told the Chicago workers that even after we, "the so-called Moscow agents," as Kaufman called us, had been elected as leaders of the union and had thrown Kaufman's Organization Committee out of the union, these grafters had the nerve to assure the bosses of the protected shops that they had nothing to worry about — that the protected shops were their territory, so the bosses gladly continued paying them their weekly graft. And I continued:

"But the grafters lost their territory. The present union leaders called the workers of the protected shops out on strike. The gangsters of Kaufman's Organization Committee attacked the strikers and beat them up murderously." I showed the Chicago workers pictures of the beaten-up strikers, with their bandaged heads, and told them that the strikers had defended themselves and the gangsters had paid a high price for their attack on the strikers. I told them how the bosses of the protected shops had come to the union with bowed heads and had signed an agreement with the union.

Then I told them about the union's successful fight for the July raises, which put an end to the system the bosses had used to cut the workers' wages each year.

And finally, I told them the chapter of history concerning the Greek workers; how the workers had slaved for years for their Greek bosses, working long hours for starvation wages, and that President Kaufman had never made the slightest attempt to organize them. I told them about the victorious strike by sixteen hundred Greek workers that the present union leadership had led.

And I finished my speech by saying that I was not accusing Kaufman of being a grafter, but I did accuse him of having surrounded himself with a band of traitors, thieves, grafters and gangsters, who terrorized the Union members and helped Kaufman to keep his power in the Union. And, for the last few months, while the present Union leadership had been deeply involved in the difficult fights against the bosses in the interests of the workers, Kaufman kept hailing insults and attacks daily on the Union leaders, calling them "Moscow agents" and enemies of the Union. And his paid organizers and their friends were hindering the Union at every step and preventing us from carrying out our important activities.

And then I asked: "How long must workers suffer, ache and bleed because of traitorous Union leaders? How long?" And I said: "Kaufman, free the thousands of workers! You are hated and condemned by the thousands of workers who are building, uniting and strengthening their democratic Union — a Union that deals fairly and honestly and is true to the interests of the workers. Kaufman, enough! If you have even a spark of conscience or a drop of human feeling, resign!"

I finished my speech and began collecting my documents and the pictures of the beaten workers which were lying on the table. Suddenly, I heard a thunder of applause. I walked down from the platform and sat down in my seat near the left-wing friends and wiped the sweat from my face. The applause kept resounding through the hall.

The chairman, who was sitting, shrunken and stiff in his seat, got up suddenly and said that now President Kaufman would answer Ben Gold.

When Kaufman appeared on the platform, he was greeted with deafening boos. When it got quiet and he started to stammer something, the boos were renewed.

I went up to the platform and asked that the workers should let him speak. Then President Kaufman said very quietly that he had recently gotten out of the hospital where he had had an operation, and that he didn't have enough strength to speak again. With weak steps, he walked off the platform. The chairman closed the meeting and the assembled workers rushed for the two exits from the hall.

I remained standing, surrounded by my left-wing comrades and Brother Sorkin, among the comrades. He was beaming with joy. A big smile spread over his face, and he almost shouted: "Hoo-Hah! (Wow), what a debate! But why did you ask that they should let him speak? Did you have pity on the lousy president?" And he burst out laughing.

I didn't answer him because I really didn't know what had come over me that I should ask the angry workers to allow him to howl more invectives against the "Moscow agents," to give him a chance for more demagoguery. This was not the first time that I had appealed to the workers to let the angry dog bark. This same drama was played out for the first time in 1924, at a mass meeting in Cooper Union in New York. At that meeting, Isidore Begoon, who was a member of the Socialist Party and a devoted servant of Mr. Kaufman, had refused to let me speak because, he explained, the executive board of the International Union had excluded me from the Union.

A stormy protest had broken out in the hall. "You excluded Gold from the Union?" the assembled furriers shouted. "We didn't exclude him! Gold will speak whether you like it or not! Ben Gold will speak!" The noise grew. The chairman sat silent, unmoving, like a clay dummy, as if the whole commotion had nothing to do with him, until one worker shouted: "I propose that if the chairman doesn't call Gold to speak within five minutes, we should all march out of here." "Seconded! Seconded!" The cries filled the hall.

And the chairman called me to speak. I spoke for fifteen minutes. When I finished my short speech, and when the applause had died down, friend Kaufman jumped up from his seat as if he had been bitten by a snake and shouted out that Gold was excluded from the Union because Communist agents of Moscow were the enemies of the labor movement.

That was all. He couldn't speak any longer. The shouts, invectives and curses hailed down on him. "Demagogue! Liar! Faker! Traitor! Gangster!" and other such pleasant compliments were hurled at him by the workers, and they didn't stop.

I jumped up on the platform, quieted the crowd, and then appealed to the assembled workers, who were angry and bitter and who hated and condemned Kaufman, to let him speak. The workers didn't want to go along with me. "No!" they carried on noisily. "Do you have pity on him? Do you have a soft heart, Ben?" I answered that perhaps Kaufman wanted to say good-bye to us and after he made his last speech, he would hand us his resignation. "Let him speak."

And Kaufman finally spoke and said that he had no intention of resigning, that he was determined to chase the Communists out of the Union. "Let them go to Moscow!" he said. Now the noise of the crowd didn't last long, because the workers marched out of the hall and left the honorable president, Mr. Kaufman, alone with the empty seats.

The workers were annoyed with me that I had asked them to let Kaufman talk. Why did I do it? I couldn't give them any reason or excuse, just as I didn't honestly know why I again begged them to have pity on Mr. Kaufman at the Chicago meeting, where he certainly had earned the hatred of the fur workers for his treasonous and criminal leadership.

A note: I feel it is necessary to explain again that the resounding applause of the workers at these meetings was not based on the fact that I was such an outstanding speaker, but rather because I had spoken about the pain and the need of the oppressed, exploited and betrayed workers. And when I spoke about the unbeatable might of the working class, which was being led by a few devoted leaders, it was only natural that the workers should feel an awakened pride and a belief in their power, which chased away their nagging feelings of helplessness. They expressed their agreement with what I said by their enthusiastic applause.

Another note: when the Chicago meeting was over, the Chicago comrades in the audience advised me not to leave the building because Kaufman would have his gangsters outside. I began to think they were right. There was a group of husky-looking men standing in front of the building. Even Sorkin did not recognize them, and began to worry. One of them approached me and asked: "Are you Ben Gold?" When I replied that I was, he told me that they were a group of steelworkers who were in town for a meeting, and that Comrade Bill Foster had asked them to come by at the meeting place to make sure that I got out safely. Then I realized why Foster had asked me for the details as to the time and place of my debate with Kaufman. It was typical of Foster's preciseness of organization to cover every contingency.

And now, back to the issues.

A Split in the United Front

The split in the United Front was the beginning of a scandalous drama which was played out at the special convention of the International Union. The reason for the split is sad, but it is also interesting.

The Furriers Union of Montreal, Canada, which belonged to the International Union, was involved in a long strike. The New York Union was helping the strikers financially. This financial aid was brought directly to the strike leaders by representatives of the New York Union — five thousand dollars every two weeks. One week before the special convention began, Shachtman and I brought five thousand dollars for the Montreal strikers.

On the train back to New York, Schachtman and I were discussing the troubled situation of the Montreal strike and other union issues. Suddenly, Shachtman let me know that it was Sorkin's ambition to become president of the International Union as soon as we would bury Kaufman at the special convention, and that that was why Sorkin had proposed that we demand that the special convention be held. I told Shachtman that I would not vote for Sorkin for president. Shachtman answered that he wouldn't vote for Sorkin either. He said he would vote for me for president.

I assured him that I would decline the nomination and that no one would be able to budge me to accept. "That means that you are leaving the way open for Sorkin," Schachtman argued. "No," I answered, "probably my left-wing comrades will block Sorkin's way; we will vote for you for president." He thanked me heartily for my faith in him and shook my hand.

A few days later, after we had returned to New York, Sorkin called a meeting of the Progressive Group and informed them that Morris Kaufman's defeat was assured and that he, Sorkin, wanted to take Kaufman's place. When Shachtman told them that he had discussed this issue with Gold and that Gold and the left-wing delegates would not vote for Sorkin, Sorkin launched a bitter attack on me: "Of course, Gold doesn't want to vote for me, because he wants the office of president himself." He complained that Gold was the "chief" everywhere in the Union: "At meetings of the shop chairmen, Gold is the spokesman, and at meetings of the locals and at mass meetings, it's always Gold! At the conferences with the bosses, Gold is the chief Union delegate, and with the Greek strikers — again Gold. We, the Progressive Group, are only rubber stamps! And I?" Sorkin complained bitterly, "I'm nothing in the Union. A janitor in the Union is all I am; no — not even that. I deserve that the Progressive Group should support me for president, not Ben Gold."

Shachtman assured the Progressive Group that Gold had emphatically informed him that he didn't want the presidency and that there was no way he would accept the nomination for president, and further, that Gold and the left-wing delegates wanted him, Shachtman, to be elected president. Shachtman's announcement started an involved discussion among the members of the Progressive Group. Sorkin argued that he did not need the votes of the left-wingers, that he had enough friends in Kaufman's camp. Shachtman argued that that would cause a split in the United Front and then Kaufman's bunch would rise from the dead and that would constitute a terrible danger for the Progressive Group. After a long and heated discussion, a majority of the Progressive Group voted that Shachtman should be elected as president of the International. Sorkin, very much upset, shouted that he would not be a janitor in the Union.

The Convention

I have already made it clear that it is not my intention to write the history of the Union. That is beyond my abilities. Philip Foner has already written the history of the Furriers' Union, which is unique in the labor movement. I am only writing short recollections of the happenings in the bitter fight of the fur workers against their brutal enemies. So I will make only a few comments about the convention which, right from the outset, became an ugly battle among degenerate union politicians.

Sorkin separated himself from the left-wing delegates, sat down with his old friends in Kaufman's camp, and renewed his old friendship with them. Shachtman knew that the delegates from the New York Union were in the majority at the convention and that his presidency was assured. So he comported himself in a calm, respectable manner, as a well-balanced person should, in order to make a favorable impression on the delegates in Kaufman's camp. The delegates of the Progressive Group behaved like guests, and so the lot fell to the left-wing delegates to fight all of Kaufman's tricks and maneuvers that were being used to curb the left-wingers. Kaufman, who was chairman of the convention, started off right at the very first meeting to announce that Ben Gold would not be seated as a delegate to the convention because the International Executive Board had excluded him from the Union in 1924.

The left-wing delegates protested loudly. I did not participate in the discussion because Kaufman had told me that I was not a delegate and therefore had no right to speak. The left-wing delegates argued: "You excluded Gold without a trial." "You ignored the constitution of the International Union." "The workers have elected Ben Gold as Union manager and now as convention delegate because they do not acknowledge such unlawful exclusions." A fight flared up. The arguments grew more bitter, and the powerful president became frightened and announced that the Executive Board would present their decision on this matter the next day.

Then Kaufman insisted that the delegates be limited to ten minutes in discussing his report. Again he suffered a defeat. It obviously pained him, but he had to report that the Executive Board had decided that a two-year exclusion was sufficient punishment, and Ben Gold became a legal member.

Finally, the secretary read the report of the International Union leadership. When he finished the report, he read a separate report, authored by Kaufman, about the leadership of the New York Union, Kaufman's report started with the explanation that in 1921, after the unsuccessful strike of the furriers in New York, the Communists and their left-wing friends took advantage of the Union's weakened condition and usurped its leadership. But in 1922, the workers threw out the Communist union. Then in 1925, they seized the Union again. In his thirty-page report, Kaufman made the most vicious, venomous, vile, libelous attack on the "Communist traitors," "Moscow agents," etc.

My answer to Kaufman's vituperative attack lasted two hours, and he didn't dare to interrupt me. I started my answer with a question: "Why did the President jump from 1921 to 1925 and not say anything about what happened in the Union in 1922, '23 and '24. Why doesn't he tell you about the 'crimes' committed by these 'Moscow agents' in the first months that they took office in 1925? President Kaufman is afraid that, God forbid, the convention delegates should discover what was going on in the Union during those few years." When I finished my answer to Kaufman's hideous report, a commotion erupted at the convention. Some members of Kaufman's camp protested against his attack on the left-wing Union leaders.

Angry and upset, Kaufman announced that the next day he would answer Gold's two-hour speech. When Kaufman opened the convention session the next day, his voice showed he was happy. "I'll show you, convention delegates," he shouted out, "facts that will substantiate my accusations that the Communist union-breakers carry out the orders of the Communist Party, which is the agency of Moscow." He then read a telegram from Charles Ruthenberg, the general secretary of the American Communist Party, which instructed the Communist delegates to elect comrades to all important offices in the International Union. Kaufman said he had gotten hold of the telegram, which had been sent to the correspondent of the Communist newspaper, the *Daily Worker*, who was at the convention every day.

Joy broke out in Kaufman's camp, and Sorkin and the delegates of the Progressive Group enthusiastically joined forces with Kaufman's delegates. They felt that they had caught the Communists in a net from which they would never be able to extricate themselves.

Shachtman was sitting not too far from me. He knew that the telegram story was a swindle. He knew that when he and I were returning on the train from Montreal to New York, we had decided that he, Shachtman, should be elected president. The Communist Party had not sent me any orders on that train. He knew that when he had told me that his Progressive Group had decided which of the New York delegates should be elected to the Executive Board of the International Union, I had quickly agreed to go along with the decision of the Progressive Group without receiving any orders from the Communist Party. Shachtman also knew that all decisions about important union matters were made at meetings of the leaders of the Progressive Group, together with the leaders of the left-wing, and without the knowledge of the Communist Party. He also knew that the leaders of the Communist Party were not idiots and would never send instructions in a telegram.

When I said to him: "Shachtman, I'm going to prove that the telegram is a swindle and you will be an important witness in exposing this swindle," he answered, "Ben, this is a pogrom! You want to discuss truth and justice with 'pogromchikes'? Not I."

He was probably right. The way I understood it, if he had helped me expose the swindle, he would have risked his chances of becoming president.

The result was that Mr. Kaufman was finally kicked out or the Union. This was certainly a great victory and made the furriers happy. Shachtman was elected president of the International Union.

Unfortunately, however, Sorkin and his "family" were elected as Executive Board members of the International Union, and also unfortunately, President Shachtman had to carry out the orders of his "cabinet of ministers," which was made up of Sorkin and his loyal friends.

CHAPTER II

The Historic 1926 Strike

Again I want to stress that I don't plan to write the history of the 1926 general strike of the New York furriers. I just want to note briefly a few recollections related to this strike.

For a few weeks, the Conference Committee of the Union and the bosses' association struggled with the problem of renewing the agreement. The demands of the Union were: a 40-hour week instead of a 44-hour week; no discharge; equal division of work; a substantial raise in wages; no contracting, and other demands. They met with stubborn resistance from the bosses, who insisted that the old agreement should remain in force without any changes.

The bosses did not deny that their profits had grown during the last few years of prosperity. They also didn't dare to deny that during the past five years, the productivity of the workers, both qualitatively and quantitatively, had increased significantly, while their wages had only increased by a tiny amount. The argument of the bosses was that in these last few years of prosperity, the seasons had been lengthened and that the workers worked longer and consequently earned more. Therefore, they insisted, the conditions of the old agreement were good enough for the workers.

The agreement expired in February, 1926. At the last. meeting, those employer representatives who wanted to avoid a strike proposed a compromise of the Union's demands:

First, taking into consideration that during the first few months of the year, when they produced their samples, the bosses had to employ their very best craftsmen, it was therefore impossible to have equal division of work. Would the Union agree that the rule of equal division of work not be applied to these two "sample months"?

Second, on the wage raise demands, they were ready to "reach a just understanding."

The bosses took the position that the Union must withdraw all of its demands. They protested most strongly against the demand for 44 hours of wages for a 40-hour week, and for raises even beyond that.

Before the last conference with the bosses over the agreement was ended, the president of their association, Mr. Samuels, came to say his piece. Samuels, who was known for his hatred of the Union and his animosity toward the workers — the same Samuels who had suggested drowning the unemployed furriers in 1920 — now, Samuels, who had not participated in any of the previous meetings and who appeared at the last hour of the last conference, delivered this lecture to the Union representatives:

"In 1912, the Union went on strike for three months and the employers' association broke the strike. But Dr. Magnes* appealed to the employers to recognize the Union and, as a favor to him, we signed a 'preferential agreement,' which meant that the Union had no say in our shops.

"In 1920, the Union struck for six months and again the employers' association broke the strike and smashed the Union, and again we let ourselves be let astray by Dr. Magnes' appeals and signed an agreement with your Union.

"But now, if your Union wants a strike, not even the most important person in the whole United States could influence us. Your demands are pipe dreams. If we were to lose our reason for one moment and give in to your demands, our businesses would be ruined in a very short time. Gentlemen, union leaders, you have one hour to renew the old agreement with us. One hour! Let your conscience be your guides!" His lecture was over.

Dr. Abelson, the impartial chairman, announced that Mr. Gold would be the last speaker before the meeting ended.

I answered: "Mr. Samuels, from 1912 to 1926, many changes have taken place in the country and also in the fur industry. Thanks to the war prosperity, the profits of the manufacturers have risen every year. In 1920, the economic crisis halted the prosperity. but in 1922, prosperity bloomed again in the fur industry and the profits mount even higher each year.

"And now the workers produce much more in the 44-hour week than they did in the 50-hour week in 1912. They do this at the expense of their energy and their health. But their wages were raised by only a drop in the bucket and their working conditions have not improved. No, Mr. Samuels, our demands will not ruin the business of the manufacturers because if they should give in to the Union's demands, they won't, God forbid, be paying the raises from their profits. They will raise the prices of the fur coats that the workers produce. And I don't believe that a customer who buys a mink coat for five or ten

_____

*The reference is to Rabbi Judah L. Magnes, who acted as an intermediary between the Union and the employers during the 1912 strike and who was impartial chairman during the 1920 strike.

thousand dollars will refuse to buy the coat if the cost is $50 more, or a cheap coat that would cost a few dollars more.

"And what will the bosses lose by agreeing to the demand for equal division of work? But for the workers, it is important and necessary to remove the terrible danger that hangs over their heads that in a crisis year, there would again be thousands of suffering unemployed, and the Union cannot 'drown' the jobless workers.

"Mr. Samuels, you are appealing to us to let our consciences be our guides. I know that there is a difference between the consciences of the Union leaders and the consciences of the manufacturers, who are concerned only about their businesses. I am telling you — let *justice* to the workers that produce your coats and bring you your profits be your guide!"

The General Strike of the Furriers

A few days after the agreement of the Union with the bosses' association had expired, the bosses declared a lock-out, and five hundred manufacturers, members of the association, closed their shops. Mr. Samuels invited newspaper reporters in and explained to them that the Union leaders were Bolsheviks, that their demands were irresponsible, and the bosses would not give in to their demands, even if the strike should last a year.

The plan of the bosses was worked out in such a manner that, according to the opinions of their experienced leaders, a victory over the Union was assured. According to their plan, the season would begin in May-June, but if necessary, they would wait until July, and the samples which they manufactured in March-April would be made by their most loyal furriers with the assistance of scabs who would be brought in by hired protectors.

In three or four months, the Union would become impoverished and the strikers wouldn't have enough money to pay their rent, their wives and children would go hungry, and the strikers would, just as they had done during the 1920 strike, run back to work without the Union.

But it didn't take long before many of the bosses began to doubt the assurances of their leaders that they would defeat the Union. Twelve thousand fur workers answered the strike call. Never before had the bosses seen such enthusiasm among the united, organized strikers. The army of special night pickets surprised the bosses. Never before had the bosses witnessed such demonstrations of thousands of workers, marching in closed ranks through the streets of the fur district. Never before had the bosses seen such warm friendship as they saw now between the workers and their Union and strike leaders.

And suddenly, the bosses were astounded and taken aback. They didn't expect, in fact, they couldn't ever imagine, that their loyal, well-paid foremen, their best workers, specialists in their trade, would leave their shops and join with the strikers. The worry of the bosses grew every day. They were no longer sure that their foremen, with the help of a few scabs, would turn out their samples. Moreover, they had hoped that their foremen, who were well known among a large number of workers, would help them find the best craftsmen who would, for attractive wages, sneak into their shops and help produce the samples. But their hopes were shattered. The foremen joined the other workers in the strike.

The worried leaders of the bosses' association, under their genial and powerful president, Mr. Samuels, decided that it was time to take necessary steps for a counter-attack against the strikers. They elected three committees: a committee to search out those workers who had scabbed in the 1912 and the 1920 strikes, a "law and order" committee to deal with the police and the judges, and a committee to hire the "guards" who would protect the scabs.

The streets along Seventh Avenue, from 27th to 30th Streets, were flooded with policemen and "guards." Gangsters led scabs into the shops.

The Seventh Week of the Strike

In the seventh week of the strike, I received some inspiring reports. The foreman who worked for one of the richest and most decent employers reported that his boss had told him that a group of the wealthy and influential manufacturers opposed the policy of reactionary bosses led by President Samuels and that they wanted a settlement with the union and wanted Motty Eitingon to negotiate with me about such a settlement.

Mr. Eitingon was the wealthiest merchant and importer of fur skins and was highly respected in the industry. He and the other fur skin dealers wanted the strike settled because they were convinced that a long strike would be detrimental to the industry. However, Eitingon made it clear to them that he would not call to a conference to negotiate a settlement until he was convinced that a majority of the members of the Board of Directors of the manufacturers' association would meet with him so that he could find out from them what they would consider an acceptable compromise with the union to settle the strike. I waited impatiently for the call from Eitingon. A settlement after only seven weeks of strike would indeed be a tremendous accomplishment. Also, the fact that the more decent bosses were ready to settle the strike, contrary to the policy of President Samuels of smashing the union, as he had stated at the most recent conference between the bosses and the union — that was indeed a blessing.

Finally, I received a call from Eitingon in which he let me know that he wanted to talk to me about settling the strike. At the very beginning of our conference, he told me that his friends, who were also the leaders of the Board of Directors of the manufacturers' association, had asked him to settle with me, and that they had assured him that if he succeeded in working out a practical and just agreement, the strike would end.

Eitingon told me that he knew that at the last conference with the bosses, I had suggested a compromise on two of the demands of the Union: the equal division of work and the raises in pay for the workers. He wanted, first of all, to know exactly what I had in mind and how far these compromises would go.

I answered him that my suggested compromise on these two demands had been made in order to avert a strike, but the bosses had declared a lock-out and caused the strike. The suggested compromise had therefore lost its meaning and its purpose.

Eitingon smiled and said that when I spoke of avoiding a strike, I certainly meant a strike that would last four or five months, but now it was only the seventh week of the strike and the workers hadn't lost anything because until now, there hadn't been a stitch of work in the trade. He stated that there was no guarantee that even if the strike were to last several months, I might not have to agree to a compromise on these two demands. Therefore, it was practical to come to an understanding now on these two demands that would help us settle the strike now, which would be a major gain for the Union.

I told him that my compromise proposal on these two demands included a condition that the bosses must agree to a 40-hour week with pay for 44 hours, as the workers then got, and that all the other Union demands be met.

Eitingon then said: "That clearly means that the major demand if the Union is a 40-hour work week with pay for 44 hours. If the bosses would agree to give on this major demand, which would certainly be the greatest gain for the workers on the history of the Furriers Union, certainly you would be able to bargain them down quite a bit on their other demands. Right, Mr. Gold?"

"That depends on what is meant by 'quite a bit,' " I answered.

"I want to tell you my opinion, Mr. Gold," Eitingon continued, "and that is that each individual demand is justified, but all the demands combined are too much of a financial burden for the individual manufacturers. In fact, you figure it out: 40 hours instead of 44 and a 20 percent raise in wages over and above that, equal division of work, and no contracting — all at once! It is no wonder that your demands produced such stubborn opposition by the bosses. Of course, they should have discussed it with you and tried to hammer out a practical agreement, but stubbornness takes the upper hand over logic. Well, so be it.

"Now, Ben, let's get to the main issue. The manufacturers want to settle the strike now! If we don't settle it now, it will go on for months," Eitingon assured me. Why the sudden change in tone? A different Eitingon, somehow. Now it was the millionaire — the successful merchant — talking. Even his voice sounded different. The pleasant softness and friendliness of his tone were gone. Now everything he said sounded like "This is it! It can't be any other way" — and it was as if he was speaking to a customer of his, telling him the price of his goods and "not a penny less."

The manufacturers wanted to settle the strike then, Eitingon told me, because a long, drawn-out strike would mean big losses for them, and for him it would be a substantial loss. He told me he had nineteen million dollars' worth of skins on ice. "The losses to the workers will be even greater," he said, "because they earn less."

"Mr. Gold, let's start from the beginning," Eitingon went on. "You certainly understood that you wouldn't win 100% of your demands. You set forth a lot of conditions because you knew that the bosses would bargain stubbornly with you. You set forth a high price because you wanted to have room to cut your demands and still come out ahead. your demand for a 40-hour work week means, first of all, shorter hours of work — a very big gain for the workers. And you also demand that for these 40 hours of work, we should pay the workers for 44 hours of work. This means a raise in the workers' wages. Very good! But you are also demanding a 20% raise in addition. And even this, in your opinion, is not enough. You add another bunch of demands. Surely you didn't believe that you could will all your demands.

"So, Mr. Gold, this is where it's at. The bosses have finally agreed to a 40-hour week with pay for 44 hours on the condition that you cut your demand for an additional 20% raise to the bone, and that you withdraw all your other demands."

Mr. Eitingon and I then discussed and bargained on each demand of the Union. I argued that the demands for no discharge and equal division of work would not cost the bosses any money and that these demands were nothing more than just and fair treatment of the workers; that the demand that the bosses should not hire any contractors was not only right but would put an end to a system which permitted a manufacturer to produce his coats in two shops — in his union shop and in the contractor's shop, where union conditions did not exist.

Mr. Eitingon kept hammering the point that it was impossible for the bosses to give in on all the demands of the Union, and that such a thing had never happened in any union. The gain of the workers on the main issue was such a giant achievement that all the other Union demands could wait until the 1928 agreement.

60

Finally, we settled the strike: a 40-hour week with pay for 44 hours; a 10% raise in the workers' wages; no discharge and equal division of work for five months (with three months under the old agreement, that came to eight months); a one-class minimum wage scale, and the prohibition of contracting.

Very well satisfied, he pressed my hand and said. "Ben, this is Saturday. On Monday, I will be meeting with my friends and we will decide to call a conference of the Union and the employers on Wednesday. The agreement with the Union can be signed there with all the points on which we have agreed. I will telephone you on Monday. In the meantime, it would be advisable that you do not disclose what we talked about. Don't worry — the strike is settled!"

Happiness Destroyed

Monday — and Eitingon didn't call. On Tuesday, he didn't call. I thought that he had probably had some difficulty with the bosses, who were choking on the terms of the settlement. I also thought that the bosses who had authorized him to settle the strike with me must have let him know which of the Union's demands they would be willing to give in on. I knew that Mr. Eitingon was no errand boy for the bosses. He was respected by a large number of bosses and, in addition, even the rich manufacturers were deeply in debt to him. But I still couldn't calm myself.

On Wednesday, Eitingon called and asked me to come to his home. I ran! I came into a large room. Eitingon was sitting in a chair in the middle of the room, dressed in his coat, with his hands resting on his cane. He answered my greeting coldly. He told me he was leaving for London on important business. It was not easy for him to make up his mind, but he had decided that before he left, he must ask me a question which had been bothering him. "Remember that Saturday when you and I settled the strike for a 40-hour work week, a 10% raise in wages, and improvements of the old agreement with the employers? And Monday, you were in Washington, and there, you, Bill Green, the president of the AFL, Shachtman, the president of the International Fur Workers Union, and Meyer London had a conference with Mr. Samuels, the president of the employers' association, and you signed an agreement for a 42-hour week and a smaller raise in wages and none of the improvements to which we had agreed! Can you possibly explain why you agreed to a different settlement with Samuels and made a fool of me?"

"Mr. Eitingon, my explanation is a simple one," I answered him. "I was not in Washington on Monday. I never talked to Bill Green and I was not present at any conference with Mr. Samuels, nor did I come to any agreement with him. On Monday and Tuesday, I was in New York, waiting for your telephone call."

Mr. Eitingon didn't take his eyes off me, and then he said: "Ben Gold, I believe you. I couldn't believe that you could do such a thing. You really didn't know — but now you do know that such an agreement was signed in Washington." We parted friends.

I went back to the Union office, very upset. Weighty questions were hammering in my head. What could be done? How could this vile betrayal be undone? What would the strikers say about this treasonous agreement? They ridiculed and condemned the *Daily Forward* for its day-in, day-out strikebreaking propaganda, that the furriers' strike was a political maneuver, that the Communists had called it, not for the economic improvement of the working and living conditions of the workers, but to gain favor with their comrades in Moscow. Many strikers held the decided opinion that the bosses were paying the *Forward* to print their strikebreaking propaganda.

The strikers were well aware that the leaders of the former Progressive Group — Shachtman, Sorkin, Winnick and the others — who were now the leaders of the International Union, had rehired the "boys" of Kaufman's Organization Committee, had surrounded themselves with strikers of the right-wing *Forward's* clan, and were spreading the *Forward's* propaganda. But they had no influence on the honest strikers, who knew that this bunch was helping the scabs and the hired gangsters who "worked" for the bosses.

But the agreement had been signed by Bill Green and Mr. Samuels. This meant that the leader of the powerful AFL had taken over the leadership of the strike. Would the strikers of the small, poor Furriers Union take on the AFL? Or would they bow their heads before the combined power of the bosses, the AFL, the *Forward's* clan, the police and the gangsters? These and other questions tortured me.

Carnegie Hall

The answer of the united thousands of striking fur workers reverberated through the entire country. The New York representative of the AFL, Mr. Hugh Frayne, and President Shachtman called the strikers to a mass meeting in Carnegie Hall to present the agreement signed by Bill Green, Shachtman and Mr. Samuels.

So we called a meeting of all the shop chairmen to discuss the Carnegie Hall meeting. The shop chairmen were aflame with angry protests against the treason of Bill Green, Shachtman and Meyer London, the esteemed leader of the Socialist Party. The shop chairmen understood that boycotting the Carnegie Hall meeting would not be a practical battle strategy because the traitors would gather together their bunch of strikers of the *Forward's* clan, together with the scabs, and they would certainly approve the treasonous agreement with songs of praise for the traitors and gratitude toward the bosses' association president, Mr. Samuels. And the *Forward* would certainly print headlines that at a packed meeting in Carnegie Hall, thousands of strikers had ratified the agreement with enthusiasm, and that the strike was over.

"No! We won't boycott the Carnegie Hall meeting. We will go to the meeting," the shop chairmen declared. "No one will sell the fur workers as if they are slaves."

When I arrived at Carnegie Hall, thousands of strikers were already standing in long lines, filling the street and all along Seventh Avenue. Not far from the entrance, the famous detectives of the Industrial Squad blocked my way. They had gotten an "order" from the AFL's Mr. Frayne to arrest me. But they said that they didn't want to arrest me. "Take my advice, Ben, and go home," said Johnny Broderick, the chief of the murderous Industrial Squad. I answered that when the meeting was over, I would go home. Broderick got very angry. "Are you blind? Can't you see what's going on here? Your whole union is here. Fifty mounted police. The slightest disturbance will turn into a blood bath. Go home, I'm telling you. Understand?"

Suddenly, there was a clap of thunder! Through the window of the hall came a mighty shout from those assembled there: "We want Gold! We want Gold!" Broderick and his helpers ran into the hall to see what was going on. Two strikers with whom I had come to the meeting grabbed me by the arms and said: "Come, Ben, it's getting too hot in there," and they literally dragged me away from the hall. The shouts of "We want Gold!" combined with the loud cries of the thousands of strikers in the streets shouting "We want Gold!" continued to be heard, even though I was already quite a distance from Carnegie Hall.

The newspapers were delighted with the dramatic Carnegie Hall events. Nothing like this had ever happened before in any strike. They wrote in great detail of how the hall was filled to capacity with striking fur workers, and how, when the representative of the AFL, Mr. Frayne, wanted to open the meeting, they didn't give him a chance. Before he could even open his mouth, the assembled strikers thundered out, "We want Gold!" and Mr. Frayne was left standing there in silence, waiting for the audience to quiet down. When the shouts of "We want Gold!" lessened, he again tried to say something, but as soon as he started to speak, the shouts of "We want Gold!" began anew. This happened several times. Meanwhile, the thousands of strikers outside the hall picked up the cry, and their shouts from outside drifted into the hall, joining the shouts within.

Poor Mr. Frayne, tired and dejected, sat down in his chair. When Mr. Shachtman, the president of the International Union, tried to say something, he, too, was met with the thundering cries from inside and outside the hall: "We want Ben Gold! We don't want you!" He tried twice more, and each time he was shouted down by the strikers. When Shachtman walked to a corner of the platform with shaky steps, Secretary Coughlin of the New York City Central Trades and Labor Council, made an attempt to speak to the strikers, and he got the same reception as Frayne and Shachtman.

Finally, Police Inspector Lyons strode out onto the stage and announced the good news that the committee had decided not to hold this meeting and that everyone should leave the hall. In the minds of the strikers, this meeting was an outstanding success, and they applauded the announcement vigorously and marched out of the hall.

The Shop Chairmen's Meeting

At the meeting of the shop chairmen held one day after the Carnegie Hall meeting, an interesting discussion developed which deserves some space in my short memoirs.

One shop chairman said in his speech that what had happened in Carnegie Hall was so clear that "not even a million words could express the issue more clearly. The demonstration by thousands of workers has expressed, in a most powerful way, the hatred for and the condemnation of the strikebreakers, and it is possible that now the traitors will back off into their holes, and the furriers will now be able to carry on their strike without further interference, until their just demands are met."

A second shop chairman almost screamed that it was "naive" and even dangerous to think that Shachtman and his bunch "will retreat like tired doves into their dove-cotes and give up their strikebreaking activities." "The furriers have learned from experience," he said, "that betrayers of workers have no conscience and no human feelings. The trials and tribulations of workers are no concern of theirs. Certainly they have principles: Swollen bank books are their holy principles." He shouted: "We have to be on our guard because the defeat at Carnegie Hall only made them more bitter, and they are burning for revenge, and we know that they are capable of the worst kinds of crimes." The shop chairmen applauded him loudly.

A third shop chairman explained that all traitors "weave false and deceptive theories and philosophies to justify their crimes," and that they use their lies and false accusations for so long that they begin to believe that their lies are the honest truth. "Therefore," he said, "we don't dare delude ourselves into believing that the strikebreakers will repent their treacherous deeds and allow us to carry on our fight with the bosses. The strikebreakers are probably working out a new plan right now to help the bosses break our strike and we must be prepared to insure the defeat of the traitors."

A few other shop chairmen briefly expressed their opinions. They

64

concurred that the "gentlemen won't give up their strikebreaking conspiracy, and we must be ready to fight them every step of the way."

When the discussion was over, I told the shop chairmen that I was considering going to Washington to speak with Bill Green about the strike and about the Carnegie Hall meeting, if he would agree to talk to me. I wanted to know what they thought of the idea — and again a discussion developed which deserves a place in my short memoirs.

The first shop chairman to speak said that my visit to Green was not practical. "The Bill Greens have a way of interpreting everything to suit their own needs. First of all, he will interpret your coming to him as a sign that you acknowledge him as the chosen almighty ruler of the labor movement, and that no one dares to be insubordinate toward him, and that you had come to him in order to ask forgiveness for the striking furriers for their sinful behavior in Carnegie Hall. Secondly, Green will interpret your visit as proof that things are not going well with the strike, that it is collapsing, and he will order the acceptance of the agreement with Samuels so that the workers can return to work. Therefore, I am opposed to the visit."

The second shop chairman said that "the leader of the Socialists, Meyer London, AFL President Bill Green, and the president of the bosses' association, Mr. Samuels, certainly created a kettle of fish with their traitorous agreement. Shachtman is only their errand boy. It is clear, even to a schoolboy, that there is a connection between the leader of the Socialists and the AFL leaders, and they are under the leadership of the bosses to fight against every honest, progressive union leader, by howling that they are all Communist agents of Moscow and enemies of the labor movement in our democratic nation. Green knows that Ben Gold is a Communist, so his attitude toward Gold will be as toward a dangerous enemy. He will tell Gold that he, Green, signed the agreement with Samuels in order to save the workers and the Union, and that this agreement is legal and binding and that no one can alter it. And that will be the end of his conference with Gold, and then the rotten, scab *Forward* will happily print that Bill Green threw Ben Gold out of his office." He finished his speech with an appeal to ignore the traitors: "Let them bark and howl! The season is about to begin. The bosses will settle with the Union better when they are losing business."

The third shop chairman did not agree with the two previous speakers. He said that he was relying on Ben Gold not to talk to Green in a subservient manner. Gold would probably tell Green about the gangsters and the graft system that had existed in the Union under the Kaufman administration, about the Greek slave-shops, and about the gangster-protected shops. Gold would probably bring along factual proof to confirm that everything he said was the truth. Gold would probably also tell Green about his settlement with Eitingon for a 40-hour week and other gains. Gold would also assure Green that the strike was going well, and he would not be ashamed to tell Green that the Carnegie Hall meeting had shown the entire world the unity and solidarity of the strikers, and that Bill Green, himself, had probably heard the cries of the strikers inside and outside of Carnegie Hall all the way to Washington. "And what will Bill Green answer? If his answer doesn't satisfy us, we'll throw it into the waste basket. In short, it is my opinion that Gold should talk to Bill Green, if it is possible." The third speaker won the debate. The shop chairman agreed and accepted the proposal that I should have a talk with Bill Green.

I telephoned Bill Green and told him that I thought it was important that we have a talk about the strike, and that I was ready to come to see him in Washington. He answered that he would be in New York the next day and would be staying at the Cadillac Hotel. He said I should call him there to decide on a time for our conference.

I was under the impression that the president of the AFL, the leader of millions of organized workers, who had to struggle daily with complex problems, would excel in intelligence, talent and experience. I soon realized my error. True, Green was a quiet man, lacking the usual arrogance of "big" leaders, who are usually quick to let you know that they are even bigger than they really are. But I was soon convinced that I was talking to a small-town politician who says one thing and almost immediately says something else, which is just the opposite of what he has just finished saying, and that he was playing a game with me in order to win my trust so I would allow myself to be led by him.

In order to forestall any arguments from me, Green talked first and let me know that he had signed the agreement with Samuels because President Shachtman had informed him that the strike was going badly and that many of the workers were going back to work.

I told him that Shachtman didn't know a thing about the strike, that he was not a member of the General Strike Committee which was in charge of the strike, that during the course of the strike, he had not once addressed a meeting of the strikers, that he didn't come to the Union office, that he had never even visited any of the halls where the strikers met every day, and that he was never on a picket line to talk to the strikers. "In short, he knows about as much about the strike as my grandmother does."

"That means that Shachtman misled me?" Green asked.

"Indeed he did," I said with assurance, satisfied that Green now recognized that he had been misled by Shachtman. I thought that now that he realized that he could not rely on Shachtman's information, he would be careful not to be misled by him again. Again I was wrong. The very next day, at a second meeting with him, he suggested that his New York representative, Frayne, should call a conference with the bosses to settle the strike. Frayne would represent the AFL, Shachtman and his vice-presidents would represent the International Union, and I and

66

other strike leaders would represent the New York Union.

The maneuver was clear: I should acknowledge that Bill Green and Shachtman and their helpers were the leaders of and spokesmen for the strike. However, it was also clear to me that if I should refuse to participate in such a conference with the strikebreakers, it would be used as propaganda by these gentlemen to show that the Communist leaders were not interested in settling the strike.

Green suggested that Frayne be the chairman of the conference. I agreed. Then he suggested that the Union call a mass meeting of the strikers and that both he and Shachtman would address the meeting. Again, I agreed.

The Mass Meeting

The mass meeting of the strikers was held in the 69th Regiment Armory at 26th Street and Lexington Avenue. The armory was packed with strikers, and thousands of strikers for whom there was no room inside stood outside. I do not know what Bill Green had in mind to tell the strikers before he came to the meeting, but I am almost certain that the reception he was accorded by the strikers affected him so strongly that he gave a speech worthy of a loyal labor leader. Miracle of miracles!

In his speech, Green praised the brave strikers who were fighting for their just demands, and he assured those assembled that he would help them win a 40-hour week and their other demands as well. His speech was full of many fine words. Of course, understandably, the strikers applauded him vigorously.

I don't know whether the ice-cold reception Shachtman received when the chairman, Mr. Frayne, called on him to speak made Green feel pity for his "partner," but Green undoubtedly understood that this was the way the strikers were expressing their contempt for President Shachtman for his treasonous deeds.

I do not know if Green felt deep regret that the Communist, Ben Gold, was rewarded with stormy applause when chairman Frayne called me to address the meeting. There was applause both during my speech and when I finished. I do believe that Green was convinced that it was Gold, not Shachtman, who held the trust of the strikers. When the meeting ended, he extended his hand to me and said: "It was a good meeting — a very good meeting." I thanked him for his speech.

The Conference With the Bosses

A few days after the mass meeting, the conference with the bosses was held. Mr. Samuels and two bosses represented the employers' association, Shachtman and his two vice-presidents represented the International Union, I and two other strike leaders represented the strikers. Brother Frayne, who chaired the conference, represented the AFL.

Frayne opened the conference by thanking the bosses for accepting his invitation to the conference and stated that he represented William Green, the president of the AFL, and that the conference had been called for the purpose of ending the strike and would not end until that objective was reached.

The first speaker was Mr. Samuels. He made a really nice speech. He said that it was an established fact that the fur workers were the best-paid workers in the needle trades, that the working conditions in the fur shops were absolutely heavenly, and that the treatment of the workers by their bosses was most friendly. Workers continued working from their youth to their old age because these shops were their second home, and when a worker needed a loan, he didn't have to run to a pawn shop with his wife's engagement ring. He could get a no-interest loan, with easy payments, from his boss.

But, Mr. Samuels continued, the present Union leaders had, in a very short time, incited the workers against the bosses and had created an unbearable situation in the trade. In July, in the middle of the season, they called shop strikes. They knew that the agreement with the bosses prohibited strikes. They had even provoked the foremen to turn against the bosses. And the demands they authorized for the new agreement — Mr. Samuels almost screamed when he talked about the Union demands. Each and every demand was aimed at "ruining our business! My respect for Bill Green and my respect for President Shachtman forced me to sign an agreement with them — an agreement which guarantees gains for the fur workers — a gift way beyond their wildest dreams handed to them on a silver platter."

He emphasized: "The agreement that I signed with Bill Green and Shachtman is a viable document." He then demanded that the Union leaders call an end to the strike. The workers should be sent back to the shops, and he gave the Union leaders 48 hours to send the workers back to the shops and announced that if his demand was not carried out, the Union would be responsible for the manufacturers' losses.

Frayne, the chairman of the conference, answered Mr. Samuels with a few short remarks. He stated that President Green was not only respected by the millions of members of the AFL, but also by a large number of manufacturers. President Green's signature on an agreement was his "word of honor," and no one could erase President Green's signature from the agreement with the manufacturers. Further, President Green would never have signed any agreement with the representatives of the manufacturers unless he was convinced that the gains for the workers would improve their working and living conditions. "When this conference is over," he concluded, "President Green will know that the strike has ended — that the agreement was approved by all parties! President Green expects this, and we will not disappoint him!"

When Brother Frayne had finished his brief remarks, he invited President Shachtman to have his say. Shachtman concocted a speech. First, he expressed his gratitude to Frayne for his active participation in the "complicated and highly responsible activities of the International Furriers Union to put an end to this tragic strike situation of the thousands of New York fur workers."

Then President Shachtman expressed his gratitude to "President Mr. Samuels" and the two other leaders of the bosses' association for coming to this conference. He assured Mr. Samuels that his signature on the agreement reached in Washington with the help of President Green obliged him to use his authority as president of the International Union to make certain that the agreement was carried out. He said he would send out letters to the strikers and explain their gains to them, and he didn't have "the slightest doubt" that the strikers would realize the necessity of ending the strike. But "before I send out the letters to the strikers, it is my wish and my hope that the present conference will produce an agreement by all parties concerned that they accept the Washington agreement and put an end to the tragic strike situation."

Chairman Frayne then said: "Mr. Gold, we are waiting for your answer." I answered: "Mr. Samuels told the conference that the wages of the fur workers are the highest in the needle trades and that the bosses treat their workers in a most friendly way — so I want to tell the conference that during the past few months, many bosses, members of the association, were forced to pay their workers back pay which amounted to many thousands of dollars. In the old agreement, there is a provision that the bosses are not allowed to pay less than the minimum wage scale, but the bosses made a point of paying less than the minimum, and for overtime, they paid less than time-and-a-half, and for holidays they only paid for half days. They scoffed at the agreement and robbed the workers. Yes, and a few of the bosses even falsified their books. Just these few facts show that Mr. Samuels' contention that the bosses treat the workers in an honest and decent way is a slight exaggeration.

"And about Mr. Samuels' argument that his agreement with President Green and President Shachtman is a viable document, and his demand that the strikers return to work because the strike is settled — I want to tell Mr. Samuels that his viable document is not an agreement!"

"What? Do you know what you're saying, Mr. Gold?" Samuels shouted out.

"Of course, Mr. Samuels, I know what I am saying," I answered. "You, Mr. Samuels, are very well aware that a deal made between the representatives of the Union and the representatives of the bosses becomes an agreement only when both parties, the membership of the bosses' association and the membership of the Union, agree with and accept the settlement, and if my side doesn't agree and rejects the offer of the conference committee, there is no agreement in the industry."

A pale and shaken Samuels then asked me: "Why aren't you telling the strikers about the agreement with President Green and President Shachtman?"

"Mr. Samuels, I told the workers about your agreement, and their answer echoed over the length and breadth of the United States. Thousands of furriers gave their answer at the Carnegie Hall meeting."

"Brother Frayne said that there was no meeting in Carnegie Hall — only the staging of a wild Bolshevist comedy," Shachtman screamed, and added that Carnegie Hall was a stigma on the Union, and his helpers screamed that a wild mob had broken up the meeting. One screamed louder than the other. I remained silent.

Brother Frayne lost his calm. He closed the conference.

The Answer of the Strikers

At packed meetings of the strikers, I reported what had happened at the wonderful conference. The strikers derived real pleasure from my report of Mr. Samuels' speech. His depiction of the "Garden-of-Eden" conditions in the shops, and his statement about the friendly attitude of the bosses toward the workers made the walls thunder with laughter.

When I told the thousands of workers who packed the five halls that Brother Frayne and President Shachtman had joined with the bosses at the conference in demanding that the strikers accept their Washington agreement and return to work, the strikers shouted *en masse:* "Carnegie Hall! Carnegie Hall!"

Then I told the assembled strikers that "Carnegie Hall" was also my answer to the bosses and the traitorous union leaders. I told them what my answer was to Mr. Samuels: "Your agreement with Bill Green and Mr. Shachtman is not a valid agreement because the strikers rejected the Washington pact at the historic Carnegie Hall meeting."

Thousands of strikers answered the claims of Shachtman and Frayne that the Washington agreement had ended the strike by forming close rows of pickets which filled the sidewalks in front of their shops. Thousands of strikers answered by marching in close ranks through the streets and avenues where the fur industry was located. Neither the daily mass arrests nor the gangsters could diminish the enthusiasm and the fighting spirit of the strikers.

The hatred of the thousands of strikers for the Shachtman-Sorkin family of traitors and the strikebreaking Socialist *Daily Forward* grew every day. At the same time, the trust and devotion of the strikers toward the Union leaders also grew. The unity among the strikers, their enthusiastic readiness to carry out their duties in the face of the real danger of the army of the bosses' gangsters and often of the policemen's clubs, astounded even our enemies.

A Chapter of History

The longer the strike lasted, the greater the financial outlay of the Union became. Each day, the Union had to pay fines that the corrupt judges meted out to the arrested strikers. The biggest expense of the Union was the weekly strike benefits paid to the strikers. Many of the strikers, the best-paid workers, refused to accept strike benefits, but the poor, needy strikers were in greater need of strike benefits every week.

We called a meeting of the workers who worked in the shops owned by independent bosses who didn't belong to the association and who had settled with the Union. The workers of the "settled" shops paid a voluntary weekly strike tax of 15% of their wages. I explained to the assembled workers that the Union was in great need of money and suggested that the voluntary strike tax be raised from 15% to 25% of their wages.

Many workers protested against this suggestion. They argued that since they were working 40 hours for 44 hours of pay and had gotten additional raises as well, it was perfectly justifiable to pay more than a 25% strike tax to help the strikers. They suggested that the least they should pay was 30% of their wages.

When my suggestion of a 25% strike tax was accepted by a majority of the assembled striker workers, the "protesters" jumped out of their chairs and shouted that they would ignore the decision of the majority and would pay 30% of their wages! And they kept their promise.

Another Chapter of History

That week, I called a meeting of shop chairmen and told them that the Union was in financial trouble and that they should ask the strikers from their shops if they would wait a few days for their strike benefits.

"Don't worry — it's no problem," the chairmen assured me. Two days later, the chairmen told me that they hadn't said anything to their workers about waiting for their strike benefits because they brought $10,000 to the Union. They told me that the highest-paid workers had provided "these few dollars" as a loan to the Union, and that a movement had started among a large number of workers to buy "Liberty Bonds" and that the money would be given as a loan, interest-free, of course, and that the Liberty Bond Committee had already sold Liberty Bonds to many of the workers and also to the foremen.

I think that these two chapters of history tell something about the devotion of the strikers to their Union and to their leaders.

The Week of Revenge

The story of the Liberty Bonds spread quickly and reached the bosses. Ridiculously exaggerated rumors about the gigantic sale of Liberty Bonds began to be circulated — that the strikers and their friends who weren't fur workers had already bought tens of thousands of dollars' worth of Liberty Bonds, and that the foremen had bought $50,000 worth — no more, no less.

The bosses were hurting. Their plan and their expectations that a strike that would last three or four months would impoverish the Union, and that the hungry workers would run back to work without the Union were destroyed. Now the Union was getting rich from the Liberty Bonds! And now their Washington agreement was a worthless piece of paper!

The worried leaders of the bosses' association decided not to depend on miracles. Their worries increased when two of the bosses, members of the association, settled with the Union, and the leaders of the association were terribly afraid lest this little crack in their ranks should, God forbid, get any bigger. They decided to employ the necessary means to break the strike. At a special meeting of the Special Committee, the top leaders made it very clear that "the strike will not be broken with 'kid gloves.' "

Certainly it was our fault — the fault of the strike leaders. During the previous few weeks, the pickets had been marching on the sidewalks, not far from the entrances of the buildings in which the fur shops were located, and had suffered only from the arrests by the police which took place every day. The gangsters who had been hired by the bosses to bring the few scabs into the shops each morning hadn't dared to use their fists against the strikers. They had learned from experience. During this period, when they parked their cars with their scab passengers, the police were already waiting for them and escorted them into the buildings where they could "deliver their scab merchandise."

We, the leaders of the strikers, never imagined that the leaders of the bosses' association would hire an army of gangsters, not for the protection of the scabs, but for the exclusive purpose of butchering the strikers. We had prepared neither the pickets nor the special picketing committee for such a possibility.

And that bloody morning, the gangsters, with the help of the police, "delivered" the few scabs just as on all the previous mornings. Then the police and the gangsters disappeared. No fights broke out with the gangsters, nor with the scabs, and no strikers were arrested. The pickets marched on the sidewalks, greeting each other happily this quiet morning. There was a holiday-like feeling.

Then suddenly, the gangsters came out of their hiding places and beat a large number of strikers mercilessly. The small group of unprepared workers that made up the special picketing committee tried to protect the attacked pickets, but they were unable to save the pickets from the brutal attacks of the gangsters. The few workers who belonged to the special picket committee came out of the gangster attack with bloodied and swollen faces, just like the beaten strikers.

The leaders of the strike understood that the bosses had not hired these murderers for a single "visit." It was also clear to us that the goal of the bosses was to chase the pickets away from their shops, and that the lives of the pickets were in danger.

The same day, more than two hundred strikers volunteered to protect the pickets and to "debate" with the gangsters. The meeting with the volunteers didn't last long. The majority of the volunteers were Jewish workers; there were also among them Greek workers, Ukranians and Russians, two Poles, and two Italians. They knew that their job was serious and risky, but they also knew that the bosses were using the gangsters to break the strike.

I warned them that the gangsters who beat up the pickets were not of the same ilk as those gangsters who "delivered" the scabs to the bosses. The gangsters that the bosses had now brought in were specialists in their trade. The Greek chairman of the committee of Greek strikers who had volunteered to confront the gangsters answered me: "Brother Gold, you are telling us that the gangsters have attacked the pickets. Here we have two hundred volunteers. Even the strongest gangster is helpless when twenty mosquitoes attack him, and each one of us weighs more than even the biggest mosquito. You don't have to worry about us, Brother Gold." All the volunteers laughed heartily.

One of the Russian volunteers said that the gangsters beat up strikers for money, but the strikers were fighting for their ideals, for the benefit of the furriers, for the interests of the working class — and "that makes our fists even stronger." His few words were applauded loudly.

A Jewish volunteer said that he had seen the beaten strikers and that he was burning with anger and thirsty for revenge for the spilled blood of the workers. "You can depend on us!" he said.

"I am depending on you," I answered and closed the meeting.

During the first confrontation with the gangsters, the police rescued the hired murderers, who paid with their blood for the spilled blood of the strikers.

The second day after that first "debate," the gangsters did not show up. On the third day, they showed up with reenforcements and again had to be rescued by the police. But this time, a few of the gangsters left the battlefield by ambulance. The gangsters disappeared. The scabs had to spend the night in the shops.

The defeat of the leaders of the bosses' association resounded through the fur industry. The mighty leaders ran to Mr. Eitingon and asked him to rescue them. He answered that after they had rejected his settlement with the Union, he had decided to have nothing more to do with the strike issue. But when Mr. Samuels came to him and asked him to arrange a conference with me for the purpose of settling the strike, Eitingon called me and informed me of Samuels' request. The thought of a conference with this gentleman made me sick, but I thought that a settlement could possibly be reached, and I agreed.

The Conference With Samuels

When I entered the designated hotel room, Mr. Samuels was already waiting for me. He greeted me courteously, and as soon as I was seated in the comfortable chair, he began to deliver his prepared speech. He wanted me to know, he said, that my leadership of the Union was a blessing for the manufacturers who belonged to the association and who had an agreement with the Union. Before I took over the leadership of the Union, he continued, there were several hundred open shops, in which union conditions did not exist, and where the wages of the workers were much lower than in the Union shops. The manufacturers in the open shops were in competition with the manufacturers in the Union shops. This competition grew stronger and stronger and went so far that the manufacturers — members of the association — were forced to compete with each other. The association had to appoint a "czar" and authorized him to use any lawful means to regulate the sharp competition among the association members. "We paid him and his two helpers $50,000 a year, but he didn't help us at all."

"But under your leadership," he went on, "the 120 Greek open shops were unionized, as well as many Jewish open shops, and the damned competition is now under control. Now you understand why the association looks upon your leadership as a blessing for the fur industry?"

I didn't say a word. I looked at him, listened to his speech, and couldn't understand why Mr. Samuels was singing these lovely songs of praise for me. But when he had finished his speech, I realized what this conscienceless gentleman had in mind.

"Mr. Gold," Mr. Samuels said. "What would happen if you would give up the leadership of your Union? Hundreds of open shops would spring up again, and again there would be the cut-throat competition with big losses for the 500 manufacturers who are members of the association and have an agreement with the Union. We do not want you to resign as manager of the Union. I want to repeat again that your leadership is a blessing for the workers and for the manufacturers. I understand that it is difficult to get along on the wages that the Union is paying you. I have already told you that we paid the lawyer and his assistants $50,000 a year, and they didn't help us. We would gladly pay you the same sum yearly to insure that you will remain the leader of the Union and keep all the enemies under union control."

I was ready to present President Samuels with the kind of answer he deserved, but I controlled my anger and calmly measured the words I used to answer him. I said, "Mr. Samuels, I am richer than even the wealthiest fur manufacturer. Let us talk about settling the strike."

About settling the strike, he said this was how things stood: the agreement that he had signed with President Green and President Shachtman guaranteed the workers the best working conditions they had ever had. This agreement had been approved by his association, and his association would never break an agreement. But because of the misunderstandings that had developed in the Union which were extending the strike into a long, drawn-out affair, and for the sake of the interests of both parties — the manufacturers and the workers — he was ready to withdraw his signature from the agreement he had made with President Green and was ready now to sign an agreement with me. He was even prepared, he said, that an agreement with me would guarantee the workers the same gains that had been written into the agreement he had signed with the president of the AFL.

I answered that his association wasn't breaking the agreement with Bill Green because that agreement no longer existed. Bill Green knew nothing about the strike of the fur workers, he was under the impression that Shachtman, as president of the International Union, represented the strikers, and he, Green, had believed Shachtman's assurances that the strikers would be happy with the conditions of the Washington agreement and would return to the shops.

"But, Mr. Samuels," I continued, "the strikers very clearly answered that Shachtman doesn't represent them, that they could not honor the Washington agreement, and that they will strike until they are guaranteed their demands: the 40-hour week with pay for 44 hours and all the other demands. And, Mr. Samuels, you know very well that Bill Green and Shachtman do not represent the strikers and are not empowered to end the strike and to send the workers back to the shops. Therefore, their agreement with you is worthless — it doesn't exist. It's only a piece of paper. The only way, Mr. Samuels, to settle the strike is by an agreement that guarantees the demands of the strikers."

Mr. Samuels now got a bit impatient and hot under the collar. He then delivered a very clever and tricky speech. He said: "Mr. Gold, you cannot deny that if I withdraw my signature from the agreement with the president of the AFL, it would be an important victory for you and your union. If I withdraw my signature from an agreement with Shachtman, who is, after all, the president of the International Union, it would be another victory for you and your union, and if I sign an agreement with you, it would mean that I recognize you as the legal representative of the Union, and that is really a major victory for you and your union. And if I agree that in the agreement I will sign with you, all the points that were written into the Washington agreement will be included, that is also a major victory for the workers. Isn't that enough? And you are asking me to give in to all your demands. Is that justice?"

I answered that of all the gains he had enumerated, not one would improve the living conditions of the workers, and if he was calling for justice and if he really wanted to settle the strike but was protesting that I was insisting on getting all the Union's demands, then I was ready to reach a compromise with him. I told him that I was ready to close an agreement with him according to the agreement that I had made earlier with Mr. Eitingon.

"No!" Mr. Samuels shouted. "My association will never agree to a 40-hour work week paid for 44 hours and with raises on top of that. Tell that to the strikers!"

The conference had ended.

My dear friends and assistants, Jack Schneider and Aaron Gross, were waiting for me in the hotel lobby. I told them of the little drama that had been played out at the conference with Samuels. We decided that when I reported on this conference to the strikers, I would not say a word about the graft offer that Samuels had made to me because it was not necessary and was ugly and disgusting.

But our decision not to tell about the graft order was not successful. In the one day until we called a meeting of the shop chairmen to report on the conference with Samuels, the story had been spread about among the bosses and among the foremen and had been picked up by many of the strikers.

When I came into the hall where the shop chairmen were assembled, a few of the shop chairmen raised me up on their shoulders and carried me to the platform. I fought with all my might to be let down, but the harder I fought, the tighter their grip became.

On the platform, I quickly wiped the ink off my jacket from my squashed fountain pen that I had kept in my breast pocket and stuffed my pulled-out shirt back into my pants, while the chairmen laughed and had a great time enjoying my "pogromized" condition.

When I finished my report on my conference with Samuels, the chairmen attacked me with questions. "Ben, why aren't you telling us everything about the conference? Why aren't you telling us that ticklish story? Are you ashamed? Ben, we know all about what happened there, but we want you to tell it to us — the entire interesting comedy." I answered that I would not talk about the affair. Let them ask Samuels.

A Talk With the Merchants

One week later, Eitingon invited me to a meeting in his office with a few of the richest fur merchants. I didn't know any of them. They greeted me with extreme politeness. They behaved toward me as if they were the owners of the entire fur industry, and I was their customer who hadn't been paying his bills.

Why, they asked me, did I negate the agreement that the president of the AFL and the president of the International Furriers Union had signed with Mr. Samuels? I answered that neither the president of the AFL nor the president of the International Union had the moral or legal right to conclude an agreement with the bosses without the knowledge of the strikers, and that the agreement they had signed was a betrayal of the interests of the workers.

And why, they asked again, was I demanding a 40-hour work week when the workers in the needle trades were working 44 hours a week? My answer was that the fur workers produced coats that sold for several thousand dollars each and that the workers had to strain their eyes and were under constant stress to the limit of their abilities and strength not to make any mistakes in their work on such expensive coats. In addition, the fur workers suffered from skin diseases, asthma, and tuberculosis, and even 40 hours a week was too long to work in the fur shops where the air was so polluted.

When they were finished with all their questions, the millionaire merchants opened their big mouths. They complained that under my union leadership, the industry had been thrown into a chaotic situation: shop strikes every day, pickets, fights, arrests, ruination for the industry!

"You say 'ruination,' " I answered them, "and Samuels told me that my union leadership was a blessing."

"What? What?" they shouted in unison, astounded.

When I told them that the Union's successful struggle to unionize the open shops had put an end to the terrible competition in the trade, as Samuels had explained it to me, and that this was the reason Samuels looked upon my leadership as a blessing to the trade, they were dumbstruck and sat there like dead dolls.

Mr. A. L. Lindheim, the lawyer and Eitingon's partner, who was the chairman of the meeting, appealed to me that I should not leave the meeting with the impression that these gentlemen, the merchants, were enemies of the Union. "The truth is, we all sympathize with the strikers," he said. "We want the strike to be settled quickly and all the conflicts between the Union and the bosses to be smoothed out in a friendly way, without strikes."

A day after my meeting with the merchants, I received a call from Mr. Lindheim asked me to meet with him. I did, and we settled the strike on the same terms on which I had agreed with Eitingon.

Settled!

Two days later, Bill Green came to New York. He had called together the newspaper reporters and had let them know that he had come to New York to bring an end to the furriers' strike that the agreement he had signed with Mr. Samuels in Washington was in force, and that both parties — the AFL and the bosses — respected their agreement.

"But Ben Gold doesn't recognize your agreement," the newspaper reporters told him.

Green answered that he had called Ben Gold and the president of the International Union, and also the vice-presidents, to a conference which would be held the next day in the hotel where he, Green, was staying. He stated emphatically that if Ben Gold prevented him from carrying out his responsible duties toward the strikers, he would have to use all legal means to remove Ben Gold from the Furriers Union.

The conference called by Green lasted for an entire day. All during this conference, a bitter war raged between me and the president of the International Union and his two vice-presidents, Sorkin and Winnick.

Green opened the conference. He said that the bosses were demanding that he respect the agreement he had signed with the association's president, Mr. Samuels, that he had been receiving a lot of mail from strikers asking him to bring the strike to an end, and that the next day, he would announce in all the newspapers that the strike was over. He appealed to me and demanded that I acknowledge the plight the strikers were in, suffering because of my stubbornness, and that I not hinder him in ending the strike in an honorable way. He said he had "waited long enough, and maybe too long" — he would wait no longer. He was determined to fulfill his duties toward the strikers.

The three "chiefs" of the International Union jumped out of their chairs and applauded President Green's speech. Then Brother Shachtman delivered a speech. He told of strikers who had come to his office and even to his home and begged him to end the strike. The few dollars that they got each week from the Union in strike benefits were not enough to feed their families. They did not want to scab! They were good union members, but they couldn't endure the strike any longer. And God, yes, God! had sent the great leader of the AFL, Brother Bill Green, to rescue the twelve thousand strikers and their families from their desperate situation.

As expected, his two vice-presidents applauded him but Green and I sat still. Green was smiling with joy and pride; I was on fire with pain and anger.

Then I spoke. "President Green," I said, turning to him, "come out on the picket line with me anywhere from 25th Street to 30th Street and Seventh Avenue. See and speak with the thousands of strikers, with the women, with younger and older strikers who are picketing the shops. You will become convinced that the high morale among the strikers is something most unusual. Ask the strikers their opinion of President Shachtman and his vice-presidents. You will hear what hateful things the strikers have to say about them and the hideous names the strikers have for them. You will become convinced, President Green, that what Shachtman says about the need to rescue the strikers is false and treasonous.

"Allow me, Mr. Green to tell you something about the weekly strike benefits that the Union is paying the strikers, which Mr. Shachtman was talking about. A large number of the best workers, specialists in their trades, who work in the best shops and earn more than all the other workers, like, for example, the foremen and the cutters, are not accepting any strike benefits.

"The strikers are divided into five separate halls. The strikers of each hall receive their benefit payments on a designated day of the week. Two weeks ago, I called a few of the shop chairmen and asked them to tell the workers of their shops that instead of Tuesday, they should come on Friday for their strike benefits, because the Union was tight on finances. Without my knowledge and without my approval, these few shop chairmen brought thousands of dollars to me at the Union — money they had collected from strikers as loans to the Union. This was accomplished in only three days. President Green, in all the years that you have been active in the trade union movement, have you ever heard of such an expression of loyalty and devotion to their strike leadership by strikers, or such readiness to help with all their capabilities so that their strike could be won? I am sure that you know that the strikers literally risk their lives when they defend themselves against the murderous gangsters that the bosses hire to butcher the pickets. They suffer from the mass arrests and from the brutality of the police, and not even that is weakening their courage and their determination to win their just demands.

"And now, President Green, I want you to know that two days ago, before you came to New York, at a conference with a very influential person in the fur industry, I settled the srike with all the provisions that had been written into the agreement that I had worked out with Mr. Eitingon. That means a 40-hour work week, a substantial raise in the workers' wages, and other gains for the workers.

"I am appealing to you, President Green. Tell the newspaper reporters who are waiting in the lobby that you have decided to leave the problem of settling the strike to the leaders of the strike, and I assure you, President Green, that in a matter of a few days, the strikers will be going back to work with their heads high, like proud victors who have achieved important victories for themselves and have paved the way for other unions for the same and perhaps even better working and living conditions."

When I finished my few words, one of the vice-presidents of the International Union, infamous among the furriers as a corrupt and cynical creature, grumbled: "A fine story for old ladies!"

Stiff and stony, as if he had just awakened from a deep sleep, Green asked me "Who is the person with whom you settled the strike? What is his name?"

"I don't know if I have the right to disclose his name," I answered.

President Shachtman and his two vice-presidents broke out into smiles, and the vice-president, known for his corrupt and cynical nature, growled under his breath: "He doesn't have a name. The man hasn't been born yet."

This arrogant and needling remark by that vice-president, whose "deeds" in the Union were no secret, really burned me up. I almost shouted: "President Green, I give you my word of honor, I swear by all that is holy and dear to me that everything I have said about my settlement of the strike is the truth — the absolute truth!"

"And I'm telling you, Ben Gold," Bill Green said in a stern voice, "that I know from reliable sources that the manufacturers do not recognize the so-called 'Eitingon agreement.' "

He got up from his chair and strode toward the exit. Near the door, he stopped and spelled out these words: "I want you to make a concerted effort to reach an understanding like responsible union leaders," and he marched out of the room.

Now Brother President Shachtman, who was chairing the conference, stated that he was sure that we could agree that one important understanding could be reached without any difficulty — that we should now go to eat lunch and come back in an hour. We voted with our feet.

Having eaten, we returned to the hotel room to continue our conference. We didn't argue, we didn't raise our voices, but for the next few hours, our conversation was a series of knife thrusts. It is impossible and not necessary, and also not nice to write down all the barbed questions and answers with which we quietly and calmly attacked each other at this conference. A few questions and answers will shed light on what transpired.

President Shachtman cynically asked if this very influential person with whom I had settled the strike the day before was a manufacturer, a banker, or maybe a messenger from Moscow.

I answered: "It is not important who or what he is, but I know for sure that he did not participate in the secret conference, and he did not sign that treasonous agreement with Mr. Samuels and Mr. Shachtman."

Vice-President Winnick asked: "Did Moscow order you to demand a 40-hour work week and all your other crazy demands?"

My answer: "No, it was not Moscow that ordered me, but my conscience. But you wouldn't know anything about a conscience."

The corrupt creature, the other vice-president, asked: "The strike has already cost hundreds of thousands of dollars. How much has Moscow quietly stuffed into your treasury? Tell us, and we promise not to tell anyone."

My answer: "During the tragic strike of 1920, you were the leader of the so-called picket committee. When the strike was near its end, you disappeared and bought a big bakery business. Maybe you would like to tell me where you suddenly got the thousands to buy such an establishment? You tell me that, and I will tell you how much money Moscow is sending me for the strike."

Shachtman said: "Ben, we are among friends here, so as a friend, I want to ask you: you know that the bosses will not give in on your exaggerated demands, and certainly not on the 40-hour week. You know this very well, just as we know it, and you know that the agreement signed by Bill Green and Samuels will not be broken. You know what the signatures of these two people mean. Why, then, are you torturing the strikers? You are committing a terrible crime!"

My answer: "Shachtman, if you and Bill Green are ready to tell the reporters who are waiting in the lobby today that the problem of settling the strike is the responsibility of the leaders of the strike, I am ready to sign a document that if I don't win the 40-hour week and a substantial part of our other demands, I will resign from my Union post."

The corrupt creature said: "Friend Gold, sign your resignation right now and we will settle the strike without you."

My answer: "I am ready to call a meeting in Carnegie Hall. Come with me to this meeting and tell the assembled strikers that you are demanding my resignation and that you'll surely settle the strike."

"A lynch party, eh, Mr. Gold?"

Enough about this interesting conference, going on while thousands of strikers were struggling with all their might against the bosses, against the bosses' murderous gangsters, and against depraved, conscienceless union leaders. It hurt me terribly, but I didn't dare leave this tragic game of mockery.

At 5:30, Bill Green came into the room and asked me to come into his hotel room, that he wanted to talk to me. His room was on the ground floor, not far from the lobby. We sat down, almost face to face.

"Brother Gold," he said to me in a serious and worried tone. "You told me that you have settled the strike with a very influential person. Have you told anyone about this?"

"Yes, President Green," I answered. "I told the two strike leaders, my assistants, about the settlement."

"Did you tell them with whom you settled the strike?" Green asked.

"They knew with whom I was meeting for a conference for the purpose of settling the strike," I answered.

"If your assistants know with whom you settled, why can't I know who it is?" Green asked, almost begging.

"President Green, the party demanded that I not make our agreement public until he telephoned me. I explained that, first of all, my two assistants knew that I was having a conference with him, and secondly, that it was my duty to inform them and consult with them about each important development. He agreed that only these two people could be told. These two, only. And I gave my promise."

"Brother Gold, I am giving you an hour," Green declared with hard determination, "to provide me with absolute and unquestionable proof that you have settled the strike on the terms of the 'Eitingon agreement' two days ago, before I came to New York. I am giving you one hour to produce this proof!"

I suddenly felt bathed in a warm glow. But only one hour? I humbly appealed to Green that he should permit me more time, because it was a difficult task and one hour was not enough time.

"One hour. That's all!" Green answered me in a tone that was more like a command.

I walked out of Green's room and remained standing not far from the door, almost in despair. Lindheim! He was the only person who could save me! But one hour? And who knew if Lindheim would agree to help me? I suddenly felt feverish.

All of a sudden, my dear friend, S. J. Zuckerman, the labor editor of *The Day (Der Tag)*, , who had, along with an army of other reporters, managed to get into the hotel lobby, waiting for Green's final word about the inflammatory strike situation, because Green, the mighty president, had to hand down the verdict, like King Solomon, as to "whose child it is" — Zuckerman came over to me, took one look at me and asked, "What happened?"

Rushed as I felt, I told him briefly: "Absolute proof! Only one hour's time! And only one person, Mr. Lindheim, can save me. I have his address. He lives on Long Island."

"So what are you standing here for, losing time? Come," my friend Zuckerman said.

Not far from the hotel, Otto Lenhardt, an active striker was waiting for me in his old automobile. Otto Lenhardt drove me every day to meetings, conferences, to the picket lines, etc. Zuckerman and I got into Otto's car and went to Long Island to see Mr. Lindheim.

S. J. Zuckerman, the labor editor of the Tammany *Day* was my friend? He was riding with me to Long Island at night to help me in a critical moment of my strike leadership? How come? How I got to know S. J. Zuckerman and why he commanded such respect and trust from me is quite interesting and deserves an honored place in my memoirs about the 1926 furrier's strike. But more about that later. Now we were riding, Zuckerman and I, to Long Island.

When we approached Mr. Lindheim's home, the tall iron gate was locked. The night watchman, who was sitting in his little booth near the door, came out and asked us what we wanted. We told him we wanted to see Mr. Lindheim. To his query as to who wanted to see Mr. Lindheim, I said, "Ben Gold."

He went back into the book, used the telephone, and then opened the gate for us.

Inside, in the courtyard, on a well-lit, paved path which led to the house Lindheim, all dressed up, was standing and waiting for us. When I explained the reason for my visit, he said that he had company. Mrs. Lindheim had invited the executive board members of Hadassah for dinner. If I could get Mrs. Lindheim's permission, he would drive back to New York with us to see Bill Green.

A few minutes later, Mr. Lindheim returned and said he was going with us. Before we got into Otto's car, Lindheim told Otto that as long as we were on Long Island, he could drive as fast as the car would go and he didn't have to stop for red lights. We didn't drive, we flew.

Finally, we were in Bill Green's hotel room and I was stunned. "Hello, Bill," Lindheim greeted Green. "Hello, Lindheim," Green returned the greeting.

What's going on here, I asked myself. Lindheim, a corporation lawyer, who, years ago, had been the lawyer for the mighty trusts in Germany — how did he come to be on a first-name basis with the president of the AFL?

I murmured, "Mr. Lindheim settled the strike with me."

"Mr. Gold, let me talk with Lindheim. I will call you when we finish our conversation," Green said.

"No!" I said determinedly. "I want to be here when you talk about the settlement."

"Ben," Lindheim said to me, "maybe it would be advisable for me and Bill to talk things over alone."

I left the room and waited, and waited. I was thinking: Why wasn't I allowed to be present while they talked? What kind of secrets did they have? Would Lindheim tell Bill Green that the strike would have been over weeks ago when I had settled with Eitingon, and that Green, with his traitorous agreement, was to blame for the strike's dragging on so long? Would Lindheim tell him that Samuels was a union-hater — that he thought he was Napoleon?

Lindheim interrupted my thoughts when he came out of the room and said, "O.K., Ben! Bill is waiting for you. Don't worry. Good luck! I'll telephone you," and he disappeared.

I went into Green's room and he told me that both of us — he and I — would walk out to the lobby and he would tell the newspaper reporters that he had handed over the task of settling the strike to me and the "general strike committee."

We went into the lobby and were surrounded by an army of reporters. Green told them that after he had a long talk with me about the strike and because he was busy with other important issues, he had agreed to hand over the responsible task of settling the strike to me.

Finally Settled!

Finally! A few days later, Lindheim telephoned me and invited me to a conference with Eitington. He said this would be the "last act of the drama."

Gross, Samuel Liebowitz and I settled the strike at this conference with Eitingon. All the provisions — the 40-hour work week with pay for 44 hours, the raises in wages, and all the gains we had agreed upon in the first agreement with Eitingon, were written into this new agreement. The strikers were wild with joy. The 1926 strike was never forgotten by the fur workers. How proud they were! They had defeated the bosses, the bosses' gangsters, the police and the corrupt judges, and the vile traitors who were the leaders of the AFL and their own International Union. These victories raised their spirits, warmed their hearts, and made them very happy.

The season went into full swing. The manufacturers were swamped with orders. The strike had been settled during the second week in June. The workers got a 10% raise in their wages, but the traditional July raises, which the workers got without difficulty, made their raises come to a lot more. The bosses needed workers and were worried lest, God forbid, some of their workers would get better-paying jobs elsewhere, so, poor fellows, they had to satisfy their workers. Many of the workers did leave their old jobs because they were able to get higher wages in other shops. The Union permitted overtime work, and the earnings of the workers rose markedly. At union meetings, the workers glowed with their successful achievements. This was the best reward for the left-wing Union leaders.

CHAPTER III
The Enemies Attack

My Mistake

In May of 1925, I had been elected manager of the New York Union, and in June, 1926, the strike was settled. At the time that I shouldered the responsibilities as the leader of a union, I did not know, nor could I even imagine or dream that in the first year of my leadership, I would be under a continuous hailstorm of problems, troubles and aggravation and that I would be nagged day and night with worry about the unnecessary troubles and suffering of the workers.

I knew that being manager of the Union would not mean smooth sledding. I knew that the bosses, who had always had a free hand and who had not been overly burdened with Union leaders before, would fight every attempt of the left-wing leadership to protect the workers.

I also knew that my determination to throw out Kaufman's gangster and grafter Organization Committee, to unionize the open shops, and to break down the fortress of brutal exploitation in the Greek shops would be a difficult, complicated and risky undertaking.

However, I also knew that the oppressed, terrorized, betrayed and brutally exploited fur workers were hoping and waiting for the blessed day when, through their united strength, they would free themselves from their hated enemies and, like freed victors, would straighten their backs and raise up their heads against their arrogant bosses.

About the workers — their devotion, their courage, their ability to carry on a struggle — about these things, I made no mistake. The strength of the workers made it possible for the left-wing Union leaders to accomplish their entire program within only six months' time. The successes of the Union inspired the workers, united them even more, and gave them strength. They had finally reached their long-awaited goal — an honest and militant union which faithfully served the interests of the workers. A warm, brotherly friendship tied the left-wing Union leaders and the thousands of Union members together in a tight bond.

It was, therefore, no wonder that the workers enthusiastically agreed with their Union leaders to ask for substantial improvements in our conferences with the bosses, like the 40-hour work week, large raises, and other improved working conditions. The workers who produced the expensive fur coats which brought huge profits for the bosses didn't underestimate their worth. They kept up their courage and strength and knew, only too well, that the bosses would not pay for the improvements they gave the workers out of their profits — that they would simply raise the prices of the coats that the workers produced.

We knew that the bosses would not hand over our demands on a silver platter. We knew that we would have to fight for them. But we had no doubt that we would be successful. If we had to strike for our demands, we were sure we would win, because there were no longer the large number of open shops that would scab, and even if there were a few dozen scabs, they would be like a drop in the bucket. We were not afraid of the gangsters whom we knew the bosses would hire. In the past few months, the strikers had shown that they were able to "argue things out" with the gangsters. Never in the history of the Furriers Union were the workers so ready, so determined, and so sure of their victory.

We were not mistaken. Our assurance did not stem from wishful thinking. Our assurance came from our real knowledge that the majority of the manufacturers could not endure a long, drawn-out strike, and that united, the thousands of fur workers were, without exaggeration, unbeatable in a contest with the bosses. The best proof that we had evaluated the situation correctly was the fact that in the seventh week of the strike, the richest and most influential manufacturers had authorized Mr. Eitingon to settle the strike with me, and that Eitingon had fulfilled his mission in a manner most satisfactory to the workers.

But I did not know that the elected, influential, powerful representatives and leaders of the AFL, who were the watchdogs of our blessed system of robber exploitation of the working class, were also the devoted servants of the bosses, and that every time the bosses cried out for help, or complained about their pathetic situation because their workers had gone too far with their demands, which they felt were putting their businesses in danger, these high priests of the American trade unions were ready to use their influence and their power and all the necessary means to save the businesses of the bosses and to discipline and fence in the workers. About this unfortunate horror which lurked in ambush against aware and awakened workers, I did not know, and there was probably nothing I could do about it.

Now about my mistakes! My first mistake, which bothered me for a long time, and which I could not excuse away by saying that "I didn't know," was that when the strike had been settled and the workers were working, earning well, and feeling good about their wonderful fight and victory, I thought that we were finished with the terrible affliction — the Bill Greens, the Fraynes and the Shachtmans — and that the Union would now be able to carry on its normal activities of protecting the interests of the workers.

After the strike was over, the Union was left with some important problems. First of all, many of the workers had been freed on bail and were in need of experienced lawyers for their defense. If we had turned to the workers for a tax, they would, without question, have approved such a tax which would not only cover the expenses, but would leave the Union with a few hundred thousand dollars.

But I decided not to rush with a tax. "Let the workers catch their breaths," I thought. "Let them first pay their own bills and their own debts. The Union will have to wait for a tax until the next season." What a mistake! That was my first mistake.

My terrible and aggravating experience with the traitors of the AFL, whose criminal acts had been aimed at breaking the strike, to discipline the outspoken fur workers and teach them that in our country, it is the bosses who decide the conditions of the workers and their unions — this sad experience should have been enough to enable me to understand that President Bill Green's deeds during the furriers' strike were neither a coincidence nor an exception, but part of a definite program of the top leaders of the AFL — and I should have prepared the workers for another possible attack on the Union by the AFL leaders. I should have paid more attention to them. I knew that the defeat of their attempt at strikebreaking was a bitter pill for them to swallow. I should not have convinced myself that we were rid of these traitors.

The result of this mistake was that when the AFL leaders, in partnership with the bosses and with leaders of the Socialist Party from the vile *Forward* crew, suddenly joined forces and began implementing their carefully worked out plan to destroy the Union, the Union was not prepared, either financially or organizationally, to close off the inroads to the "pogromists" at the very beginning of the "pogrom." The bloody fight lasted ten years, until the heroic fur workers finally broke the assault of the bosses, got rid of the hordes of gangsters, and chased the AFL and the Socialist agitators from the battlefield. They — the top leaders of the AFL and those in the Socialist Party who were in partnership with the enemies of the awakened working class — were the enemies of justice and the enemies of humanity. And even now, more than fifty years later, when I am writing my short memoirs and recollections, notwithstanding the enormous world events that have taken place, that foul partnership of the persons of those camps is still an unholy alliance. The history of the fur workers and their struggle against these traitors will probably be given a place of honor in the history of the American labor movement.

The heroic struggle of the fur workers and their substantial achievements resounded throughout the entire labor movement and created a real concern among the manufacturers, especially those in the needle trades. A 40-hour week and considerable raises in wages — this disease could, God forbid, spread to their workers as well. It was necessary to take steps against the possibility of such an epidemic.

The top leaders of the AFL assembled in the AFL building in Washington to review this important question. Matthew Woll, the AFL's first vice-president, who was more renowned for his intelligence and ability than any of the other union chiefs — the most gifted demagogue and the most gifted servant of the employers — called the event "the tragic fur strike."

First of all, Woll informed the assembled leaders of the AFL that he had information from very reliable sources that Stalin had ordered the American Communist Party to have the Communists agitate among the American workers to get them to fight for a shorter work week and higher wages in order to give strength to the class struggle and to organize the workers for a Communist revolution in the United States; and that in the New York Furriers Union, the Communists had seized power and had called the strike in accordance with Stalin's orders.

In the second place, Woll said that the scandalous Carnegie Hall meeting, where thousands of strikers had gathered to hear the report of the "practical and just settlement" that President Green had reached in a friendly manner with the president of the Fur Manufacturers Association, was a stain on the record of the AFL leadership, because it was widely known that President Green had not even dared to go to the meeting since the assembled strikers started a storm of wild screaming: "We don't want Green! We want Ben Gold!" which lasted a long time.

"And what is even worse," Woll continued, "is that the agreement with the manufacturers that President Green signed with his own hand was worthless! The Communist leaders of the Furriers Union forced the bosses to give in to their demands which will ruin the industry."

"We must not remain silent," Matthew Woll shouted. "If we remain silent, the whole country will look upon us as puppets. We must crush the Communist fortress in the Furriers Union and chase out all the Moscow agents from all the unions. We must protect our blessed democratic freedoms from the Communist conspiracy."

The leaders of the Socialist Party were wild with joy. The Feinstones and the Shiplacoffs and the Beckermans* were jubilant. Now they had

---

*The reference is to a group of right-wing Socialist leaders in the needle trades' unions — Abraham Shiplacoff and Morris Feinstone of the International Ladies Garment Workers' Union and Abraham Beckerman of the Amalgamated Clothing Workers.

powerful allies in their fight against the Communists — the leaders of the AFL with their unlimited power — to force the Communists out of the trade unions, and with enough influence to put an end to all Communist propaganda and all Communist demonstrations. Finally, their dream had come true. The call of "All the enemies of Communism, unite!" that would be heard all over the land heartened them. Their certainty that the Communist plague would be rooted out filled them with joy.

The Attack

Early in 1927, Matthew Woll called a meeting of reporters from all of the New York newspapers and informed them that he had definite proof that the Communist leaders of the 1926 furriers' strike had paid weekly graft to the officials of the New York City Police Department, to the Industrial Squad, and to the detectives, in order to remove all legal interference with the "criminal methods they used to enforce their domination over the fur workers." He told the reporters at this meeting that the AFL had expelled the New York Furriers Union and had decided to organize a democratic Furriers Union in New York.

How happy the *Forward* was to print this important news that there was already a democratic AFL union, that the bosses had already broken their agreement with the Communist union and had signed an agreement with the AFL union; that the bosses had ordered the workers to take out union books from the new union, and that Ben Gold had been accused of paying graft to the Police Department.

We called a meeting in Cooper Union. I explained to the workers that the Union was in deep debt due to the long strike, that we had to pay large sums to our well-known lawyers, George Z. Medalie and Frank P. Walsh, to defend the workers who had been arrested during the strike, and that the fight with the dummy-union, which was supported by the AFL, the bosses, the *Forward,* and the Socialist leaders, was going to be a long and bitter one. All the furriers present at this meeting, as well as those not present that day, would have to decide whether to fight until our enemies were crushed, or lock the doors of the Union and let the traitors rule.

I couldn't continue my speech because of the storm that broke out in the hall: loud, angry cries of "They won't live to see that day," "We will destroy them," and "Fight! Fight!" Hands were raised all over the hall; the workers were demanding their chance to speak their minds.

The first worker, a quiet, modest man who had made a name for himself through his energetic union activities, put a fire under the meeting with his words: "What are you talking about, Ben? What are you saying about shutting down our Union? Have you, God forbid, lost faith in the furriers? In May, 1925, when the left wing took over the leadership of the Union, we got rid of the underworld from the Union. That was a difficult and a bloody fight, but we won!" he shouted.

"In June," he continued, "we unionized a large number of open shops. In July, we broke the resistance of the bosses and got decent July raises, and in September, we unified, organized and called the Greek furriers out on strike and freed them from slavery and won all the union benefits for them.

"About the 1926 strike, I don't have to tell you. Whom are they threatening by announcing that the AFL, the bosses and the *Forward*, with its Socialists, have joined forces against our Union? Until now, haven't they been united? Our answer is clear: Traitors, strike-breakers, swindlers, lackeys of the bosses — we will fight you and crush you just as we did in the 1926 strike!"

A storm of applause broke out in the hall. When it quieted down, a second worker made a short speech. He said that he agreed with everything the previous speaker had said, but he wanted to propose that the workers consider a voluntary tax to help pay the strike debt and to pay the lawyers. "Let each worker decide how much his tax would amount to, and let the workers bring their voluntary contributions to the Union. We can depend on our furriers." He said he was sure that they would gladly help their union, and that he would be the first one to bring in his voluntary tax of $20.

Once again, there was a storm of applause. All the other workers who had wanted to participate in the discussion waived their requests to speak. One after another, they declared that they agreed with the first two speakers and that the meeting should take a vote on both proposals: to fight against the traitors, and for a voluntary tax.

"All those in favor, raise your hands," the chairman of the meeting called out. I saw a magnificent picture of thousands of raised workers' hands. "Who is opposed?" Not one hand was raised. Again the applause resounded.

The enthusiastic decision of the assembled workers in Cooper Union to fight rang out like a bell and spread to the fur shops and even further.

The Bloody Attack

Representatives of the bosses' association and officials of the AFL went from shop to shop and instructed the bosses to employ only those workers who would register in their AFL union. Many of the bosses who were angry that they had to pay their workers such high wages and had to follow all the conditions set by the Union, were more than happy to order their workers to take out books in the right-wing union, because the left-wing union was "dead, finished." The workers answered with strikes.

90

Shop strikes, picketing, bloody fights with the gangsters of the AFL union and daily arrests followed. The members of the "Organization Committee," who had always fomented trouble under the Kaufman administration, who had terrorized the workers and protected the bosses against the Union for their weekly graft from the bosses, who had been kicked out by the left-wing leadership in 1925, now regained their "honorable" position in the AFL union.

At an elegant banquet which the leaders of the right-wing union held in honor of the underworld characters who were invited to help the new union destroy the Communists, "Big Alex," "Big Abe," "Moishe the Babe," "Bullet-proof Harry," "Billy the Yak," "Sheenie Mike," "Chinaman Charlie" and other long-time underworld figures were praised for their loyalty in the speech that the Socialist union-manager, Charlie Stetsky, Kaufman's adjutant, delivered. Friend Charlie declared: "Those who aren't with us are against us! And he who is against us is our enemy. And the enemy are the Communists and the left-wingers who are infected with the Communist poison! And they should get a full measure of what they wish us!"

And Edward F. McGrady, the most able organizer of the AFL, who was appointed by Bill Green and Matthew Woll as the direct boss of the right-wing union, praised Charlie for his genial leadership. Charlie knew, McGrady said, that serious union problems were not solved with sweet medicines. In unions where small Communist opposition groups appeared, they were quickly stifled before they had a chance to grow. The government, McGrady said, had helped the AFL to clean the Communist plague out of the trade unions. He added that very soon, Ben Gold would be deported from the United States.

Wild shouts and applause greeted this good news.

The Beginning

Encouraged and refreshed by the magnificent banquet, the "organizers" of the right-wing union began their "noble" activities. They escorted a few scab-workers from the *Forward* group to work and beat up the strikers who insulted the scabs. For several days, every morning, there were strikers beaten up.

One of those mornings, the fur workers were standing near the large buildings on Seventh Avenue, waiting for the bosses to open the shops. Unemployed furriers, who were looking for work, packed the corner of 30th Street and Seventh Avenue. On both sides of Seventh Avenue, between 29th and 30th Streets, strikers were marching near their shops.

Irving Potash, Jack Schneider and I were standing near one of the buildings talking to the strikers. Suddenly we heard shouts across Seventh Avenue. "Scabs! Gangsters! — and masses of fur workers made a dash to "greet" the gangsters. Potash, Schneider and I made an attempt to run with the workers, but a group of the strikers barred our way and kept us like prisoners.

I saw the tight ring of the workers; I saw the police run over and tear into the ring, and in only a few minutes, the ring opened wide and I saw the bloodied gangsters being led away by the police. Their faces bloody, their clothes torn to shreds, they followed the police with the shaky steps of drunkards.

Potash, Schneider and I freed ourselves from our "imprisonment" and ran toward the workers' ring, which had closed around a few of the strikers, who were wiping their faces with bloody handkerchiefs. "Let's get to the doctor," I said to them. "No, it isn't necessary — it's nothing," they answered me. "So come to the Union office," I said. "No, we are not running from the battlefield," they answered.

The Frenchie Gang

For two weeks, the gangsters of the right-wing union didn't dare to show up in the fur market. But when they got considerable reinforcements, they reappeared to continue their "principled" duties.

The Frenchie Gang worked for Abe Beckerman, who was at that time the manager of the cutters' local of the Amalgamated Clothing Workers. Friend Beckerman was fulfilling his socialist debt and helping the right-wing furriers union by sending in the Frenchie Gang to encourage and add strength to the weakened gangster forces of the Socialist-AFL union.

The Frenchie gangsters, after surveying the battlefield thoroughly, used careful methods. They waited until the workers were inside the shops at work and the mass of unemployed workers' ranks had thinned out after one o'clock in the afternoon, when there was no longer any hope of getting a job. Then, they and the gangsters of the right-wing furriers union attacked the strikers, beat them up murderously, and ran as from a fire.

In order to protect the strikers from any more such attacks, we, the leaders of the left-wing Union, organized a defense committee from among the fearless active members of the Union, and they marched with the pickets. Enthused by their clear "hit-and-run" tactics with which they had been successful for a few days in a row, beating up more strikers without any interference, the gangsters and the right-wing scab union believed that they would succeed in chasing all the pickets away from the shops, thus opening a free road for the scabs.

And it happened on the very first day that the defense committee marched with the pickets. The gangsters never expected the welcome they received. The gangsters of the right-wing union ran away after the very first "sholem-alechem" that the defense committee greeted them with. The Frenchie gangsters, who had not had any experience with the angry fur workers, tried to make a heroic stand. They did not run away. They were driven away in abulances.

The fur market became quiet. The pickets weren't being beaten up. The bosses were making peace with their workers who were picketing their shops, with many workers going back to work with the understanding that their bosses would no longer dictate to them which union they had to belong to. The *Forward's* bunch of scabs lost their nerve.

We, the leaders of the left-wing Union, understood that this quiet would not last long. We were sure that Charlie Stetsky, the manager of the right-wing union, and the boss director, Organizer McGrady, would not accept the disgrace of the defeat of their gangsters quietly. So we lost no time in preparing an even larger defense committee. The committee had more members than we had expected. Workers came to me complaining that I hadn't called them to the special meeting for enlarging the defense committee. In one week's time, over a hundred workers pledged to protect the strikers. And an error in our plan saved a good number of workers from the well-planned gangster attack. We thought that after experiencing such a defeat, they would try in their future attacks to avoid the crowded ring of pickets and the unemployed workers who joined them in their tight ranks, by attacking in several places, and that such a tactic would confuse the unemployed workers, break them into small groups, and then the gangsters would have the strength to "handle" the pickets and the small numbers of unemployed workers who would run over to help protect the pickets. We thought that would be the plan of the generals of the right wing: Friend Charlie, Brother McGrady and Mr. Frayne.

That is why we divided our defense committee into four groups. Each group had its specific place among the pickets and had instructions that, no matter what happened in any other place, it had to remain in its own position, guarding the pickets of its assigned territory.

But something quite different happened. The gangster-generals worked out a plan that, by all rights, should have led to the butchering of a considerable number of workers who would be caught in a helpless condition. After one o'clock, when the workers were already back in the shops after their lunch hour, a large gang of gangsters attacked the pickets in only one place. When the shouts of "Gangsters! Gangsters!" were heard all over Seventh Avenue, the unemployed workers surrounded the gangsters and helped the pickets "argue things out" with them.

The other defense committees remained in their positions, ready to defend the pickets in their territories. Suddenly, they saw a group of gangsters rush out of their hiding places and attack the outer side of the ring of pickets — the backs of the workers. They were helpless and defenseless, with no possible way of escaping from the gangsters' fists, which were hammering on their bodies.

You can well understand that the defense committees did not remain in their assigned positions. In a matter of a few seconds, they were hammering at the gangsters. There were eight gangsters and forty enraged workers of the defense committees.

The gangsters did succeed in beating up many of the pickets before the unemployed workers ran over to protect them. The luckier workers only received "dry blows." Others survived the gangster attack with bloody, swollen faces.

For this, the Frenchie gangsters paid a bloody price. Not one of the gangsters was able to escape the fists of the enraged workers. When the police, who "happened to be" not far from the fighting, finally approached, it was all over. And also "by chance," several detectives from the 30th Street Precinct "happened" to show up. The detectives stopped passing taxis, and, with the help of the police, stuffed the exhausted gangsters into the taxis and ordered the drivers to take their bloodied passengers to their AFL union.

The Shapiro Gang

The Frenchie Gang disappeared. It became quiet again in the streets of the fur industry. Strikes were being settled on the condition that the workers, and not the bosses, would determine to which union the workers would belong. New shop strikes broke out when the bosses demand that their workers "register" in the AFL union. Representatives of the bosses' associations and the business agents of the right-wing union were running into the shops, demanding that the bosses stick to their agreement with the right-wing union to hire only those workers who belonged to their union. Here and there, a clash between strikers and scabs did take place, but there were no gangsters, and fights were avoided.

Friend Charlie and Brother McGrady were worried; the accusation that Matthew Woll had given out to all the newspapers that the Communist union had paid graft to the police and to the Industrial Squad came to trial, and after a few days, it was thrown out of court. McGrady's promise that Ben Gold would be deported from the United States did not materialize. Gold was still there in the left-wing union.

In addition, the defeat of the gangsters, those most important helpers on whom the chiefs of the right-wing union built their hopes for success, constituted their most serious worry.

The "generous gifts" that the bosses were quietly giving the right-wing union were not enough to pay their Organization Committee and the outside gangsters for their "union activities," not to mention to pay for the sick and beaten gangsters until they were well again.

What was eating at them the most was that it was almost a year since they had started their union with such fanfare, and it was still an empty "house of study." As soon as their union was formed, the Socialist fur workers of the *Forward* bunch took out union books. Then the scabs in the 1926 strike took out union books. And that was all! No new customers showed up for the AFL union books.

The truth was that the scabs had really been wronged by the left-wing Union. When the 1926 strike was over, these people remained jobless, excluded from the Union, and they waited for the Union to punish them for their sins and then issue union books to them, so that they could work in the shops. But the Union was in no hurry. The bosses asked the Union to have pity on these sinful people, and the Union leaders argued that it was a Union matter, and that the bosses had no right to interfere. The discussions between the bosses and the Union ended when Dr. Paul Abelson, the impartial chairman of the conference committee, brought out his verdict:

First, the Union should take the scabs back into the Union, and they should pay no more for their union books than the other workers had to pay — no more than $100.

Secondly, the punishment for the scabs must be a just one.

Thirdly, since the workers who worked in the "settled" shops of the independent manufacturers had paid 15% and later 25% of their wages as a strike tax, the scabs had to pay the same tax.

The Union and the bosses had to accept this decision of the impartial chairman. But the scabs didn't like it at all. Their wages for scabbing had been $200 a week. Those scabs who had stayed in the shops overnight had worked seven days a week, with overtime in the evenings. Their earnings came to at least $300 a week. $100 for a union book, $100 fine for scabbing, plus the strike tax that they owed — all came to $600 or $700 for each scab. In addition, they were hated by the workers, who treated them as if they were dogs with fleas. So it was no surprise that the scabs ran to join the right-wing union. First, it gave them a chance to get revenge on the left-wing Union; secondly, they felt more at home with the people of the Socialist *Forward* bunch; thirdly, they could now scab with the blessings of the right-wing union leaders. For the scabs, the right-wing union was a real "Garden of Eden."

But the whole "bag of refuse" — the *Forward* bunch and the scab family — only came to a few hundred members for the right-wing union. They had no other members. This was a terrible defeat for the leaders of the right-wing union.

McGrady ran to Washington often to discuss the problems of his AFL union with Bill Green and Matthew Woll. When he returned to New York, he would complain to his friend, Charlie Stetsky, that Woll was always giving him the same lecture: that McGrady must be well aware that every undertaking is difficult at the beginning and is plagued with complicated problems. Further, that he, McGrady, must know from long experience that the fighting mood of the workers wouldn't last long and that sooner or later, they would tire of a long struggle, which was holding back their ability to solve their most pressing problem: "making a living." And as for the defeat of the Frenchie Gang, Woll's answer was: "When a light bulb burns out, you screw in a new bulb." There really was no problem.

And the manager of the right-wing union, Friend Charlie Stetsky, calmed him down and told him that he didn't really expect Bill Green or Matthew Woll to have the remedy for all their problems — but that they did have the remedy but didn't want to "disclose their secret." "They are depending on you, Mac," he told McGrady. "When Matthew told you about the burned-out light bulb, I am telling you that he was recommending a gang that would undertake the job of 'making dust' of the Communist gangsters. I haven't hired them yet. I was waiting for you, Mac."

And the Shapiro Gang, which was led by two very "gifted" brothers, did very well in their first attack. They succeeded in beating up a large number of pickets in a few locations. During the weeks and months of the truce that had reigned in the fur market, the defense committee had almost ceased to exist. Almost all of the committee members were working in the shops. The strikers were not in need of their help, because after the Frenchie Gang had disappeared, no other gangsters had taken over their "work."

So we had organized a small defense committee, made up of strikers and unemployed workers. It was small in numbers, but capable of protecting the strikers — not, however, against a new gangster assault like that which came from the Shapiro Gang.

But the Shapiro Gang didn't show up for a few days, and we made use of the time to enlarge the defense committee. In the shops and among the unemployed workers, the word was spread quickly that the Shapiro Gang had beaten up strikers, and workers stopped work, took half-days off, and joined the defense committee.

When the Shapiro Gang tried to carry out its planned surprise attacks against the strikers, they got quite a surprise themselves — one that they had "honestly earned."

They attacked the workers in three different locations. Everywhere, the gangsters, for the first time in their cursed lives, had the honor of meeting up with workers who were fighting for their rights and who didn't even consider the possibility that their lives might be in danger as they protected their sisters and brothers who were fighting against the murderers who were hired by the bosses and the degenerate betrayers of the working class. They, the mighty gangsters, ran, but they couldn't escape.

Only one of the gangsters managed to get away. He ran into a garage and hid between the cars that were parked there. He was one of the two Shapiro brothers, one of the leaders of the gangsters. When the workers chased him and entered the garage where he was hiding, he grabbed a brick that was under a wheel of a car and hurled it at the worker closest to him. But the brick missed the worker and flew back to the anointed king of his gang and made a "terrible impression" on him.

The Industrial Union

In 1929, the furriers union, the left-wing cloak and dressmakers' union, the knit goods and white goods unions, and the millinery union united under one name — "The Industrial Union of the Needle Trades Workers." Louis Hyman was elected president and I was elected secretary-treasurer of the Industrial Union.

Joseph Borochovich, Abe Weiss and Jack Goldman, all capable and devoted servants of the interests of the workers, were the leaders of the New York cloakmakers' union. Rose Wortis, one of the most capable labor leaders, and Israel Weisberg were the leaders of the dressmakers' union. Charles "Sasha" Zimmerman, who had been a respected leader of the left-wing dressmakers' union, left the left-wing labor movement along with his friends, Jay Lovestone, Benjamin Gittlow, and other "principled moralizers and informers" who helped the government condemn many Communists and send them to jail.

Joe Rappaport was the leader of the knitgoods union. Gladys Zukovsky was the leader of the millinery union.

Aaron Gross was elected as manager of the furriers' union and Sam Liebowitz was elected assistant manager.

I was besieged with problems from the industrial unions in Philadelphia, Boston, Cleveland and Chicago. President Louis Hyman gladdened the hearts of the workers at mass meetings, but he came to the Industrial Union office only once a week — to collect his meager weekly wages.

The 1929 Furriers' Strike

The situation for the workers in the fur shops got worse. The appetite of the bosses became insatiable. They never tired of cutting wages, and in many of the shops, union conditions no longer existed. It became necessary to show the bosses that the fur workers were neither powerless nor helpless. Despite the weak financial situation of the left-wing Union, despite its involvement in a few shop strikes, despite its fights with the AFL "organization committee" and the arrests of the strikers, we decided to convince the bosses that the fur workers were not their helpless slaves. We called the workers of over two hundred shops out on strike. The strike surprised both the bosses and the AFL union. Seeing over two thousand picketing strikers really frightened them.

When I arrived at the battlefield, the war was already over. I saw the police busy with the horribly beaten gangsters. Despite my burning hatred for these wild, professional murderers, it makes me shudder to write about their dreadful appearance. They had succeeded in beating up a large number of workers, and many workers were arrested. But the Shapiro Gang, like the Frenchie Gang before it, disappeared from the fur market without a trace.

The fight between the left-wing Union and the bosses with their AFL union continued, but no outside gangsters appeared for a long time. The leaders of the right-wing union had to be satisfied with the efforts of their own "organization committee," which dared to provoke fights only when the police were on hand to help them.

There were shop strikes that lasted for weeks, clashes with the scabs who were members of the right-wing union, arrests, and unemployment. The union workers' situation was bad, and the bosses took advantage of this by lowering wages again and again. The big-hearted bosses then made concessions to the workers: they stopped demanding that the workers take out union books with the right-wing union; they only wanted the workers to "register" in that union. Many workers were driven by need to register, but when, under pressure from the AFL union, the bosses again demanded that union books be taken out in the right-wing union, the workers left their shops. So again there were shop strikes, clashes with the scabs, fights and arrests. The number of workers in great need grew larger. Many of these needy workers were unable to pay their Union dues. The financial situation of the Union grew worse every week because of the expense of paying lawyers and hundreds of dollars daily for fines inflicted by the judges on strikers who had been arrested, who had, according to the interpretations of the judges, and according to the gifts the judges received from the bosses, broken all kinds of laws.

But the devotion of the thousands of workers did not diminish, and their hatred for the AFL became only stronger.

We knew that in many of the shops, the workers only had a few days' work each week, but we looked upon this as a normal occurrence. We did not recognize this as one of the signs, the portent of the impending economic crisis which devastated the entire country. The first victims of this disaster were the needle trades' industries. The fur manufacturers were not besieged with orders, so they were not interested in settling the strikes. When they finally did settle with the Union, the gains achieved by the workers were not what we had expected. But even an unsuccessful strike has an effect. The arrogance of the bosses was curbed, and the AFL scab union was, to a great extent, paralyzed.

Jack Schneider

Jack Schneider deserves an honored place in my short memoirs. Not all the leaders of the left-wing Union were physically strong enough to withstand the exertion and the aggravation caused by the long and bitter struggle. Aaron Gross became ill and left for Los Angeles. Sam Liebowitz got sick and went away to Washington, where he worked in a fur shop for a short time. Later, with the help of his family, he bought a small grocery in a poor neighborhood in Richmond, Virginia, where he and his devoted wife worked from early morning to late at night in order to feed their two gifted daughters.

The Union needed other leaders to replace Gross and Liebowitz. At a meeting of active Union workers, I recommended that Jack Schneider, who had distinguished himself in his Union activities as a rank-and-filer, be elected as a business agent in the Union.

Jack protested and fought against my suggestion. He complained that he was not capable of assuming such a high and responsible position in the Union, that his English was poor, and that he didn't have any experience at all in dealing with the bosses about workers' problems. He literally begged his friends at the meeting that, in the interests of the workers, this complex and responsible position should not be forced on him. He appealed to them that the work involved was such that he would not be capable of carrying it out in a manner that would be satisfactory for the interests of the workers.

But Jack Schneider was unanimously elected as business agent of the Union. And Jack Schneider had grossly underestimated Jack Schneider's abilities. In the very first few weeks, his God-given talents were developed and unfolded. Jack was quickly acknowledged to be the most capable business agent in the Union. He fought untiringly for the shops that were in his jurisdiction to insure that all Union conditions were enforced and that the wages of the workers were not only not cut, but raised. All the dirty, underhanded tricks that the bosses used to hide or justify their methods of robbing the workers were of no avail against Jack's staunch and successful defense of the workers. Jack also distinguished himself by his organizational capabilities. He soon became beloved by the workers and hated by the bosses.

A few times, the bosses, with the help of the leaders of the AFL, tried to send Jack to jail, and once they did succeed in doing so for a year. The charges against him were serious ones:

One morning, in one of the big shops, a foreman marched in dressed up in a Nazi uniform. At noon, the workers came to the Union and told Jack about this lovely incident. Jack demanded that the boss get rid of his Nazi foreman, and the wealthy Jewish boss answered that America is a democratic country, and that the foreman had a right to his convictions, and further, that the Union had no right to tell a boss whom to employ as foreman in his shop.

The workers did not return to work. The shop was declared on strike. On the second day, the Nazi again came to work in his Nazi uniform. The strikers chased him away from the shop. On the third morning, the foreman came to work accompanied by a group of Nazis who tried to teach the strikers respect for the Nazis. The strikers, with the assistance of many other workers, did not chase these Nazi gangsters away; they were led away in ambulances.

Jack had not been present at this "debate" between the workers and the Nazis, but both bosses — brothers — swore in court that they had seen how Jack butchered their foreman. Jack was sent to jail for a year. When he was released from jail, the workers carried him on their shoulders into the Union office.

For twenty-five years, Jack Schneider maintained an important place in the leadership of the Union. Fifteen times, the workers elected him to serve them, and always with the largest number of votes. He was unable to get his American citizenship papers, because the *Forward* informers swore that they had proof that he was a member of the Communist Party, but until the last moment of his richly honored life, Jack remained a highly principled and devoted citizen of the class-conscious, huge segment of the working class which fought for freedom and for justice.

The Conference With Matthew Woll

After Matthew Woll had spread the news to all the newspapers that he had absolute proof that during the months of the 1926 strike, the Communist union leaders had paid many thousands of dollars in graft to the police and to the detectives of the Industrial Squad, the government conducted a thorough investigation of these charges.

I sat in the witness box in court and answered all the questions asked of me by the district attorney. McGrady, the boss-director of the AFL scab union, sat in the courtroom and listened closely to all my answers. When my interrogation was over and I left the courtroom, McGrady stopped me and, as if he were an old friend of mine, said: "Ben, Matthew lost. That doesn't bother me. What I'm sorry about is that you won."

I answered him that this was not the first, and surely not the last defeat that the big shots of the AFL would suffer for their vile conspiracies against the fur workers. McGrady smiled and said in a most friendly tone: "Ben, you can't win in a contest with the mighty AFL. Take my advice and talk to Bill Green to reach some sensible understanding. If you want, I'll arrange a conference between you and President Green."

Of course I agreed. But I waited weeks and months until I gave up hope that such a conference would ever take place.

And what was happening in the struggle between the left-wing Union and the scab-and-gangster union? First there were some quiet days. Then, once again, there were fights between the workers and the "organization committee" of the right-wing union, and, naturally, arrests of workers.

One morning, I had the pleasure of meeting up with Brother McGrady, who was standing, flanked by two policemen not far from the marching pickets. When I approached him, he shouted to me: "Ben, the conference is in the works!" I did not stop and I did not answer him but kept walking past him. For one moment, I did not understand what he meant, but then I thought that perhaps he meant the conference with Bill Green that he had promised to arrange, and I didn't take his words seriously.

But without warning, two judges — Rosenblum and Brodsky — suddenly invited Matthew Woll and me to a conference for the purpose of bringing an end to the war between the two unions. Rosenblum was a faithful servant of the bosses. True, he had never sentenced any strikers to jail terms, but equally true, he also had never let strikers go without paying heavy fines. Brodsky, on the other hand, had always released the arrested strikers without any punishment.

At the conference, Woll explained to the judges that, after a thorough investigation and factual proof confirmed by reliable witnesses, the AFL had come into the fur market to free the thousands of fur workers from the tragic circumstances in which they found themselves under the leadership of Communists who received their orders from Moscow. The only solution was to organize a truly American democratic union.

He told the judges that in 1926, at a conference with the Communist union leaders, the bosses had offered substantial gains for the workers, but the Communists had insisted on a strike, in accordance with the "holy orders" of Lenin and Stalin, for the goals of the class struggle and the revolution.

He also told the judges that during the eighth week of the strike, President Green had settled with the bosses, obtaining huge gains for the workers, but the Communist strike leaders had shouted down and condemned this agreement as a betrayal and had made the strikers wait for weeks, and that the strikers, driven by need and by hunger to scab, had been crippled. He added that after the strike was finally settled, the Communist leaders had demanded that the scabs pay thousands of dollars in fines, which, of course, they could not pay, so they were left jobless, and they and their wives and children had suffered hunger and privation. And he went on and on and on, until he finished his terrible accusations against the Communist union leadership.

My answer: I explained to the judges that none of the stories that

Woll had told them could be proven to be true, while all that I would tell them I was ready to back up with facts, documents and reliable witnesses. Briefly, I told the judges that the present Union leaders, who had been elected by the largest number of votes in the history of the Union, had, with the assistance of the workers, chased the gangsters and the grafters out of the Union, that we had organized hundreds of "protected" shops and over one hundred open Greek shops and had achieved better working and living conditions for the workers. "Moscow did not order us to fight for and win these improvements for the workers," I said. "We simply fulfilled our duty to the workers, as honest union leaders should do."

"Matthew Woll said," I continued, "that in 1926, the bosses offered substantial gains for the workers, but that the Communist union leaders wanted nothing short of a strike. Well, first of all, it is not true that the bosses offered any gains for the workers. The truth is that the bosses turned down all of our demands. Secondly, it is not true that the Communist union leaders wanted nothing short of a strike. The bosses had caused a lock-out, and we were forced to declare a strike."

"As to the story Woll has told you that President Green settled the strike with the bosses with enormous gains for the workers, and that the Communist leaders condemned that agreement as a betrayal," I went on, "Woll certainly read in the newspapers that thousands of strikers who packed Carnegie Hall when called by the AFL, and who packed the streets outside the hall as well, stormily protested against the secret agreement that President Green had concluded with the bosses. That agreement may have satisfied the bosses, but it did not satisfy the workers. Did President Green really think that the twelve thousand furriers are helpless idiots who would say 'amen' and shout 'hurray' when their leaders went against their interests? Green's secret deal prolonged the strike, and Woll probably knew that when I brought concrete proof to Bill Green that the workers could win their just demands if he did not interfere, he withdrew from his involvement in the strike, and a few days later, we settled it with gains tha the workers agreed to and accepted with joy and enthusiasm.

"And the story that scabs were crippled is also not true. I personally know all the scabs. They scabbed during the 1912 strike, the 1920 strike, and also in the 1926 strike. I challenge Matthew Woll to come up with one scab who was crippled by the strikers. It is true that the strikers didn't feed candy to the scabs, but the story of crippling — that, to put it mildly, is bunk!

"And the story Matthew has told you that after the strike was settled the Union punished the scabs with $1,000 fines that they could not pay, and that they remained jobless and they and their families suffered hunger and privation is another one of the series of false accusations against the Union.

"The true story about this issue is that Union representatives held conferences with representatives of the bosses' association in order to try to come to a satisfactory solution to this problem. Together, we agreed to let the impartial chairman, Dr. Abelson, decide what should be done, and he decided what the punishment for the scabs should be. Both sides — the Union and the bosses — accepted the verdict of the impartial chairman. If Woll believes that the fines imposed on the scabs were too high, he should complain to the impartial chairman, not to the Union."

I finished my short speech with the statement that by presenting all these lies, fabrications and frame-ups, and by shouting "Communists! Moscow's orders! Orders from Marx and Lenin!" they sought to justify their attempts at splitting the Union and their bloody assaults on the workers, whose only crime was that they dared to fight for the truth, for justice, for their rights, and for their life interests.

"Mr. Matthew Woll and Ben Gold," Judge Brodsky addressed us, "what was, was. All this belongs in the past. Leading a union is not an easy job. The leaders of the AFL, who carry the responsibility of millions of workers, deserve the respect of every decent person. But even the greatest leaders sometimes make a mistake. Maybe it is possible that in the Furriers Union, a few mistakes were made by both sides. The practical way to correct these mistakes, which belong in the past, is to start a new chapter of a united union where friendship and brotherhood among the workers can be established. I know that you, Matthew Woll, occupy an important post in the AFL and are in a position to unite both unions and end this war. That would be a blessing for the workers and an important contribution for the president of the AFL. You, Matthew Woll, have the power to free thousands of workers with only one word — 'peace.' "

"With all my energies and all my ability, I serve the workers," Woll said. "My greatest pleasure is my contribution to the welfare of the workers. What the AFL is fighting to do is to remove the internal enemies and provide a democratic union for the fur workers. The AFL is not responsible for the state of affairs among the furriers. Ben Gold and his Communist lieutenants are responsible for the unnecessary suffering of the workers. Ben Gold can put an end to the conflict if he is truly interested in the welfare of the workers. First, Ben Gold has to close his union office and instruct all the furriers to become members of the AFL union. Secondly, we have a list of 32 Communists in Gold's union. They will be allowed to work in the trade, but they will never be allowed to become members of the AFL union."

In a soft, quiet voice, Judge Rosenblum asked: "Matthew, and if Ben Gold would, as you demand, close his office and instruct his union members to join the AFL union, who would be the leaders of the united union?"

Woll answered that the current leaders of the AFL union were capable union organizers. It would take time to establish order in the Union. In a year or two, elections would be held, and the workers would then elect Union officers.

Now, Judge Rosenblum's tone was a bit agitated: "The workers in the united union will have to wait two years until they get the opportunity to elect their officers? For two years, the workers will have to be subjected to officers whom they did not elect? And what if the workers are not satisfied with the current officers? And furthermore, Mr. Woll, 32 union members, who you claim are Communist comissars will be excluded from the Union without a trial? Without the opportunity of the accused to defend themselves? This, Matthew, is the system of justice practiced by the Bolsheviks in Russia. Here in America, an accused man is innocent until he is found guilty. If they are thieves, traitors or grafters, bring them to court or before an impartial judge where they might be able to prove their innocence. No one can be allowed to be both the accuser and the judge. This can happen with the Bolsheviks, not with us in the United States."

I broke the silence that fell over the room where the conference was being held. I made use of the powerful speech Judge Rosenblum had just made. Each sentence of that speech hit at Matthew Woll mercilessly and paved the way for me to present a just and practical plan for ending the bloody war. I was in a hurry to speak, to head off Woll and prevent him from opening his mouth. I briefly unfolded my proposals.

"I am ready to close the office of the so-called left-wing union," I said, "and I am ready to give my pledge that I will appeal to the workers to join the AFL union, but only on the following conditions: first, let the 'strong men' whom the AFL leaders employ be removed from the Union. Secondly, three months after the unification, elections must be held for union officers under the supervision of an impartial committee. Thirdly, the 32 Union members whom Matthew Woll has decided to expel from the Union should be judged by an impartial committee, and I suggest that Judges Rosenblum and Brodsky be the judges.

Matthew Woll had a terse answer for my proposal. He said that the conditions he had set forth for ending the present situation among the furriers had been decided upon by the AFL leaders and would not be changed under any circumstances.

Then Judge Rosenblum declared that neither he nor Judge Brodsky could, with clear consistence, agree to the conditions that Woll had demanded as a price for peace among the furriers. He appealed to Woll to seriously consider Ben Gold's proposal, and in the name of justice, to let them put an end to this war which was a disgrace to the trade unions in our democratic country.

On this note, the conference ended.

104

Soldier Bartfield's Gang

A week after the conference, the right-wing union opened a bloody offensive against the strikers and against those workers who dared to protect the strikers, while the police, in accordance with a predetermined plan, gave the impression that they were trying to stop the fighting. In reality, however, they helped the gangsters to carry out their bloody objectives.

Just before a fight would start, the police suddenly appeared at the exact spot where the fighting was starting, and instead of stopping the fight they used all their strength to push away the workers who had come running to help defend the attacked strikers. Then, a few minutes later, the policemen threw themselves on the gangsters, pulled them away from the fight, arrested them, and on the way to the police station, let them go. And the strikers and workers who had been beaten up wiped their bloody, swollen faces.

We soon realized that in those locations where the police suddenly happened to turn up, the strikers were in danger. The members of the defense committee knew what to do. Quietly and carefully, they changed places with the strikers, who slid, unnoticed, out of their ranks to make room for the defense committee. Then, five gangsters came to do their duty. The police were busy pushing away the workers who had come running to the spot. The five gangsters met up with twenty members of the defense committee, and they paid for every drop of workers' blood that they had spilled, "with interest."

We already knew from experience that these gangsters, like those before them, would return to get their revenge on the workers who had dared to "insult" their brothers, so we prepared ourselves for a meeting with our "honored guests." Patrol committees guarded the street corners which were the most likely places for the gangsters to appear and surprise the strikers with a quick attack. And the gangsters did us a real favor. They were in no rush to visit us. Perhaps they thought that if they waited a whole week, we would think that they weren't ever going to return.

But we used that week to make better preparations, and when Soldier Bartfield's Gang appeared with reenforcements of experienced, strong men, they found out that in a contest with a hundred organized, prepared, angry workers, they were neither strong enough nor very lucky, and neither Matthew Woll, nor McGrady, nor even President Green had the power to rescue them. And the police "happened to come along" too late to do them any good.

It is not a pleasant task to describe the battle or even to report briefly on how the heroes of the underworld remained lying on the sidewalks, helpless and bloodied, when the battle was over. But I expressed my satisfaction with the Union leaders and the heroic workers who had risked their lives to defend their brothers and sisters in the bitter struggle for their rights.

After that famous battle, things were almost quiet in the fur market. There were no fights. The Bartfield Gang had vanished. The bosses stopped ordering their workers to join the AFL union. Gradually, the number of shop strikes diminished. Here and there, relatively unimportant clashes occurred between strikers and scabs who were escorted to work by the "strong boys" of the right-wing union. There were no arrests.

And suddenly! Despite our past experiences, we, the strike leaders, did not anticipate, nor did we ever even dream of such a possibility — that the gangsters of the AFL-Socialist union would dare, even for a very high price, to carry out such a murderous order — *a massacre of the Union leaders in their offices!*

The generals who planned this undertaking obviously knew that between twelve noon and one o'clock in the afternoon, the unemployed workers were in the fur market where they hoped to find jobs, and that only the Union officials remained in the Union offices, where they were busy with only a few individual workers who came to them with important problems or important information. It was, without doubt, the best time of day for the gangsters to carry out a massacre of the unprotected Communist union leaders.

Luckily, some furriers spotted Soldier Bartfield and his gangsters marching in two's toward the Union office, and they ran and told Jack Schneider that "company" was coming. On Jack's instructions, these workers ran to the workers who filled Seventh Avenue during their lunch hour and sounded the alarm: "A gangster attack on the Union!" In only a few minutes, under Jack Schneider's leadership, the fur workers blocked the entrance to the Union building. Not far from the entrance to the Union building, there was a small restaurant. All the Coca Cola bottles and other soft drink bottles from the restaurant were in the hands of the fur workers.

The daring underworld heroes did not anticipate the "welcome" they received. They tried to push through the tight ranks of workers who were blocking the entrance to the Union building with the help of their blackjacks, but Coca Cola bottles hammered at their heads and bodies.

The famous leader, Soldier Bartfield himself, tried to run away, but he didn't have enough strength left to run and remained lying unconscious on the sidewalk in a pool of blood. This time, it was not workers' blood, but his own. The police and ambulances arrived quickly, but not for the workers. Not one worker had been beaten up, and there were no arrests.

The furriers were jubilant. In the shops, in the fur market, wherever fur workers got together, the defeat of Soldier Bartfield and the failure of his planned massacre of the Union leaders were the main topics of conversation. The workers blessed Coca Cola bottles. Those workers who had blocked the entrance to the Union building were designated the "Koysl-Maarov" (The west wall of the temple in Jerusalem), and Jack Schneider was given the title, "Miracle Worker" for building the wall of workers which had accomplished miracles and for getting it done in only a few minutes.

All three underworld gangs — the Frenchie Gang, the Shapiro Gang and the Bartfield Gang — which had been hired by the AFL-Socialist union leaders to help them build their union and destroy the left-wing Union, were smashed and crushed by the workers. The left-wing Union leaders had no doubt that a fourth underworld gang would appear in the fur market. But the economic crisis which had flared up even before it burst into flames, paralyzed the fur industry, and the bosses were too busy struggling with their serious financial problems, heaped on them by the economic crisis in the land, to be able to provide the AFL union with the thousands of dollars needed for "gangster expenses." The gangster union was also paralyzed.

But we, the leaders of the left-wing Union, had to give up our plans of mounting an offensive against the bosses for higher wages and union conditions for the workers. The 1930 season shrank terribly. Large numbers of unemployed workers were unable to find even one week's work in the middle of the season. Those workers lucky enough to be employed worked only a few days a week. Workers' wages sank. Working conditions became unbearable. We had to postpone our planned offensive against the bosses for better working conditions for the workers with the hope that in 1931, the situation in the fur industry would improve.

In 1930, I travelled to the Soviet Union for a short visit, which became considerably extended. More about my visit to the Soviet Union later, but meanwhile, a short remark: The months that I spent in the Soviet Union were the best months of my life. I was not only in another country, I was in another world — my world.

When I returned to New York in 1931, the economic crisis had already devastated fat, rich America. The millions of unemployed were already going hungry. The wages of the fortunate employed workers were cut by the bosses in all the industries, and especially in the needle trades. These cuts were made both with and without the consent of the unions.

Weak, but Healthy

The left-wing furriers union was weakened and poor. (The AFL union was moribund). The condition of the workers in the fur industry was unbearable. The jobless were going hungry. We decided not to wait for the economic crisis to have mercy and disappear. We knew that the fur workers were hoping and waiting for the left-wing Union leaders to help them and to protect them from the arrogant and brutal bosses. And we did not disappoint them.

We understand that in the critical state the fur industry was in, our plan of action meant employing methods different from those of the prosperity years and different from those when the Union was not plagued by the underworld-AFL affliction. For our first contest with the bosses, we chose, after making the necessary preparations, to call out the four hundred workers who made the trimmings for the coats made from dog skins. We knew that these workers were devoted union members and determined fighters. We did not make a mistake. In 1930, in the middle of the season, in the middle of the day, at the call of the Union, the workers marched out of their shops. The bosses had two alternatives: to go bankrupt or to settle with the Union and save themselves from the financial difficulties imposed on them by the crisis. They didn't wait long — they settled with the Union, and the gains the workers won were even higher than they had expected.

Three days after this strike was won, the Union called nearly three hundred young women — the "pointers" — out on strike. These young women slaved for long hours for starvation wages. The enthusiasm of these youthful strikers brought a holiday spirit into the Union. For two weeks, these young workers surprised their bosses with their enthusiasm and determination. The strikers won a 40-hour work week, their wages were doubled, and they won other union conditions as well.

This signal to the fur workers awakened, refreshed and encouraged them, and it strengthened our decision to let the bosses know that we weren't going to let them protect their profits at the expense of the living and working conditions of the workers. We made all the necessary preparations to ensure the success of our plan to punch holes in the organized might of the bosses and to convince them that the Union had the power to protect the workers.

The manufacturers who produced fur coats belonged to the rich manufacturers' association, and those who produced the fur trimmings for cloth coats belonged to the Fur Trimming Association. Both associations were joined. Our plan was to first split the Trimming Association from the larger association, and then, when the leaders of the Trimming Association had signed an agreement with the Union, to deal with the bosses of the high and mighty manufacturers' association.

We knew quite well that it would not be easy for us to accomplish our goal, but we also knew that the hatred of the thousands of furriers for the half-dead AFL union would never die out, and that their confidence in their principled left-wing Union leaders could not be destroyed by anyone. We were convinced that the united and organized furriers would break the resistance of the bosses.

108

But suddenly, a disappointment! Just when we were prepared to call the workers of the trimming shops out on strike, the season suddenly started to die, even before it had gotten started. We had to postpone our undertaking until the 1932 season.

The End of the Wait

When the 1932 season began, three thousand workers walked out of the shops of those bosses who were members of the Trimming Association, in response to the Union's strike call.

The strike made the Union feel elated, while it threw the bosses into a turmoil. Matthew Woll shrieked, McGrady growled, and the *Forward* howled that "the Communists are forcing the workers to strike on orders from Moscow." And the strikers, with pride and with happy laughter, marched on the sidewalks and picketed their shops.

The bosses were not prepared for such an enormous blow. They trembled with fear that they would lose the season, which would mean certain bankruptcy for a good number of trimming manufacturers, who were struggling with grave financial difficulties due to the economic crisis.

The bosses could not hold out for more than four weeks of strike, and for the first time in its history, the Trimming Association negotiated independently with the Union for a collective agreement. The negotiations were pleasant for the Union representatives. The representatives of the bosses — the president of the Trimming Association and its paid representative — treated the Union representatives with respect at the conference called for settling the strike. They did not express any regret over the fact that they were breaking their agreement with the AFL. They recognized the right of workers to belong to the union of their choice, and they discussed each of the demands of the Union in a friendly manner.

The conference did not last long, and we concluded an agreement with the Trimming Association providing for, first, a considerable raise in the wages of the workers; second, for all the conditions won in the 1926 strike, and third, weekly payments to an unemployment fund. It was also decided that neither the Union nor the bosses had any further need for a permanent, salaried impartial chairman. If a need should arise, both parties could find a person they could entrust with the responsibility of arriving at a just verdict in any arguments between the Union and the bosses.

The economic crisis in the land was getting worse. Millions of hungry, homeless workers roamed the streets. Wages of those lucky enough to have employment were being cut mercilessly. But in the fur trade, three thousand workers had won an increase in wages and other improvements in their conditions after a four-week strike, under the leadership of the "Moscow agents." Thousands of fur workers were ablaze with joy.

1933

As soon as the first signs of the start of the 1933 season appeared, and the bosses gleaned the first rays of light in businesses that had been shut down because of the economic crisis, we decided to carry out the second part of our planned program — to punch holes in the mighty bosses' association. We told the bosses that we were not asking for any written agreement because their signed agreements were worthless. We were simply demanding higher wages for the workers and the conditions won in 1926.

We let the Forward-Socialist adherents know that they didn't have to accept the honor of becoming members of the left-wing Union—but we demanded of them that they not scab. The strikers picketed and watched their shops. There was not one scab! There were no gangsters! No strikers were arrested!

We had prepared ourselves for a long struggle with the mighty Fur Manufacturers' Association. But, miracle of miracles! — the strike lasted only one week! And another surprise — the bosses negotiated with the leaders of the "Communist" union like gentlemen. Each one of the gentlemen bosses denied that he had ever demanded of his workers that they join the right-wing union. The Union settled the strike with the bosses without any difficulties. The poor bosses had to agree to raise the workers' wages and to enforce all the conditions of the 1926 agreement.

The workers in the other shops became terribly impatient. They came to the Union and demanded: "Our shop next!" So we had to alter our plan: instead of selected shop strikes, we called "building strikes." All the shops in a building owned by bosses who were members of the association were declared on strike. A whole series of building strikes started. The angry, agitated leaders of the bosses' association tried to breathe new life into the dead AFL-gangster union, but with no success. Matthew Woll and McGrady did do something to help the desperate manufacturers. They obtained the consent of the chief of police to flood the fur market with policemen, but there were no gangsters, and no scabs came running, and there were no arrests.

The bosses had no choice but to settle with the "Communist" union. As soon as one boss in a building settled with the Union, the other bosses of the struck building lost no time in quickly settling with the Union, and with a show of magnanimity, agreed to raise the wages of their workers and to ensure all the union conditions set in the 1926 agreement. And, as soon as the shop strikes of one building were settled, the bosses of the other struck buildings settled their strikes in only a matter of hours. Many bosses sent their foremen or their shop chairmen to the Union to tell us that their boss was ready to settle with the Union without a strike. The blessed hour had finally arrived! The overwhelming majority of the manufacturers who belonged to the association had settled with the Union. Their shops were now under the control of the left-wing Union! And this was accomplished without the association!

The Conference With the President

Bright, warm summer days shone and brought joy. A rumor was being spread that the corrupt, reactionary, union- and worker-hating Mr. Samuels had suffered a "nervous breakdown." Mr. Scheidlinger, who was the leader and spokesman of the conference committee of the bosses' association, was elected president of the association. Mr. Scheidlinger was a somewhat modest man and a smart manufacturer. When it was necessary, he had the ability to deal with problems concerning the workers in a fairly decent way. I received an unexpected phone call from him. He asked: "Mr. Gold, you know that I was elected president of the association, and you didn't find it necessary to congratulate me?" I answered that if he wanted me to, I would congratulate him the next morning by calling a strike in his shop. Strikes, Mr. Scheidlinger explained, were not healthy for the fur industry, which was suffering so badly from the depression. And it was this issue of the strikes that he most wanted to discuss with me.

At the appointed time, I met with President Scheidlinger and the lawyer for the association, Mr. Filmore, in the lobby of the Pennsylvania Hotel. President Scheidlinger spoke. I was quiet and heard him out. He reminded me that when he had been the chairman of the bosses' conference committee, he had settled many complicated workers' grievances with me justly and had carried out honestly all the agreements he had made with me. He said that the shop strikes which were being called every day were adding to the chaos in the industry, which was suffering so badly during this depression that it meant that there had to be losses, not only for the bosses, but also for the workers. "We must find a way to avoid further chaos in the trade," he said.

He then made his proposal: The agreement with the AFL would not be broken by the bosses' association under any circumstances, but this agreement expired in 1934, and he assured me that at that time, he would call a conference of the bosses and the left-wing Union for the purpose of concluding a new agreement — but *only on one condition:* that we immediately stop the strike epidemic. All grievances of workers should be settled by the business agents of the Union and the representatives of the association. Complicated problems, which the representatives of the Union and the association could not settle, would be

111

referred to him and to me. There must be an end to the strikes.

When President Scheidlinger had finished, he turned to the association lawyer and asked his opinion of the proposal. The lawyer, Mr. Filmore, a tall, proud gentleman with a thick shock of snow-white hair, answered in a sad voice: "It smells bad — very bad to me."

Scheidlinger answered him that he, Scheidlinger, was sitting in a dirty, bloody swamp. "You, Filmore, can't stand the smell of the swamp," Scheidlinger said, "but I am sitting in that swamp."

Mr. Filmore didn't reply. I didn't say a word, either. Scheidlinger then asked me if I agreed with his proposal. I answered that in order to rescue him from that dirty swamp, I was ready to undertake his plan. The conference ended in a friendly mood.

I walked out of the hotel lobby and met Jack Schneider and Irving Potash, who were waiting for me not far from the hotel. I told them about Scheidlinger's proposal which I had accepted without any changes. Their eyes shone — their faces glowed. It is hard for me to describe the joy felt by these two principled, beloved, capable Union leaders who risked their lives daily in the interests of the workers.

Things got quiet in the fur market, as if by magic. No strikes. No picketing demonstrations. No gangsters. No fights and no arrests. Scheidlinger's peace plan was being carried out. All grievances of workers against the bosses were being settled peacefully by the Union business agents and the representatives of the bosses' association.

One problem remained — the problem of unemployment in the fur trade kept bothering us. We had hoped that when the season got into full swing, the jobless workers would be able to get at least a few months of work. That wouldn't make them rich, but it would at least save them from hunger. But our wishes did not come true. The season was a victim of the depression that plagued the whole country, and the hopes of the jobless to find work did not materialize.

At a special conference with Scheidlinger, I insisted that every manufacturer hire at least two unemployed workers. The president of the bosses' association almost shocked me when he agreed that, in his opinion, the bosses must acknowledge that it was their duty to help the unemployed fur workers. But he wanted me to know that the bosses were carrying a grudge about the upset caused by my leadership of the Union: the 40-hour work week, the almost doubled salaries, etc. Therefore, he felt certain, he explained, that the association's Board of Directors would regard my demand as an attempt by the Union to dictate to the bosses how many workers they should employ.

His proposal: that this not be a union demand, but an appeal to each manufacturer to hire at least one unemployed worker as a voluntary act. He would help to see that his plan brought successful results. In addition, he felt it would help to establish an atmosphere of peaceful cooperation between the Union and the bosses.

My answer: I said I was willing to try his plan, but if it did not bring results, we would have to resort to other methods.

"Ben Gold," Scheidlinger said to me, "it will work. It will bring results! You should understand that a joint appeal from the association and the Union for a voluntary act could not be turned down by even the meanest boss."

Scheidlinger's plan worked. In the first week, the Union business agents and the representatives of the bosses' association visited dozens of shops and found that over a hundred unemployed fur workers had been provided with jobs. Yes, the plan worked.

1934

1934. The economic crisis was even worse. Millions of hungry, homeless, desperate and hopeless people wandered the streets, lay around in the parks, and crowded into filthy "Hoovervilles." President Roosevelt's attempts to help the helpless millions of hungry workers were not helping. The NRA, the WPA, and the other federal programs did not help the bankrupt, rotten capitalist system. The mighty leaders of the AFL were deaf, dumb and blind and sat trembling because their holy capitalist system was in danger. Rumors were being spread that their was talk in high places in Washington that shorter working hours might be the blessed cure for the crisis because it would significantly decrease the numbers of unemployed.

The New Agreement With the Trimming Association

The leaders of the furriers union didn't want to wait. They felt they couldn't wait for President Roosevelt to bring "salvation," and we decided to go ahead with our program of improving the condition of the workers and helping the unemployed. The 1932 agreement with the Trimming Association was to expire in January, 1934. During the almost two years that this agreement had been in force, almost all the arguments between the workers and the bosses had been settled without any difficulties. Only once, when several complicated arguments between the Union and the association had accumulated, did we call in Roger Baldwin of the Civil Liberties Union to act as impartial chairman and to arbitrate between the Union and the association.

At the conference between the representatives of the Union and the Trimming Association for the renewal of the agreement, the Union demanded a 35-hour week with pay for 40 hours, a raise in the workers' wages, and an increase in the payments into the unemployment fund. We asked that the bosses now pay two-and-a-half percent instead of one-and-a-half percent, as they were paying up till then. We also asked for the continuation of all the other conditions contained in the old agreement.

113

Of course, the representatives of the bosses were more than a little surprised by the demands of the Union. They fought these demands, but without affrontery or hatred for the Union. They argued that since the economic crisis had begun, they had not had one good season. Even the wealthier manufacturers who were members of the bosses' conference committee were not ashamed to talk about their financial difficulties, and they insisted that the demands being made by the Union would force them to raise the prices of the manufactured trimmings, and that would shrink the so-called season even more, which, in turn, would result in losses to the manufacturers and less earnings for the workers.

But the bosses did not deny, when presented with the arguments of the Union representatives, that the 1933 season had been better than in the three previous years, and that they had already raised their prices without hurting the season at all.

At the second conference, we reached an agreement: The Union won the 35-hour week with pay for 40 hours, a smaller raise than was originally asked for, and the continuation of only one-and-a-half percent payment into the unemployment fund.

I don't intend to try to describe the joy of the workers. A 35-hour work week with pay for 40! And a raise in wages, too! And despite the crisis! And without a strike! The joy of the workers was enormous.

President Scheidlinger's Promise

President Scheidlinger kept his promise. As soon as the agreement between the Fur Manufacturers' Association and the AFL expired, he instructed Dr. Abelson, the impartial chairman, to call a conference of representatives of the left-wing Union and representatives of the Association. Dr. Abelson carried out his instructions quickly.

The last conference between the Union and this association had been held in 1926. Now, eight years later, we Union leaders were once again sitting at the "long table" with these "fine gentlemen" — the conference committee of the giant bosses' association.

They had not changed. Smarting from their terrible defeats and the defeat of their AFL union, and embittered that they had been forced to bow their heads to the victorious "Communist" union, they poured out an ugly attack on the Union which dared to present them with such outrageous demands as a 35-hour week with pay for 40 hours, increases in wages on top of that, and payments into an unemployment fund. Finally, they let me know that I was not dealing with the trimming manufacturers, who were mortgaged to the cloak manufacturers, and that they represented manufacturers who employed more than sixty percent of the fur workers, even then during the depression. They emphasized that they were doing everything in their power to

114

save the fur manufacturing industry from the terrible economic crisis, *and to save the jobs of the thousands of workers employed by the 500 members of their association.* Therefore, they maintained, the Union should be helping them, not trying to force conditions on them that would bankrupt the majority of the manufacturers.

Then they let me know that if they were to close their factories until the economic crisis was over, they wouldn't be losing a thing, because their profits, during the last three years of the depression, had not amounted to enough to fill the eye of a needle. And if I did not withdraw the Union demands, it was not out of the question that they would shut down their factories, and then the responsibility for their thousands of workers who would be unemployed would fall on the leaders of the Union.

And then: "Why, Ben Gold, did you gang up on the manufacturers of the fur industry? In 1926, you called the workers out on a strike that lasted twenty weeks until we had to give in to your Union's demand for a 40-hour week and pay for four more hours in which they didn't work. Now your Union is demanding that the workers put in a 35-hour week and we should pay them for five hours of not working? And if we should suddenly lose our minds and agree to your Union's demands, two years from now, you will demand a 30-hour work week. What does your union want? Do you want to drive the fur industry to suicide?"

The conference became heated. One member of the bosses' conference committee cooled off the atmosphere. In a quiet, modest manner, he said: "Mr. Gold, I want to ask you one question. You know very well that in the cloak industry, the union leaders permitted the bosses to reduce the wages of the workers, and in the men's tailoring industry, the union leaders also agreed to let the bosses lower the wages of the workers. Why? Because the depression is impoverishing the manufacturers.

"In the fur industry, the depression has caused devastation. Still, we did not come to this conference with demands to reduce the wages of our workers. But you have brought demands to us that are impossible for the bosses to swallow. Mr. Gold, you are always talking to us about justice. Well, Mr. Gold, where is *your* justice."

I answered as follows:

"Mr. L., your question deserves an answer. It is true that in the cloak and dress and in the men's tailoring industry, the bosses reduced the wages of their workers with the consent of their union leaders during these crisis years. But you are very well aware that in 1927 and 1928 and 1929, when prosperity boomed, these workers received higher wages without any difficulty. But what did you gentlemen fur manufacturers do in those years of prosperity, when the fur industry and your profits grew 'like from yeast?' In 1927, you broke off your agreement with the Union and helped to build another union. And as soon as your union was born, in 1927, you gentlemen cut the workers' wages. In 1928, you cut the workers' wages again, and in 1929, you cut their wages again.

"Our demands constitute only part of the sum that you took away from the workers in the years of prosperity. In the name of justice, you should, without the slightest resistance, accept the just demands of the Union and —"

"But, Mr. Gold," he interrupted, "you have forgotten that in 1926, the workers won a 40-hour work week and doubled their wages."

But still, I answered him, their 1926 season was the best one they had ever had, and their profits had also doubled.

Now President Scheidlinger spoke, short and clear: "We have called this present conference for the purpose of coming to an agreement with the Union, to establish order in the industry, and to avoid strikes which are no blessing either to the bosses or to the workers. It is useless to get involved in discussions about the events of the last ten years. What was, was. The fact that we are assembled here at this present conference is proof that we are ready to begin a new chapter, that we are concerned with the problems of today, not of yesterday — about tomorrow, not the past. The demands of the Union are not realistic," he intoned, "and the manufacturers will reject them without any discussion. We must reach an agreement which will satisfy both parties — the Union and the association. Despite the critical situation in the industry, we are not making any demands on the Union. We are prepared to sign an agreement with the Union with all the provisions that had been written into the 1926 agreement, with no changes. I am glad that we had a chance to talk things over at this conference, and I suggest that we meet again in a week and come to an agreement."

The Conference With Scheidlinger

A few days after the conference, President Scheidlinger invited me for an important talk. We met in the lobby of the Pennsylvania Hotel. He told me that the board of directors of the bosses' association had rejected the demands of the Union. He appealed to me to withdraw our demands because he had been notified that his board of directors members were negotiating with the AFL union about concluding an agreement, and that the AFL union had agreed on a 35-hour week with pay, not for 40 hours, but for 35. "And Ben, as God is my witness," Scheidlinger said to me, "it makes me sick to sit at a meeting with the leaders of that union!"

"But still, Mr. Scheidlinger, you will probably put your signature on the agreement with those disgusting people," I smilingly gave him a dig.

He was quiet and looked at me for a long moment. Finally, he asked me: "And you, Ben Gold, have never done anything against your will?"

"No," I answered him.

"No — hah?" Scheidlinger asked. "And when you are arrested and they take your fingerprints, do you reach out your hands willingly?" We both had a good laugh. "And now, Ben, come to an agreement with me here, now," Scheidlinger appealed to me. "Thirty-five hours a week, O.K.! But pay only for those thirty-five hours, and one-and-a-half percent for the unemployment fund! Listen to me. Come to an agreement with me and let's outmaneuver 'that' union!"

I answered him that the bosses of the Trimming Association and the "independent" bosses had accepted the just demands of the Union, and that the bosses of his association would not be an exception. Of course, I would like to outmaneuver "that" union, but not at the expense of the workers' interests. We parted cordially.

A few days later, the Fur Manufacturers' Association signed an agreement with the AFL union: 35 hours of work a week and 35 hours of pay, and one-and-a-half percent for the unemployment fund.

The Union sent out letters to the manufacturers who belonged to the Fur Manufacturers' Association, in which it explained that "you know that thousands of workers employed in the trimming manufacturing shops and in the independent companies are working 35 hours a week and are paid for 40 hours of work. If you will pay your workers for only 35 hours, you will force your workers to strike; *and we will pay the workers for every day that they will strike.*"

The Union's Plan

We decided that this struggle with the bosses would focus on the one demand: a 35-hour work week with pay for 40 hours. The demands for higher wages would be tabled until the first indications that the new season was about to begin. We decided, too, that we would start the fight for our one demand with a small number of shop strikes.

We called out the workers from twenty shops which belonged to manufacturers who had distinguished themselves by their brutal treatment of the workers and by their loyalty to the AFL.

But our plan did not go exactly as we had expected. Workers from many other shops demanded that we call their shops out on strike, too. They didn't want to wait, they said, not only because they wanted their bosses to give in to the demand of the Union, but because the bosses had become nasty and arrogant again, boasting about their agreement with the AFL union. So instead of the twenty shops we had planned to call out on strike, there were now over forty shops striking.

And a group of fur workers, members of the Socialist Party and their right-wing friends who had been members of the AFL union when that union was first born, now joined the left-wing Union and participated actively in the strikes and in all the other Union activities.

117

The bosses were thrown into turmoil when their workers went out on strike. The crisis in the fur industry had lowered their profits by quite a bit. They could not afford a struggle with the Union that was supported by the thousands of fur workers. Neither their leaders of the association nor their AFL union had the power to rescue them. And in a matter of a few days, all the strikes were settled; and in a matter of a few weeks, all the fur workers were working 35 hours a week and getting paid for 40 hours of work.

Now the victorious left-wing Union had another task to accomplish — a raise in the workers' wages. We called a meeting of the shop chairmen and discussed with them whether we should demand a raise then, in the month of May, or wait for the traditional July raises.

The shop chairmen's meeting was a festive one. The chairmen reported that conditions in the shops had been greatly improved, that the relationship between the bosses and the workers and the respect of the bosses for the chairmen were again like what they had been in 1925-26, when there had been only one union. The discussion on when to demand the raises was lively, and it was decided to wait until July and to ask for substantial raises.

A Conference to Save the Association

It was "Tishe b'ov," a day of great mourning, in the bosses' association. The paid officers of the association, who had been busy daily settling grievances of the workers against the bosses with the business agents of the Union, now sat in their offices and played cards because the Union had severed relations with the association and refused to deal with its representatives. A number of manufacturers resigned from the association, which had lost its power and its prestige.

President Scheidlinger called in fifty successful and influential bosses, members of the association, to discuss ways and means of restoring the power and prestige of the association. At this meeting, manufacturers, for the first time in the history of the association, protested against the policies and methods its leaders had used which had gotten the association into this scandalous situation. "We broke off our agreement with the Union in 1927 and made an agreement with the AFL leaders and obligated ourselves to organize their union," the manufacturers argued, "and our association supported the AFL union with many thousands of dollars, given ostensibly as loans, and we forced our workers to buy books in the AFL union." This, they argued, had caused strikes and fights and arrests. "For eight years, we have been suffering from this misfortune," they complained, "and it is high time to put an end to this scandalous situation" and conclude an agreement with the Union that had thousands of members.

President Scheidlinger stated that it was advisable to quickly break

118

off their agreement with the AFL, and he proposed that he call a conference with Matthew Woll about this matter. His proposal was unanimously accepted.

The Conference With Woll

Scheidlinger invited the powerful AFL vice-president to an important conference with the board of directors of the bosses' association. Matthew really suffered at this conference. Scheidlinger told him everything that had been said at the conference of the influential manufacturers, and he finished his report by stating that his association must sign an agreement with the left-wing Union if it hoped to save its power and prestige. He concluded that the association didn't have the strength to endure more than eight years of this fight.

Matthew Woll answered that a lost battle does not mean the war is lost. And Scheidlinger answered that when one side had neither an army nor ammunition, it was useless to undertake a war. Woll countered with "armies aren't born, armies must be built."

Then Scheidlinger asked him why, in all those eight years, the leaders of the AFL union had failed to organize enough furriers for a baseball game.

And Matthew, obviously pained, answered: "Because the bosses did not fulfill the point of the agreement with the AFL to employ only those workers who held union books from the AFL union."

To which Scheidlinger answered that this accusation was not based on fact. The truth was that the bosses had demanded that their workers join the AFL union, and the workers had answered with strikes which had caused enormous losses for the manufacturers. "The workers struck for weeks and months and refused to become members of the AFL union," he declared. "The thousands of fur workers remain members of the left-wing union."

Matthew Woll then delivered one of his short demagogic speeches: that the fight in the fur industry was a struggle against the Communist conspiracy, which was a serious danger for our blessed system of democratic freedom. "Under no circumstances," he cried, "must the Bolshevik conspirators be allowed to triumph in the fur industry."

Scheidlinger answered that it was a pleasure to hear Matthew's views on the struggle between both unions and the fur industry. Unfortunately, however, the thousands of workers did not agree with his ideas. They, the workers, argued that it was their democratic right to belong to the union of their choice. And he closed the conference.

The Murderous Attack

Of course, we knew from experience that the Socialist and AFL leaders were capable of committing the worst crimes in order to achieve

119

their ambition of destroying the left-wing Union. But it seems that we were also sure that the AFL union was dead and would not suddenly rise from the dead. They were not getting any money from the bosses, and that was why, for the past three years, they had been unable to hire any underworld gangsters to beat up the strikers. And their own gangsters, from the so-called "Organization Committee," had left their impoverished "business establishment." Thus, during these three years, the left-wing Union had led many shop strikes, unhindered, and the paralyzed AFL union did not have enough strength to even cry out loud enough for their pain to be heard. That was why we, the left-wing leaders, and the thousands of workers believed it was finished and that we were finally free of this misfortune.

But suddenly, the leaders of the paralyzed, impoverished union were restored to health. Thousands of dollars streamed into their treasury. And they proceeded to plan and organize a wholesale murderous attack on the leaders of the left-wing Union.

AFL and Socialist union leaders murderers? Unbelievable! A frame-up! A lie! Communist propaganda! But read the facts that were described in the capitalist press and take a look at the photo that was printed in the New York newspapers, showing the bloodied murderers after their attempt. Read and be astounded!

The offices of the Union's business agents were located on the second floor of the building occupied by the Union at that time. My office was on the fourth floor. Each week, on the same pre-arranged day, I held a meeting with the Union leaders in Jack Schneider's office on the second floor. On that fateful, historical morning, the able, energetic, devoted and beloved Union leaders were waiting for me in Jack's office on the second floor to begin our weekly meeting.

Suddenly, a band of murderers sneaked in to the second floor of the Union building. First they shot at the workers who happened to be not far from Jack's office, killing one worker and wounding a second. Then they emptied their revolvers into the glass upper walls of Jack's office in which they must have been told that the Union leaders were all assembled and that they were there, waiting for me. The gangsters obviously knew when and in which office the Union leaders met. The following Union leaders were to have been in that office: Irving Potash, Jack Schneider, Joseph Winogradsky, Sam Burt, Max Kochinsky, Herman Paul, Maurice Cohen and Isidore Gru.

But a very lucky coincidence! That moment, when the bullets shattered the windows of Jack's office, the Union leaders were not in that office, but in my office on the fourth floor. Because of a special important matter that I wanted to discuss with all the leaders, I had asked them to please come up to my office where we would be able to discuss this matter without being disturbed. They did me the favor and came up to the fourth floor to my office. They had just seated

120

themselves, when, before I could even open the meeting, the telephone rang and Shirley Koretz, the secretary of the Complaint Department, which was located on the second floor, shrieked hysterically: "Gangsters! Gangsters!"

We all ran down the stairs to the second floor. By the time we reached the second floor, it was all over.

When the gangsters had emptied their guns of bullets, they threw down their revolvers and headed for the exit, but the angry, embittered unemployed workers who were on the second floor blocked their way.

Unemployed furriers would carry their tools with them in hope of finding work. The finishers carried their scissors, the operators and cutters their sharp knives, and the nailers their steel pinchers.

When the police arrived, they carried six punctured and cut-up gangsters out of the Union building and laid them out in a row on the sidewalk. They did not call for ambulances. They called the captain, the lieutenants and the detectives of the 30th Street police station.

Like a plague of locusts, newspaper reporters and photographers, with their cameras ready, flew into the area. The photographers took pictures of the gangsters who were lying quietly, barely breathing, huddled close to each other on the sidewalk, holding their ripped open bellies. The street was flooded with fur workers.

And the Socialist *Forward* wrote, "We are sorry to say, but 'inexperienced gangsters....' "

The "Inexperienced Gangsters"

When friend Kaufman had finally been thrown out of the furriers union, he became a salesman for a fur dressing and dyeing establishment where the cheap furs were dyed and sold to the manufacturers of cheap coats and trimmings for cloth coats.

When the AFL, with the help of the *Forward* Socialists, began their scab-gangster union in partnership with the bosses, they invited friend Kaufman to help build the new union and help destroy the Communist union. But he didn't stay with them long.

When his friend Abe Beckerman was fired as manager of the cutters' local of the Amalgamated Clothing Workers, both men, who were old friends, organized an association of the owners of the dressing and dyeing firms and of the merchants who dealt with these cheap furs. Kaufman and Beckerman decided how much each plant could produce and also the price they would charge, and they also set the price that each coat could be sold for and what each merchant must get.

And woe to any employer or any merchant who did not wish to belong to the Kaufman-Beckerman "Fur Dressers' Factor Corporation" and wanted, instead, to carry on business in their own way and not in accordance with the orders of Kaufman or Beckerman. Bosses were beaten up and their shops were shattered by bombs during the night. One merchant named Schechter, who had refused to become a member of the Kaufman-Beckerman corporation, had acid thrown in his face and became blind. My friend, the progressive lawyer, Schwab, who was married to Schechter's daughter, told me that Kaufman and Beckerman got only a few cents for each skin, but that twenty million skins were dressed each year. In addition, the members of the "Corporation" paid a thousand dollars for bombing a shop whose owner did not wish to become a member of the racket. Lawyer Schwab, who had made a thorough investigation of the racket's activities after his father-in-law had had acid thrown on him, also told me that the strongest and most murderous gang, the Lepke-Gurrah gang, worked for the Kaufman-Beckerman racket.

The gangsters, those "inexperienced gangsters," as the Socialist *Forward* had called them in tones of regret because they hadn't succeeded in killing the leaders of the "Communist" union — belonged to the Lepke-Gurrah gang. Who had ordered the wholesale murder? Who paid Lepke the necessary thousands of dollars for this job of killing workers and getting rid of all the leaders of the "Communist" union? Who had decided that it was important, essential — a "holy commandment" — to murder the left-wing Union leaders and thus get them out of the way? Who had hired, first the Frenchie Gang, then the Shapiro Gang, and then the Soldier Bartfield Gang to butcher strikers and workers who were fighting for better working conditions and for their right to belong to their union and who had refused to join the AFL scab-gangster union? Who paid the underworld bandits the thousands of dollars for their murderous work?

And who hired the murderers who killed Morris Langer, the young, energetic, beloved leader of the workers of the dressing and dyeing industry? Who?

As I write these lines, I recall that when I arrived in the Soviet Union in 1930, the Soviet court had just found 48 people who opposed the Communist government guilty of a "small crime." The 48 people worked in a corned-beef cannery and were found guilty of poisoning the corned-beef which millions of workers would eat.

And how many big union leaders, here in America, betray, sell out, rob, oppress, terrorize and poison the minds of millions of American workers?

And leaders of the Socialist Party — the Shiplacoffs and the Pankens — were active partners in a conspiracy to help the bosses exploit and rob the workers. Leaders of the Socialist Party were active partners in a conspiracy to employ underworld gangsters to beat up strikers and to murder their elected, devoted beloved union leaders; to kill union leaders because they were Communists or because they were left-wingers and served the workers with all their strength and ability.

122

Norman Thomas

Norman Thomas refused the honor of being a part of this conspiracy against the thousands of furriers and their leaders.

A group of fur workers, members of the Socialist Party, who had been among the first to join the AFL union, returned to the left-wing Union because, as they told it, that other union was a scab-underworld union, and the AFL leaders, Woll and McGrady, together with the Socialists who were in charge of the union, were traitors, criminals and lackeys of the bosses.

These furriers, all members of the Socialist Party, went to Judge Jacob Panken and to Norman Thomas and told them what kind of an organization this AFL union actually was. From their conversation with Judge Panken, they left disappointed and embittered. He listened to their accusations against the right-wing union and answered them with a venomous attack on Ben Gold, "the Moscow agent," the enemy of the Socialist Party and of the labor movement, and the enemy of the democratic freedoms of America, which must be protected and guarded by every loyal member of the Socialist Party.

From their conversation with Norman Thomas, they left full of joy. Thomas listened to them and then informed them that he knew about the terrible injustices that were being perpetrated against the fur workers. Fur manufacturers, long-time members of the Socialist Party and his old friends, had told him what was going on in the fur market. He said that he intended to investigate this matter, to gather all the facts, and to speak out about this black mark on the Party's record. He told the furriers that he would call them in a short while, and that they should prepare written statements about all that they knew from their experience about this matter. The furriers, loyal members of the Socialist Party, were heartened by Norman Thomas's words, and especially by his decision to investigate the matter and speak out about it.

But he never called them and he never "spoke out" about the "terrible injustices" that he knew about, and he remained silent about the "black mark on the record of the Socialist Party." And the Pankens and the Shiplacoffs fulfilled their Socialist obligations with pleasure and contributed their share to the uniting of the AFL leaders with the bosses, who hired one underworld gangster after another to beat up strikers and murder the Communist and left-wing leaders of the progressive and militant left-wing Union.

CHAPTER IV

One Union!

The Call for One Union

I n 1934, cruel winds were blowing across "the home of the brave
and the land of the free." The number of lynchings of Negroes, the
number of murders of progressive, militant workers, the number
of attacks on unions and on strikers increased greatly.

The Klu-Klux-Klan, revived and revitalized, issued its program:
"against strikers, Communists, Negroes and Jews." The "Order of '76"
was organized to work the with the Nazis to spread anti-Semitic
propaganda. In New Jersey, the "United States Fascists, Inc." was
conducting its campaign to destroy all Communists, Socialists, anar-
chists and all other racial elements. In Alabama, the "White Legion"
was formed with the main function of organizing "pogroms" on the
homes of striking mine workers and other strikers as well.

The "Silver Shirts" organization proclaimed its goal that "no Jew
would remain in the United States." Father Charles E. Coughlin
organized his "National Union for Social Justice" with a fascist program. And Adolf Hitler, with the support of the American, British and
French capitalists, was carousing in Nazi Germany.

In a significant number of unions, the workers protested that their
leaders were turning a deaf ear to the existence of these Nazi and
Fascist terrorist organizations, which were growing and spreading
their propaganda and their activities across the entire country.

The Communists and the left-wingers did not remain indifferent to
this serious menace. They knew that the united, informed and organized workers in the trade unions were capable of mounting effective
resistance against the Nazi and Fascist organizations, which were
supported by the reactionary capitalist corporations. "Unity in the
workers' ranks" became the call-words of the day for the progressive
organizations.

The left-wing leaders understood the importance of uniting the
members of all the trade unions to fight the Nazi and Fascist menace.

124

We knew it was our duty to mobilize the energies of the united, militant and successful Furriers Union for this fight. But, unfortunately, we were entangled in the fight with the AFL and Socialist leaders of their union, which had been revived with the help of thousands of dollars poured in from the bosses and from other AFL unions. We understood that their failure to murder the "Communist" leaders of the left-wing Union would not deter them from their decision to destroy the left-wing leadership and force their gangster power on the fur workers.

To do battle on two fronts — one with the bosses and their AFL-gangsters union, and at the same time conduct a fight against the Nazi-Fascist organizations — was beyond the capabilities of the small left-wing Furriers Union. How could we free our Union from the burden imposed by the wretched AFL union? After long discussions, we, the leaders of the Union, decided that in spite of our hatred for the Matthew Wolls and the *Forward*-Panken Socialist leaders of the gangster-AFL union, we must begin to struggle to unite the two unions into *one united Furriers Union.*

We had strong doubts about whether the thousands of workers would agree with our decision because we knew that their hatred for "that union" burned strong and would never be completely extinguished. So we first called a meeting of over two hundred Union members — Communists and left-wing, class-conscious, principled Union activitists. We knew that they were all aware of and deeply concerned about the KKK and the criminal Nazi-Fascist activities that were going on, so we felt almost certain that, with the exception of a few extremists, the overwhelming majority would agree with our plan — *for one union.*

But we made a mistake! We were simply shocked by the sharp protests raised by our comrades at that meeting. Not one word was expressed in favor of our recommendation for one union. All those who participated in the discussion screamed that unity with the criminal traitors, murderers and lackeys of the bosses would be a tremendous blow, not only to the thousands of fur workers, but to the workers of all the trade unions who were fighting for their freedom from the traitorous AFL leadership. The vote was not encouraging to us — the leaders of the Union. A small majority voted for our recommendation, a small number voted against, and many of those present abstained from voting.

But our resolve to fight for our recommendation for one union did not weaken. We were convinced that a united union was necessary, not only to fight against the Nazis and Fascists who were running rampant in the land, but also in the interests of the thousands of fur workers. We called a meeting of one hundred influential shop chairmen in the hope that they would acknowledge that our recommendation to fight for a united union was essential. But the shop chairman didn't show any enthusiasm for our recommendation either. They argued that "when we will destroy the damned AFL union, the fur workers will have one union." They also argued that "that union" would not exist much longer. They stated that they knew that the membership of the AFL union was made up of a small group of Lovestoneities, a small group of corrupt *Forward* Socialists, and some old professional scabs, and that they were doomed to destruction. The majority of the shop chairman voted against our recommendation.

So we called a meeting of all the shop chairmen, and Webster Hall was filled with hundreds of them. For the first time since we had assumed the leadership of the Union, a recommendation of ours met with powerful opposition from the shop chairmen. They screamed that there was no difference between the AFL leaders and the Nazis and Fascists. "The Nazis and Fascists and the KKK butcher strikers and break strikes, and the AFL leaders do the same thing. Their hired gangsters butchered the fur workers. They even hired murderers to kill our Union leaders! The Matthew Wolls and the McGradys are a greater threat than the Nazis because they parade under the masks of union leaders."

They also argued that our fight against the traitors who were leading the AFL was an important contribution to the struggle against the Nazis and the Fascists. They shouted that to give up their union and join the AFL union meant that they recognized the Matthew Wolls and the Bill Greens as their leaders. That, they maintained strongly, would be a terrible blow not only for the thousands of fur workers, but also for the progressive workers in many other trade unions who were fighting against the corrupt AFL leadership.

They argued that the 40-hour week won in 1926 and the 35-hour week we had just won, together with the raises in wages, were gains no other union had been able to accomplish, and that we had achieved all this because we had driven the traitors out of the Union. "To unite with that union? Never!" There were more and more such expressions of protest by shop chairmen who opposed our recommendation for unity.

Suddenly, a surprise: Jack Schneider, who rarely spoke at these meetings and whom it was very difficult to persuade to address a mass meeting for even five minutes, let me know that he wanted to say a few words to the shop chairmen. And Jack Schneider spoke thus: "You are so embittered against the AFL strikebreakers, union breakers and enemies of the workers, that you don't even want to think seriously about this recommendation for unity. A united, democratic union does not mean that Matthew Woll or Bill Green will decide who the leaders of this union will be. The furriers will elect their own leaders. And you know whom the furriers will elect! Not Matthew Woll or the *Forward*-Socialist Charlie Stetsky. And a 'united union' means that we remain united — the thousands of fur workers and Ben Gold with us. Yes, it is true that one 'united union' would also include the *Forward*-Socialists and their friends, the professional scabs. So what? A drop of filth doesn't foul up the whole ocean. The furriers will keep away from them like from dogs with fleas. The main thing is that a unified union will belong to the workers, and the Matthew Wolls and the McGradys will be driven out of the furriers union. That would be our greatest victory. It will not be easy, but we will win. I am sure we will win our fight for one democratic union!"

The shop chairmen applauded him warmly. The recommendation that we fight for one union was accepted unanimously with one condition: that as soon as a united union was organized, elections for union leaders must be held.

And when, at a series of meetings, the thousands of fur workers approved the recommendation of their leaders for "one union," we began our struggle for unity. We postponed our plan to organize the many open shops that had sprung up in these few years when we had been occupied with the fight with the bosses' association and with the AFL, and we concentrated on our fight for "one union."

The leaders of the AFL answered us by telling us that we would have to shut down the offices of the left-wing Union and order its 9,000 members to take out books from the AFL union and pay dues to that union — then there would be only one union in the fur industry. As for elections for union leaders, they answered that Matthew Woll would decide when they should be held.

Some Happenings

During the months that we were carrying on our struggle for one union, a few things happened that deserve mention in my recollections.

Norman Thomas, at the meeting of the Central Committee of the Socialist Party, protested against the "dirty doings" of the Socialist leaders of the AFL union, who, he said, were "working hand in hand" with the bosses against the interests of the thousands of fur workers. He told the Central Committee that according to the agreement between the AFL and the bosses' association, the bosses had to employ only those workers who were members of the AFL union. But the thousands of workers were members of the left-wing Union and did not want to join the AFL union. So the leaders of the bosses' association had advised the Socialist leaders of the AFL union to get a court injunction that would prohibit the bosses from employing workers who belonged to the left-wing Union. But the AFL union didn't have enough money to pay the lawyers who would have to fight for such an injunction in the courts. The bosses' association then gave the AFL union enough money to pay for the lawyers.

Despite this disclosure, the Central Committee of the Socialist Party of New York voted 53 to 16 to support the conspiracy of the AFL and the Socialist union leaders against the thousands of fur workers.

The Civil Liberties Union requested from the national committee of the National Recovery Administration (NRA) that a referendum be held among the fur workers to decide who should represent them at the conference with the bosses. Robert Wagner, the famous senator from New York, was the chairman at the meeting where the discussions of such a referendum took place.

The AFL-Socialist union brought three lawyers to defeat the proposal of the Civil Liberties Union for a referendum among the furriers. The three lawyers — Samuel Markewich, Samuel Null and the leader of the New York Socialist Party, lawyer and judge Jacob Panken — fought bitterly against the referendum proposal. Senator Wagner explained that a referendum was a democratic and practical way of bringing the tragic situation among the furriers to an end.

And Judge Panken, practically screaming, insisted that when a union made an agreement with an association of employers and the union controlled even only five percent of the workers employed, the other 95% must accept the agreement.

And Senator Wagner answered him: "Mr. Panken, that is Fascism and not democracy."

Brother McGrady, the director-boss of the AFL union and Matthew Woll's right hand, became Assistant Secretary of Labor and went off to Washington, D.C.

Mr. Samuels, the former president of the bosses' association, committed suicide.

And Charlie Stetsky, who had been raised by Matthew Woll to such a high position that only he and McGrady, the two top leaders of the AFL union, dealt directly with the bosses and worked out the strategy, tactics and methods needed for the objective of destroying the Communist Union — Charlie Stetsky committed suicide.

Matthew Woll sent in William Collins to take McGrady's place. President David Dubinsky of the ILGWU sent in one of his co-workers, Sam Shore, who had been the manager of the white-goods union, to take Stetsky's place. The AFL union was in deep mourning and remained "sitting shiva" for a long, long time.

The Fight for One Union

The tragedy that befell the AFL union, and also the bosses, did not weaken our resolve to do our utmost to achieve our goal: one union. It was necessary to talk with the few "visitors" in the empty AFL "klayzl." We turned to the president of the International Fur Workers Union, Pietro Lucchi, with our recommendation for "one union." We knew that the international union was weak and impoverished and barely able to stand "on chicken's feet." We knew that the international had 1,800 members and possessed neither the finances nor the ability to help the weakened local unions all over the United States and Canada. Therefore, we thought that President Lucchi, who had been an organizer under former President Kaufman, and who had been elected president of the International Union mainly to guard its empty offices, would perhaps enjoy this opportunity to become the president of a revitalized international union, with thousands of workers.

We made a mistake. Pietro Lucchi answered us that as long as he was president of the International, he would not deal with the leaders of the Communist union. The weakened locals from all over the country sent telegrams to Lucchi, demanding that he take advantage of this golden opportunity to have one union and thereby save the locals from doom. But Mr. Lucchi answered that he would remain faithful to the brilliant leaders of the AFL and would have nothing to do with the Communist union leaders.

So we decided to call a conference of representatives from locals all over the country. The conference was held in New York at the same time that the International was holding its eleventh biennial convention in Toronto, Canada. Irving Potash went to Toronto to find out what was happening at the convention and to chat with friendly delegates. Potash telephoned me from Toronto and told me that I must come there immediately because the issue of "one union" had already come up and was causing quite a stir at the convention. He let me know that only a small group of Lovestoneites and the *Forward*-Panken delegates were fighting against the united union.

When I arrived in Toronto, the discussion about one union was no longer burning, but it was still glowing. In the lobby of the hotel at which the convention was taking place, a few of the delegates who knew that I was coming, were waiting for me. I told them that I wanted to say a few words to the convention.

In a few minutes, almost all the delegates, with the exception of the Lovestone-*Forward* group, came out to me in the lobby and surrounded me, and we continued the convention discussion in the lobby of the hotel.

Suddenly, President Pietro Lucchi appeared in the lobby. He greeted me cordially and invited me for a face-to-face talk. We moved over into a corner of the lobby, and he said to me: "Ben, I believe you. I think you are sincere about a single, united furriers union. I have made up my mind. I agree with you. I am going back into the convention and I give you my word that the resolution for a united union will be approved and that a committee which will work out our plan for unity, as you have suggested, will be elected at the convention. I will do everything in my power to help unite the union." We pressed each other's hand and parted.

When I returned to New York, the delegates from all the locals that had put together the New York conference already knew that the International Union convention in Toronto had approved the resolution for a united union and had elected a committee which would work together with a committee from the left-wing union on a plan to unite the workers into one union.

As can be imagined, the delegates from the locals were very happy. Finally, the ten-year bloody battle was ended. The fight for a united union had finally been won. But they protested strongly that the International Union convention, which represented less than 2,000 members, should not elect the president and the general executive board, who would be the leaders of the International Union for the next two years, until the next convention, without the consent of the thousands of fur workers of the left-wing union.

Some of these local delegates argued that a few months after unity became a reality and after the elections for Union officers in New York were carried out, a special convention should be called to give the thousands of New York members an opportunity to elect their leaders of the International Union.

The discussion at the conference became heated. The main argument was that a convention representing 2,000 workers could not force its elected officers on 10,000 union members.

Others argued that a few of the New York delegates, who represented the small number of members of their AFL union, had been elected to the general executive board of the International Union. These few were connected with the leaders of the bosses' association, had been involved in the bloody war against the workers of the left-wing union, and were the bitter enemies of our democratic union. They would certainly use their power as leaders of the International Union to disrupt the responsible task of uniting the thousands of fur workers into one union.

Most of the delegates argued that if we demanded a special convention then, as soon as unity was achieved, our big victory in achieving one union would be smashed. It was wise to wait for the unity of the New York union to become a reality. Then elections for leaders of a united union would be held, and the thousands of furriers would certainly elect their experienced, able and dedicated leaders who had led them in the ten years of bloody struggle in which they had achieved victory over the combined forces of the bosses, the AFL "czars" and the *Forward*-Panken Socialists.

They also argued that without the help of the bosses and without the help of the underworld, these few leaders of the International were "no more than bed bugs, and we will clean them out at the very first opportunity."

130

The Agreement

The committee that had been elected at the convention of the International Union to work out the plan to unite all the furriers into one union met with a committee from the left-wing Union and agreed on the following points:

1. All the excluded Communists were to be reinstated into the Union.

2. The left-wing Union would close all its offices.

3. All members of the left-wing Union would take out books in the united AFL union and pay four weeks' dues.

4. Forty days after unification, elections would be held to select the leaders of the united union.

5. The business agents of the left-wing Union would help carry out the unification and deal with the bosses on all worker grievances.

The decision of the International convention to form one union upset, confused and angered the top leaders of the AFL. It punched holes in their belief that they were the "chosen" and had "divine right." They quickly let President Pietro Lucchi know that they were resolutely opposed to the "tragic decision" of the International convention to "unite with the Communist-Moscow agents into one union."

President Lucchi was called to a conference with Matthew Woll, Sidney Hillman, David Dubinsky and William Collins, the AFL boss who had replaced McGrady. All these famous and lofty union leaders complained and appealed to President Lucchi to, without fail, for God's sake, correct the tragic error and void the convention's decision to unite with the Communists.

President Lucchi answered them that he did not know the difference between Communism and Socialism or the conflicts between them. He said he knew that Ben Gold was a Communist; Ben Gold did not deny this. When Gold was elected in 1925 as manager of the New York Furriers Union, there had been a terrible to-do in the International Union. Morris Kaufman was president at that time and he, Lucchi, was one of Kaufman's organizers. "So what happened to the Union under Gold's leadership? Hundreds of open shops were organized. Over a hundred Greek sweatshops, which had never been unionized, went out on strike under Gold's leadership and won higher wages and union conditions. That is what happened in 1925."

"You know very well what happened under Gold's leadership in 1926," Lucchi told them. "The Union went out on strike and won the 40-hour work week with pay for 44 hours. And for the last few years, the furriers have been working 35 hours a week and the bosses are paying them for 40 hours of work. That is why, after ten years of bitter struggle, the AFL union has only a few hundred members, the International has only 2,000 members and the left-wing union has eight or nine thousand members. That is why," Lucchi finished, "We must unite with the left-wing union."

Matthew Woll was the first to break the silence that followed Lucchi's speech. "President Lucchi," he said, "I assure you that the AFL will assist you financially and in every other way necessary to strengthen the International Union — an American, democratic union — but without the Communists, who are enemies of the trade unions and of our democratic land."

Sidney Hillman also assured President Lucchi that he would give him financial help. David Dubinsky told Lucchi that he would not only help him financially, but that his organizers would help him strengthen the weak furrier locals all over the United States and Canada, and that he would help the New York AFL union to win the fight against the Communists.

And President Lucchi answered them that, as Matthew Woll well knew, in the past ten years that the fight with the left-wing union had been going on, the AFL union had spent many thousands of dollars and had employed all possible methods to defeat the left-wing union. "And the result is that each week, the left-wing union gets stronger and richer, and the AFL union gets smaller, weaker and poorer. I gave my word of honor that I will help to build one united AFL union, and I will keep my promise!" President Lucchi finished his answer, and the conference of the high and mighty union leaders was, unfortunately for them, over.

One Union!

The doors of the left-wing union were closed, and thousands of members of the left-wing union flocked to the AFL union to take out their union books. Three business agents, leaders of the left-wing union — Jack Schneider, Gus Hopman and Herman Paul — worked every day until late at night, utilizing all their skills, their experience and the devotion and confidence of the workers, to unite all the furriers into one union.

The *Forward* and the Lovestoneites and the united *Forward*-Socialist group began an "honorable" propaganda campaign for one united union, but without the Communists. Almost every day, these gentlemen howled in their circulars that:

If the Communists and their left-wing followers would get into the leadership of the united union, the AFL would once more exclude the union, and the furriers would have to suffer again from the renewed battles between two unions. And they appealed to the Communists, in the name of the life interests of the workers, their wives and children, not to permit their names to appear on the ballot when the workers would be voting for their leaders, in order to save the united union.

They even published a "fine" cartoon which showed Ben Gold receiving his orders from Moscow. The bosses distributed these circulars and the cartoon in their shops and agitated for one union — but without the Communists.

The daily howls of the *Forward* and the *Forward*-Panken-Socialist group that the AFL had decided to exclude the united union and would organize a second union if the furriers elected a Communist leadership, confused many of the fur workers.

We, the left-wingers, decided to include a minority of delegates to the Joint Board from the more or less decent right-wingers and two right-wing business agents on our slate for the election. When the votes of the workers who participated in the election were counted, 5,000 workers had voted for the slate of candidates which the left-wingers had distributed among the workers, and 2,000 had voted for the Socialist slate.

The *Forward*-Panken-Woll family cried with pain over their terrible defeat. They agonized most over the fact that the Communist Ben Gold had once more been elected to be manager of the furriers union.

At the first Joint Board meeting, the left-wing union leadership made two more concessions to the Socialist "family." Despite the fact that Begoon had been the secretary-treasurer of the AFL scab-and-gangster union, the left-wing Joint Board delegates elected him secretary-treasurer of the united union. And, truly against their will, the left-wing delegates elected the much-hated Hyman Sorkin as assistant manager of the union.

But even though the left-wing union leaders helped elect exalted and beloved *Forward*-Socialists to high union positions, and included them in the leadership of the union, the *Forward,* with its group of traitors, never stopped hammering on the point that the Communists, the Moscow agents, had once more grabbed power in the furriers union and that, unfortunately, the mighty leaders of the AFL were remaining indifferent to the tragedy of the fur workers.

Again the Left-Wing Leadership

In these short memoirs, it is impossible for me to describe all the successes of the united furriers union under the left-wing leadership. The elected leaders again distinguished themselves by their indefatigable activities, and they were again rewarded with the warm, devoted friendship of the workers.

The building where Matthew Woll's union had "done its unioning" was too small and too cramped for the broadly branched-out activities of the united union. Only two weeks after unification, the union purchased a building for $86,000 — an amazing bargain. Now, all these years later, as I write my memoirs, I can still see the union occupying

133

that building.

In the new, spacious building, union activities bloomed every day and late into each evening. There were shop meetings, meetings and conferences with shop strikers and with unemployed fur workers. The united union lived and fought and served the workers with all its strength.

The two anti-Communist and anti-left business agents who had been on our slate and had been elected because of our backing, fulfilled their responsibilities and duties to the best of their limited abilities.

My assistant manager, Brother Sorkin, used to come to my office once a week. He would come every Friday, sit for a while in my office, collect his wages, and go home happy. Neither I, the business agents, nor the workers knew that an assistant manager existed in the union.

Begoon, the long-time devoted member of the Socialist Party, who had been secretary-treasurer of Matthew Woll's AFL union, and was now elected as secretary-treasurer of the united union with our support, faithfully carried out all his tasks and responsibilities. Every day of the week, he came to his office in the financial department of the union. Every day, he came to my office with problems he wanted to discuss with me, such as, for example: A worker who, because of illness, had not paid dues for a long time, or workers who had managed to get out of Hitler's Germany and brought their union books from the German furriers union, etc., etc.

But I never knew whether Begoon was even a little friendly toward me or not, because he did not know how to laugh or even how to smile. And even when some important issue got him upset and angry, to the point where he must have been burning up inside, it didn't show in his voice — the only outward signs were a few drops of sweat on his forehead. When he came to report something that he was unhappy about or dissatisfied with, his quiet, calm voice remained unchanged. "A cold lung and liver" is the expression Bessarabian Jews use to describe such a person.

But suddenly, something happened, and what an event it was! And when it was over, Begoon surprised me by something he said which sounded almost friendly. The entire story of this event deserves a place in my memoirs.

One morning, Begoon came into my office and informed me that the AFL union — the Matthew Woll union — had not paid its debts when it went under. The rents owed to the Socialist Rand School, for example, could wait, but the debts still owed to some of the members of the so-called Organization Committee must be paid as quickly as possible by the union, because these people didn't want to wait any longer and they held him, Begoon, responsible.

I suddenly felt feverish. He was asking me, I thought, to authorize payments to the gangster "Organization Committee — members who had been hired by the AFL union to butcher strikers. And to take such money out of the dues paid by the workers of the united union? And unintentionally, I blurted out a question to him: "And if you won't pay the Organization Committee?" He didn't rush to answer me. Carefully and slowly, he flicked his cigar ash into the ashtray and when this carefully executed task was completed, he answered quietly: "Gold, you know the answer to your question yourself."

Of course I knew that the answer to my question was that if the "strong boys" of the "Organization Committee" didn't get the wages they had "honestly earned," they would, without a doubt, send the former finance minister of their former union for a long vacation in the hospital. So I told Begoon to supply me with a list of the debts owed to the "boys" of the "Organization Committee."

He took a list with the names of eight "gentlemen" from his breast pocket. He had been paying them only half of their weekly wages for many weeks now, he told me. Rapidly and with disgust, I looked over the list of the "principal builders of the Socialist-AFL union" — names with which I was quite familiar — and I told Begoon that I would take up the problem with the Board of Directors of the union.

But I did not call a Board of Directors meeting to decide on this question because I was sure that Begoon and my assistant manager, Sorkin, would come to such a meeting, and I was also sure that members of the Board would rake up the entire history of the "Organization Committee" and would show their contempt and their hatred, and would not be ashamed to tell those who had hired to gangsters to pay these back wages themselves. I wanted to avoid a possible split in the union leadership.

Therefore, I called a meeting of the influential left-wing leaders of the Joint Council, who were the rank-and-file leaders of the union, instead. Neither Begoon nor Sorkin would be there. Well, what a meeting it was!

"Let Matthew Woll pay the money he owes his gangsters!" my left-wing friends argued. "Let David Dubinsky, let the *Forward* pay their organizers!" "Let Begoon pay them!" Such outcries were followed by angry protest speeches against the "chutzpah" (gall) that Begoon had in even asking that the union pay "his gangsters." And they demanded to know why I hadn't told Begoon straight out that the union didn't want to have anything to do with this matter.

I answered that the left-wingers had helped elect two business agents who were not our friends, that we had elected Begoon even though we all knew that he had been an important leader in the gangster-union, and that we had allowed them to elect the corrupt Mr. Sorkin as assistant manager of the union because we wanted to remove any obstacles and win our fight for a single union as quickly as possible. "We have the support of President Lucchi, and it looks as if we have driven Matthew Woll out of the union. The new union is growing and blossoming, and every day we are realizing successes in our struggle for the interests of the workers."

"My opinion," I told them, "is that we pay the debts of the gangster-union and get rid of the gangsters — they must have no access to the union; and then to let Begoon know that in the union, under the left-wing leadership, there is an unwritten law that when a union official is found to have a friendly connections with underworld characters, he will be removed from his office. The union is not as yet sufficiently fortified," I said. "Don't forget that we don't have any friends in the General Executive Board of the International Union. We must wait until the union is strong enough to bar all roads to the union to our enemies. Only then will we no longer have to make such compromises." The decision was that the union should pay.

I could have handed the few thousand dollars to Begoon and let him have the honor and the pleasure of rewarding his union "organizers," but I decided that I should present the underworld heroes with their "earned wages" so that they should know that in the united union, Begoon was not one of the top leaders. And on the appointed day at the appointed time, the gentlemen to whom Begoon had extended the invitation arrived at the union building, and one at a time, they came into my office and I personally handed each one his "back wages."

In my office, not far from the desk, Begoon and Sorkin sat as witnesses, to see for themselves that I paid each one the money due him. As soon as this spectacle was concluded, Sorkin walked out of my office. When Begoon was alone in the office with me, he said, "I understand how you feel, but it had to be done."

And yes, Begoon became almost friendly toward me and all the left-wing business agents, and also to all the other active union workers. He was finally convinced that a democratic union, under devoted, principled and capable leadership, is a blessing for the workers, and the unions that had been headed by his bosom pal, Kaufman and later by Matthew Woll and McGrady, were a blessing for the bosses and a curse for the workers. And Begoon continued in his post in the union led by "Communist-Moscow agents" with pride and pleasure until his death.

The activities of the new union began to bear fruit. With the assistance of the large number of active union members, the open shops were brought under the control of the union, and within a short time, the union had over 10,000 members. The left-wing union leaders did not want to wait for the so-called organizers of the International Union to perhaps get around to organizing the open shops in New Jersey and Pennsylvania. Again with the able help of the dedicated union members, we soon obtained successful results without any difficulties.

In the small out-of-town shops, the foremen and the cutters were workers from New York, and at the call of the union, they returned to New York, and those out-of-town sweatshops ceased to exist. In the larger shops in Pennsylvania, the main craftsmen were also New York workers without whom the shops would have had to close down. At the call of the union, these New York workers helped the union organize the rest of the workers in their shops. After a strike that lasted only a few days, the bosses had no other choice but to settle with the union. Many of the workers who, until they met the union organizers, had no idea what a union was, found it hard to believe, once the strike was settled, that they had really won such substantial wage increases and other improvements that the union had demanded.

The prestige and power of the united union grew, and the power of the bosses' association soon diminished. The bosses had to pay the workers tens of thousands of dollars in back pay for unpaid holidays and for wages that had been cut. They also had to pay tens of thousands of dollars into the unemployment fund in accordance with the 1934 agreement, an obligation which they had completely ignored for the past few years.

For the first time in the history of the union, the union organized the young unskilled workers whom the bosses hired as "floor boys" and who worked very long hours for starvation wages. The bosses did not want to recognize the union of the "floor boys," but in a short time, Local 125, made up for the floor workers, grew and became a gem in the union. The bosses had to recognize the union of these young, spirited workers, raise their wages, shorten their hours, and provide them with all the other union conditions.

Disregarding the successes of the united union, the small bunch of *Forward*-Panken-Shiplacoff Socialists never stopped howling against "the Communist Moscow agents" who were conducting union activities "on direct orders from Moscow. They kept warning the furriers that the AFL would not tolerate Communist leaders in the furriers union.

The union leaders ignored the propaganda and the threats of the *Forward*. Moreover, at membership meetings, I had to appeal to the assembled workers to let even one or two of these gentlemen pour out their venomous, arrogant speeches. When they would finish their speeches, which were often a mish-mash of idiocies, the workers would reward them with suitable "compliments." But the hatred and contempt shown them by the workers didn't have the slightest effect on these characters. They continued their propaganda, which gave comfort and hope to the bosses.

A Little Incident

One little incident, which really shouldn't deserve a place in my memoirs, is included here perhaps because it is necessary to show what kind of irresponsible and idiotic methods the *Forward* and its followers used to try to undermine the activities of the Communist union leadership.

In February, 1936, the agreement that the union had with the bosses' association expired. The economic crisis had devastated the fur industry. The seasons had shrunk, and the army of unemployed workers had grown and grown. Bankruptcies among fur manufacturers were on the increase. Yet, despite the crisis, the union demanded a raise in the wages of the workers and other improved conditions. The bosses were demanding a cut in wages, the cessation of payments into the unemployment fund, and other such demands. After several conferences between the union and the bosses, the latter stated to the union representatives that they would not conclude any agreement with the union unless the union bowed to their demands. We answered the bosses that we did not need a collective agreement with the Association and that the union would deal with each boss individually.

This statement made by the union representatives broke the obstinacy of the bosses. They knew that the union had the power to clip the wings of their association, and they withdrew their demands and settled with the union. The workers accepted the gains they achieved with great satisfaction. The union had won a 7½% wage hike, weekly payments into the unemployment fund, better regulation of contracting, and the assurance that the shop chairmen would be the last workers to be laid off when the season ended.

The Attack

The *Forward* opened fire on the Communist, Ben Gold! The attack was written by one of the *Forward* group in the union who was a members of the General Executive Board of the International Union. He carried on about how Ben Gold had deceived the workers — that Ben Gold had told a story about what the union had won for the workers which didn't have a gain of truth in it!

I didn't make a fuss over the nonsense he scribbled in the *Forward*. Attacks on me and lies about the Communist leaders of the union were almost daily occurrences in the *Forward*. So I ignored their wild accusations against me. Encouraged by my silence, the writer got bolder and began ranting in the *Forward* daily that Gold had swindled and deceived the furriers with his report on the gains achieved in the new agreement, and he challenged me to show proof that my report on the gains in the new agreement had not been falsified by me.

Many workers demanded of me that I answer the attacks. So I finally decided that it might really be necessary to act out this challenge-comedy, to completely expose this fool's nonsense and let the workers enjoy the performance.

138

The huge Manhattan Center hall was packed with fur workers. I opened this comedy meeting with a short speech, in which I complained that the writer had acted unfairly. Instead of printing his attacks against me in the *Forward,* he should have brought his accusations against me before the Joint Council.* Moreover, I argued, the writer was himself a member of the General Executive Board of the International Union, so he should have brought me up on charges before the Board which was, after all, the highest directional body of the union, and given me a chance to defend myself. I finished my short speech by stating that the writer was not interested in my defense, that he was only interested in dirtying my name, and that that was neither fair nor just and was counter to every concept of the responsibility of one who occupies a high position in the union.

The foolish writer was visibly heartened by my short speech and delivered a fine answer to my criticism of his actions: "Ben Gold is making a mistake," he assured the assembled workers, "if he thinks that he can distract me. I am not a schoolboy. I am an expert in Ben Gold's techniques for diverting the meeting from its main road. Ben Gold wants to save himself from these serious accusations. Does Mr. Gold think I will permit him to slide out from under the main issue — that he deceived the thousands of furriers with a falsified report about the gains in the new agreement? I exposed Gold's deceit in the interests of the workers and in the interests of truth. No! No! Gold won't get out of it this time! The point! The main point! Why did Ben Gold fool the workers and tell them that in the new agreement with the bosses, he won all sorts of improvements for the workers when he knew it wasn't true? Let Mr. Gold answer that!"

His friends, the *Forward*-Panken-Socialists jumped out of their seats and applauded loudly and happily for their heroic leader who had finally crushed the Moscow agent. He sat down on a chair on the platform, beaming with joy.

The End of the Comedy

I walked over to the lectern on the platform and asked him to come over with me. When we were standing shoulder to shoulder, with our faces turned toward the assembled workers, I presented a document to him and suggested that both of us, he and I, should read it aloud together so that the assembly would hear each word that was written in the document. So we both read. First we read that the document was signed by Dr. Paul Abelson, the impartial chairman of the conference

---

*After the establishment of one union, the organization of the fur manufacturing workers took the name of the "Furriers Joint Council" — the name which the AFL union had had before unity.

committee of the Fur Manufacturers' Association and of the Furriers Union. Then, together, we read each word that was written in the document, that:

1. Both parties, the conference committee of the Manufacturers' Association and the conference committee of the union, agreed that the following points will be included in the renewed agreement for 1936 and 1937:

2. The wages of the workers will be raised by 7½%.

3. The manufacturers will pay 1½% of the amount they pay in wages to their workers for the unemployment fund.

4. A higher fine for employing contractors.

5. The shop chairmen should be laid off last when the season ends.

That was the end of the document. I had wanted to say a few words after we had finished reading the document, but it was impossible. A storm broke out in the hall. Shouts! Very ugly, dirty words and curses filled the hall and hailed down on the writer, the *Forward*, and the small group of Panken-*Forward*-Socialists. Disappointed and degraded, as if they had been spanked and spit upon, they and their unfortunate hero ran from the hall as from a fire.

They suffered quite a bit from their defeat. It really hurt them that the "Communist" union leaders had managed to wangle higher wages from the bosses while, because of the economic crisis, wages were being cut in all the other industries. It hurt them that in 1936, the Communist leaders of the union were reelected by the workers to continue their leadership. And they were really struck by thunder when, in 1937, at the convention of the International Fur Workers' Union, Ben Gold, the Communist, was elected president of the International Union. At that convention, it was also decided that the International Union would pull out the AFL and join the newly-formed CIO.

They suffered, but the thousands of fur workers celebrated. Salvation at last! The hoped-for and prayed-for day, when the united conspiracy of the leaders of the AFL and the leaders of the Socialist Party, together with the bosses, against the fur workers, would be totally crushed, had arrived. And ten years of bloody warfare that these enemies of the workers and of the working class had carried on against the furriers were finally over! The victory of the heroic fur workers was sealed!

The Left-Wing Leaders of the International Union

It is certainly somewhat interesting and also important to briefly note the successes and the growth of the International Fur Workers' Union under the leadership of the "Communists and Moscow agents." But I repeat that I am writing only my recollections and not the history of the Furriers Union. I just wish to briefly present a few facts to show

140

once again how the conscienceless demagogical high priests — the top leaders of the AFL and many Socialist trade union leaders — were a curse for the American working class. Maybe, maybe, now that the Bill Greens, the Matthew Wolls and their ilk, and the Socialist leaders — the Pankens and the Shiplacoffs — have already completed their noble work, new union leaders will appear who will bring a ray of light into the darkness and a spark of hope into the home of the brave and the land of the free.

And now to the main matter here. The office of the International Fur Workers' Union had been located on Long Island. I was in that office only once, when I was first elected president of the International. It was impossible for me to move into such a far corner, out of contact with the thousands of workers and their problems. So the office of the International was moved to 20th Street and Fourth Avenue, which made it possible for me to have daily contacts with the leaders of the New York union and with the workers.

My First Undertaking

While I was involved day and night in the bloody battle with the bosses and with their lackeys of the AFL in the fur manufacturing industry, I did not know that 60% of the dressing and dyeing industry — the factories that prepared the most expensive fur pelts, that were not under my jurisdiction — were not under the control of the union at all. Why hadn't the former presidents of the International, who had presided over the union until 1937, when I was elected president, ever organized the open shops in the dressing and dyeing industry? Why? Why had the Socialist union leaders in the manufacturing industry never even made the attempt to organize the Greek workers? From 1914 to 1930, the fur industry grew and bloomed, thanks to the war and the post-war prosperity. So why didn't the union leaders take advantage of the opportunity, when the bosses were besieged by orders, to organize the open shops? And why didn't the mighty leaders of the AFL take advantage of the prosperity years to try to organize the millions of workers who slaved in the open shops? Because this family of vile, conscienceless so-called labor leaders was ruled only by their own ambition, their power, and their pocketbooks.

But Communists, left-wingers and progressives are separated from that vile family — there is a huge spiritual gulf that separates them. They belong to a different tribe, a tribe of idealists, whose strivings and whose goals are to serve the working class. That is why the newly-elected left-wing leaders of the International Union decided that their first objective was to organize the workers of the open shops in the dressing and dyeing industry.

We knew that our undertaking was a difficult one because the millionaire firm of A. Hollander & Son — which had a huge plant in Newark, New Jersey, another one in Middletown, New York, a third in Montreal, Canada, and a fourth in Paris, France — would mobilize its entire strength to fight the union. But we also did not underestimate the power of the Furriers Union under the left-wing leadership. Our biggest problem was that we had no contact with the workers in the factories owned by this firm.

But we, the newly-elected left-wing leaders of the International, were not going to rely on miracles. In a few days, we mobilized the energies of the union. At a conference of all the union leaders of all the locals in New York, Brooklyn and New Jersey, the right-wing union leaders were astounded by our daring to undertake this task and were amazed even more by the certainty expressed by the newly-elected left-wing leaders of the International Union that we would break the open shop fortress of Hollander. I informed the assembled union leaders at this conference that the strike against this wealthy firm would not be settled in one day, and that the International must be financially prepared, with a hundred thousand dollars. Within minutes, the assembled leaders pledged to contribute the necessary sum.

Just a few remarks about the International Union organizers. The former president, Pietro Lucchi, had had two organizers. When I was elected president, I did not send these organizers away. They themselves understood — they disappeared from the offices. So I supplied organizers who had grown up and distinguished themselves by their devotion and their abilities in the struggle for the interests of the workers.

I don't intend to write about the tactics and the methods that the left-wing union leaders used to prepare for the fight against the mighty open-shop firm. But I do want to tell about a few of the successful preparations that assured the union of an unbeatable assault against this giant of the industry.

First of all, the left-wing organizers made contact with the most highly skilled workers, without whom the factories would be paralyzed. In Middletown, New York, priests visited the homes of the workers and forbade them to have any connection at all with the Communist union, but the workers ignored the representatives of God and got more closely connected with the union organizers.

On a nice day, at 12 o'clock — lunch hour — thousands of workers from the manufacturing shops, at a huge open-air meeting on the corner of 29th Street and Seventh Avenue, decided that when the union would call the workers of Hollander out on strike, the manufacturing workers would not touch any skin that had been prepared by that firm. That was a terrible blow for the firm. Against such a battle tactic, the mighty boss of Hollander was powerless. The shop chairmen let their bosses know about the decision of the workers; the bosses ran to Mr. Mike Hollander to let him know about the catastrophe that was about to hit them.

Mr. Motty Eitingon, the richest merchant in the world of fur skins, was also Hollander's best friend. In addition to being friends, they were also business associates. Each year, Eitingon sent hundreds of thousands of skins to Hollander to be dressed and dyed. When the International Union began its struggle to organize the Hollander workers, Mr. Eitingon advised his friend, Hollander to settle with the union and avoid a strike. But Mr. Mike Hollander laughed at his friend's advice. Hollander explained to Eitingon that first of all, his workers would never join the union, and secondly, he paid the union organizers more than the union paid them.

Mr. Eitingon told his friend, Hollander that the present organizers of the International Union could not be bought, that the present union leaders had defeated the bosses' association and the leaders of the AFL as well, and that, in his opinion, Hollander should not wait until the union called his workers out on strike, but should settle with them right away. But Mike Hollander remained steadfast in his conviction that his workers would never have anything to do with the union.

What a surprise it was for Hollander when he found out that a large number of the most important workers of his factory in Middletown, New York were in close contact with the union organizers! Politicians and priests were running to the homes of the workers, warning them to cut all their connections with the Communist union. But neither the politicians, nor the church, nor the mighty Knights of Columbus, who were Mussolini patriots, had the power to reduce the influence of the union. And in a short time, the most highly skilled workers of the Middletown factory were ready to fight for union conditions. Without these highly skilled workers, the factory could not exist. Before we decided to call the workers of the Middletown factory out on strike, we called the thousands of New York workers to that open-air meeting at which the decision was made not to work on Hollander-dressed-and-dyed fur skins if a strike were to be called.

Mr. Mike Hollander knew that the thousands of workers in the fur manufacturing shops would not back down from their decision, and that Hollander would have to close its shops. Now Mike Hollander asked his friend, Eitingon to help him settle with the union. I had only three conferences with Mr. Hollander. Without any difficulty, he came to an agreement with the union for the following conditions: 15% and 7½% increases in the workers' wages; a 35-hour work week; time-and-a-half for overtime; equal division of work, and no discrimination against active union members.

For twenty years, the Hollander firm had never even dreamt that a day would come when its open shops would become union-controlled shops. But that bright day for the workers finally came when those "damned Communists" were elected to the leadership of the International Fur Workers' Union.

Telegrams from other unions streamed into the union with enthusiastic congratulations on its achievement. John L. Lewis sent a telegram which said: "Ben Gold. I congratulate you on the fine agreement with the Hollander firm. Let your fine progress continue."

After the victory over the Hollander firm, eight bosses of other smaller open shops in the dressing and dyeing industry rushed to sign agreements with the union. In only eight weeks after the election of the left-wing leadership, the International Union could point to important achievements which the dishonest right-wing leaders didn't achieve in the twenty years that they had dominated the International Union.

A few weeks later, Mike Hollander and I signed an agreement which brought the workers of the plant in Montreal, Canada considerable gains.

The organizers of the International Union — those able, dedicated union members who had grown up in the progressive movement and developed during the long, bloody struggle against the enemies of the Furriers Union — did an outstanding job in fulfilling their objectives. Open shops were organized. New locals were organized wherever a fur industry existed; weak locals were strengthened. Fur workers worked 35 hours a week. Their wages were raised, and union conditions were maintained and enforced in the shops.

The wages of the International Union organizers were meager, but their successful achievements for the workers were their highest reward. On Saturdays and, when necessary, on Sundays as well, I met with the organizers to plan the activities of all the organizers and to work out the special tactics or methods needed to handle the specific problems faced by each organizer.

The organizers from cities far from New York could not come to New York, so I went to them. In those outlying areas, the problems were more complex. The organizers in Chicago were not blessed with the necessary qualifications. Principled, progressive comrades took their places, and in a very short time, the locals in the mid-western states were revived. In Los Angeles and San Francisco, I had to remain for several weeks until conditions in those locals had improved and the old organizers were replaced by competent leaders.

There was a friendly camaraderie among the thousands of fur workers. Their giant victory over their hated enemies and their achievements were uplifting and encouraging. Each fur worker was proud of his decision to uproot the gangsters and their AFL and Socialist leaders. Now it was their union! They, the workers, were the union! And they, the workers, elected the union leaders who fought for the interests of the workers. And in their democratic, free union, they, the workers, had the last word on all important decisions. At meetings,

144

there was no longer heard the thundering command of the gangsters: "Sit down or I'll knock you down!"

And the conscienceless demagogues who ruled the trade unions stopped ranting and raving "Communists! Moscow agents!" They had suffered their greatest defeat at the hands of the small Furriers' Union. Now the free, progressive, militant Furriers Union blossomed. Our friends were happy with our success — our enemies were badly hurt.

In the CIO, the small Furriers Union occupied an honored position. John L. Lewis was proud of the Furriers Union which had smashed the attacks of Matthew Woll and Bill Green, whom he hated. He regarded the decision of the International Fur Workers' Union to pull out of the AFL and join the CIO as an important victory for the CIO. He looked upon the successes of the Furriers Union as achievements of the CIO. Not only did he send a telegram of congratulations when we concluded the Hollander agreement, but he expressed his happiness over all our other achievements and our growth. But more about the relationship between John L. Lewis and the Furriers Union later.

1938

Among all those who were hurt by their defeat, the ones who were hurt the most were, of course, the bosses. Why did the 500 members of the rich and mighty bosses' association help to build the AFL-Socialist-gangster union? They didn't stint in either energy or cash outlays to rescue their AFL union from every crisis, because they were certain that their investment would finally pay off for them many times over. And suddenly — such a defeat! All the assurances of the chief general, Matthew Woll, that the AFL would carry on the fight against the "Communist union" until victory, and all their hopes, melted like a heap of snow in the sun.

And the embittered leaders of the mighty Fur Manufacturers Association decided that they had to defend themselves against the militant Furriers Union on their own, without any "partners." The economic crisis got worse and was ruinous for the fur industry. The seasons became shorter. The number of bankruptcies grew each year. For months on end, thousands of workers were jobless. And those who did work couldn't save enough from the short seasons to have enough bread for their families. The amount of money that the union paid the needy workers from the unemployment fund each week did not help much.

And the bosses thought: in the cloak and dress industry and in the Amalgamated Clothing Workers Union of the men's tailoring industry, bosses were cutting the wages of the workers all the time. Only in the fur industry were the bosses punished with a union that demanded

July raises, weekly payments into an unemployment fund, and complete adherence to every point in their agreement. And the leaders of the bosses' association decided to use the sharp crisis in the fur industry as their strongest weapon to fight the union.

In the month of February, the agreement between the union and the bosses' association expired. At the conferences held on renewing the agreement, the bosses demanded a return to the 40-hour week, a cut in wages, no July raises, no payments into the unemployment fund, and more.

The union rejected all the demands of the bosses and set forth its demands: a raise in wages, higher payments into the unemployment fund, an additional week's paid vacation, and more.

The conferences between the union and the bosses did not bring any results. The bosses were sure that the union was in a critical condition. They reasoned that they could close their shops for a long time without losing very much, because until the start of the meager season, they didn't receive much in the way of orders for fur coats anyway. They figured that the union was in no position to carry on a strike that might last a long time.

The bosses knew that during the 1926 strike, several hundred independent manufacturers who did not belong to the Association had settled with the union, and that the workers who were employed in the settled shops had paid a strike tax every week and had thus helped their union to pay the strikers strike benefits and to cover other expenses incurred by the strike. But in 1938, there was a depression and a terrible crisis in the fur industry. The independent manufacturers would not be needing workers for a long time. The leaders of the Association were convinced that if the leaders of the union would dare call a strike, the union treasury would be emptied in a matter of a few weeks, and the union leaders would beg the bosses to settle the strike. And in February, when the agreement expired, the Association declared a lock-out and closed the shops.

The General Strike

We, the union leaders, did not rush to answer the lock-out tactic with a strike call. At mass meetings, we explained the strategy of the leaders of the bosses' association, and the workers voted unanimously that the union leaders should call a strike when they decided it was practical and necessary. We were sure that the fur workers would not work in any shop that was not controlled by the union.

In the month of February, the bosses declared the lock-out. Six weeks later, on March 31, the union called the workers out on a general strike in the fur industry. The leaders of the bosses' association understood that their plan to provoke the union into a strike which would

146

impoverish the union and cause hunger among the workers, had been smashed by the union's tactics. There was no way that their devoted friends, Bill Green and Matthew Woll, or the Pankens and the Shiplacoffs could help them this time. These friends of theirs had vanished, and their devoted lackeys, the once high and mighty leaders of the International — the Shachtmans and the Sorkins — were now totally powerless. There were no gangsters around — there were no arrests — only closed ranks of strikers marching on their picket lines — an invincible workers' army.

When the first weak signs of the start of the season appeared in the month of May, the leaders of the Association instructed the impartial chairman, Dr. Paul Abelson, to arrange a conference of the union and the Association to settle the strike.

The first conference lasted four hours, from 9 in the morning until 1 o'clock in the afternoon, and brought no results whatsoever. The representatives of the bosses claimed that they were ready to withdraw their demands on condition that the union withdraw its demands, and that no changes be made in the agreement which had expired in February, 1938. But the union representatives did not withdraw the union's demands. At one o'clock, both sides went to eat lunch and planned to convene again at two-thirty to continue the conference.

I didn't have the slightest doubt that the union would be able to break the obstinacy of the bosses. I was more than certain that after one more week of strike, or two weeks at the outside, the victory of the union would be assured. But one important problem! The union did not have enough money to finance two more weeks of strike and would need a loan of fifty thousand dollars. Who would help us?

Suddenly an idea — John L. Lewis! Maybe? I quickly drank up the last bit of coffee in my cup and ran to telephone John L. Lewis in Washington. I was lucky. Lewis was in his office. I told him that I was conferring with the bosses about settling the strike and that I was certain that if the strike lasted one more week, or at most two more weeks, we would win all our demands, but that I must have a loan of fifty thousand dollars. And John L. Lewis answered right away: "President Gold, the miners' union has half a million dollars in the Amalgamated Bank. Go there tomorrow morning. On the manager's desk there will be a telegram authorizing you to get fifty thousand dollars. Good luck!"

When the second conference began, the bosses spoke. We remained silent. Again and again they complained: the crisis had ruined the industry, the seasons were very short, their profits were negligible, and if they gave in to the union's demands, the number of bankruptcies would increase and the number of unemployed would also increase. That was why it was impossible to accept the demands of the union. And they also argued that they had had to lower the prices of fur coats

147

every year and that the demands of the union would force them to raise their prices, and that would drive them out of business in no time at all, etc., etc.

Finally I spoke. "I know," I said, "that in these crisis years, your profits are lower than in the prosperity years. But there is a Jewish saying: 'One doesn't get poor from lower profits.' Certainly, lower profits are a serious problem for the manufacturers, but for the workers, their meager earnings are an even bigger problem — a problem of paying rent for their homes, of buying bread for their families. You gentlemen bosses know that what I am saying about the conditions of the workers is true. That is why the union must get higher wages for the workers. Bread! A glass of milk for the children! But you gentlemen ignore the bitter problems of your workers! So there is no point in continuing this conference." I then proposed that the conference be closed.

The conference committee of the bosses froze when they heard my proposal. They did not support it. There was dead silence in the room. Then suddenly Mr. Manheimer, one of the rich, aristocratic manufacturers, who had not uttered even a single word during the entire conference, said to me: "Ben Gold, if you want to settle this strike, come with me!"

Mr. Manheimer and I walked into a side room and in one hour, we had settled the strike. Mr. Manheimer opened this private conference with a short explanation that all the conditions that the bosses had set forth for signing a new agreement were being withdrawn — they no longer existed. He now wanted to work out a wise and just agreement with me.

I answered: "That means the 35-hour week instead of the 40 hours the bosses are demanding?" "Yes," he answered. "And a raise in wages instead of a cut in wages?" I asked. "Yes," he answered, "but how much? How much?" he asked himself. "This is a bitter pill to swallow. Ben Gold, I give a 10% raise in wages, and don't bargain with me. More than 10% is impossible! Don't haggle. I give you my word that this is my last word on this matter."

"And July raises still have to be fought about?" I asked. "Yes," he answered, "but you must recognize the justified complaint of the bosses that you have ignored the agreement and have been calling shop strikes for the July raises."

I answered him that when the representatives of the union and the representatives of the Association would help to settle the disagreements between the bosses and the union, strikes would not be needed. "Good," he answered. "I agree."

We agreed on higher fines for manufacturers who hired contractors, and that the workers had the right to refuse to work on furs that were imported from Nazi Germany or that came from scab shops. We

148

agreed on a two-week trial period. And we agreed on a collective bargaining agreement for the floor workers and for the shipping clerks — a 40-hour work week, a minimum wage scale of $18 a week, July raises, and nine paid holidays.

When we had gone through almost all the points of the new agreement, Mr. Manheimer called the impartial chairman into our room so that he could write out all the points on which we had agreed. A nice little thing happened which deserves a few lines in my short memoirs.

When Dr. Abelson, the impartial chairman, heard Mr. Manheimer tell him to write down the point that workers had the right to refuse to work on furs from Nazi Germany and from scab shops, he almost shouted that this point must not be written into agreement because "boycotts are illegal."

In a quiet, polite tone, Mr. Manheimer said: "Mr. Chairman, Dr. Abelson, we are not asking you for advice. We called you in to write down all the points that Mr. Gold and I have agreed to." And Dr. Abelson remained silent and wrote.

When we returned to the conference committees who were waiting for us with impatience and curiosity, the impartial chairman read the points that he had written to the assembled committee members. When he finished reading the document, the room was shrouded in a dead silence. The bosses seemed to have lost their power of speech.

One of the bosses finally broke the silence and asked Mr. Manheimer if all the points of the old agreement would remain without changes. And Mr. Manheimer answered, "Yes, we didn't make any changes. We only made clarifications and improvements."

"And the 10% raise? Is that also one of the clarifications and improvements?" one manufacturer asked.

"Yes," Manheimer answered. "The 10% raise is a clarification, an improvement and a guaranteed remedy for a sick situation. That is my opinion."

There were many more questions and answers but not of any importance. The most important thing was that the agreement was accepted by both parties and the strike was ended. The union no longer needed John L. Lewis's loan of fifty thousand dollars.

The successful strike of the fur workers became the topic of the day among masses of workers far and wide. In the midst of the bitter economic crisis, with millions unemployed, with wages of those lucky enough to be working at all being cut again and again by the bosses, with workers' earnings sinking lower and lower — the furriers were once again victorious. The fur workers fight, and the bosses have to raise the wages of the fur workers!

Among the telegrams from friends congratulating the union on its victory, John L. Lewis's telegram is worth noting. It said: "Just heard of your splendid victory. The CIO congratulates you and your members for your fine work. The settlement in your industry will go a long way in stopping the downward trend of wages. Yours for continued success. John L. Lewis."

Gold (second from left in the front row) at 14 years of age with a group of fur workers active in the 1912 strike.

Gold with Louis Weinstock (left), former leader of the Painters Union and a pioneer in the struggle for unemployment insurance and the late William Z. Foster, former chairman of the Communist Party of the U.S. and an early organizer in the steel and packinghouse industries.

Gold with John Brophy, Director of Organization of the CIO.

To

BEN GOLD

President

International Fur & Leather Workers Union of United States & Canada

With love and deep appreciation for your tireless and everlasting devotion to the fur workers and their families.

Your brilliant leadership, your warm human understanding, your staunch and steadfast loyalty enabled us to build a strong powerful union, a progressive union in the forefront of the labor movement.

From you we draw continued inspiration to overcome all obstacles and to march forward so that our workers and our nation may enjoy the fruits of peace, progress and democracy.

We Salute You, Ben Gold

in deepest affection, and look forward to many, many years of working side by side with you as our leader and friend.

Scroll presented to Gold by the delegates to the 15th Biennial Convention of the International Fur & Leather Workers Union held in Atlantic City, N.J. in May, 1944.

Gold chairing an 80th birthday reception for Dr. W. E. B. DuBois at which the world-renowned scholar was presented with all of his works, specially bound. In the background is author Shirley Graham DuBois.

Gold greeting Paul Robeson at the 1944 convention of the International Fur & Leather Workers Union at which Robeson was made an honorary member of the Union.

Ben Gold (center) with Cleveland Robinson, secretary-treasurer of District 65; the late Ruth Siegel Lerner, leader of the Hollander Joint Board; Ewart Guinier, then secretary-treasurer of the United Public Workers of America and now director of Black Studies at Harvard University; the late Alpheus Hunton, then executive director of the Council on African Affairs, and Clifton Cameron, then a leader of the United Electrical Workers.

Ben Gold addressing a meeting of the Joint Board Fur Dressers & Dyers Unions in 1952.

Ben Gold marching in the 1950 May Day Parade, flanked at left by Furriers Joint Council President Samuel Mencher and at right by Pietro Lucchi, then Secretary-Treasurer of the International Fur & Leather Workers Union.

Gold with two Black leaders of the Fur Dressers & Dyers Joint Board — Lyndon Henry (left) and Gladstone Smith.

Exhibit for Negro History Week prepared by the Educational Department of the International Fur & Leather Workers Union, featuring Ben Gold's statement: "Every time a Negro is lynched, I feel the noose around my neck. Every time I read in the newspaper the lying, demagogic, criminal agitation against the Negroes, I feel the whip on my back....We must demand that these crimes be stopped and demand the complete unity and respect of every national minority, regardless of race, color or creed."

Gold flashes a typical smile as he acknowledges the delegates' applause at a convention of the International Fur & Leather Workers Union.

CHAPTER V

Fur and Leather Unite

In 1939, we were entangled in a jurisdictional dispute with the leaders of the Leather Workers' Union. A leather manufacturer who employed a few hundred leather workers also employed a small number of fur workers who worked on cheap fur skins. When the Furriers Union organizer began organizing the fur workers in that factory, the leather workers also began to move. And when the fur workers went on strike because the boss refused to accept the union's demands, the leather workers went on strike with them. When the strike was settled, the leather workers, who also enjoyed the gains the fur workers had made, joined the Furriers Union.

The leaders of the Leather Workers Union came to me with a justified complaint. They felt that the leather workers of the plant should join their union — the Leather Workers Union — even though it had been organized by the fur workers' union. But the leather workers replied that they wanted to remain members of the Fur Workers Union. Why?

I am only writing my own short recollections. The tragic history of the leather workers is described in Dr. Philip Foner's wonderful history, *The Fur and Leather Workers Union*. The fact that the leather industry employed over fifty thousand workers and the Leather Workers Union had only about five thousand members made me suspect that the leaders of the leather union, who were carrying on this jurisdictional dispute with me, lacked either the power or the ability to organize the thousands of leather workers, and I told them that the best way to solve the jurisdictional dispute between the Furriers Union and the Leather Workers Union was to merge into one union.

They were overjoyed at my suggestion, but they said they had to consult with John L. Lewis, and that without Lewis's approval, they would not make even the first step. So we went to Washington to consult John L. Lewis.

When we came into Lewis's office, he greeted us warmly, and even before we even sat down, Lewis congratulated me on the victory of the

Furriers Union in the 1938 strike. I thanked him for the loan that the union did not need to use but that was nevertheless very helpful in settling the strike. Lewis answered me that the interest he had gotten on that money that had remained in the bank came to more than the loan was worth.

The leaders of the Leather Workers Union told him about the jurisdictional dispute with the Furriers Union and about my proposal to merge the two unions, and that his opinion would be their decision.

John L. Lewis moved his chair closer to his desk and spoke to the leaders of the Leather Workers Union as if he was lecturing a group of children: "For fifty years, the AFL tried to organize the leather workers and suffered one defeat after another. And despite all our efforts, the CIO has not succeeded in breaking through the bastion of company unions and the open shops. I look upon this plan for merger as a blessing for the thousands of leather workers who are being brutally exploited by the bosses. The Furriers Union is a truly democratic American union. The Furriers Union successfully defeated the false saviors of the AFL. The Furriers Union has won every battle against the bosses. The wages of the fur workers are the highest in the needle trades industries. Carry out the merger of the two unions as quickly as possible. You have nothing to lose and a great deal to gain. Good luck!"

At the 1939 convention of the International Fur Workers Union, the resolution to merge both unions brought forth a heated debate. After the debate, 100 delegates voted for the merger, and only eight voted against. The fur workers unanimously approved the decision of the convention.

The Leather Workers

We, the leaders of the Furriers Union, were not aware that a group of incurable anti-Semites were spreading their venomous anti-Semitic propaganda among the members of the Leather Workers Union, and that portraits of the arch anti-Semite, Father Coughlin, hung on the walls of all the offices of the company unions. This anti-Semitic group unfurled a broad propaganda campaign against the merger of the Leather Workers Union with the "Jewish-Communist Furriers Union." In Boston and in Peabody, the priests in twelve churches warned the leather workers not to merge with the "Godless Communist Furriers Union." Just as the mass of fur workers had ignored the rantings of the *Forward* and its Socialists, the leather workers now ignored the rantings of the anti-Semites and the priests and happily voted for the merger of the two unions. Moreover, in the battle against the depraved anti-Semitic group, a united, almost progressive group of leather workers — Irish and Jewish — was born. They fought the anti-Semites and won the confidence of the workers.

152

Once again I find it necessary to stress that I am not writing the history of the union, but rather only my short recollections. Dr. Philip Foner's book is filled with facts, letters and documents which confirm that everything he wrote is the truth, and noone is able to deny it. I only want to point out that in fifty years, the AFL was unsuccessful in trying to organize the leather workers, and that even the CIO did not succeed in overcoming the difficulties and obstacles they encountered in their attempt to organize the leather workers. But the poor and small Furriers Union accomplished this task! It sounds unbelievable, doesn't it?

It did not take very long before the Furriers Union won the trust of the leather workers. Finally, the workers in the leather tanneries, who had been robbed and betrayed by the AFL organizers and brutally exploited by the bosses, began to feel that the day of their liberation was in sight, and they were happy to welcome the organizers of the Furriers Union. The bosses threatened the workers that if they dared to join the union, they, the bosses, would close down the tanneries. The anti-Semitic and anti-Communist groups stepped up their activities. The AFL carried on its usual misleading and union-busting activities. But the energetic, able, experienced organizers of the Furriers Union did not let any of these obstacles stand in their way, and they unfurled their broad-based plan for organizing the leather workers.

Each leather tannery had some capable, courageous workers who helped unite, organize and prepare the workers for a fight for higher wages, shorter working hours, and other union conditions, and they also helped to combat the anti-Semitic and anti-Communist creatures.

The AFL traitors, upset by their defeats, turned to the courts for an injunction against the union, but there, too, they met with defeat. The court threw out the case and made the AFL pay the court costs.

There were more and more successes. Bosses settled with the union, and the workers were happy with the gains they made. Membership in the union kept growing. Even the company union fortresses were smashed. Dedicated, able and active leather workers were selected as organizers. They developed quickly and soon distinguished themselves by their untiring determination to organize the leather workers and combat all their foes.

The sun was shining now on the thousands of organized leather workers. New breezes refreshed them. Every gain, every successful strike, every defeat of their enemies raised their spirits and strengthened their belief in their power as part of the International Fur and Leather Workers Union. The pictures of Father Coughlin disappeared from the walls of the offices of the former company unions. The anti-Semitic, anti-Communist gang was condemned by the leather workers.

A minor event which tells much is worth a few lines in my memoirs. The fur industry in the state of Massachusetts employed only a few workers. There was only one local of fur workers in Boston. When the thousands of leather workers who were employed by factories all over the state of Massachusetts were organized, it was necessary to appoint a district manager to supervise the activities of all the locals. I called a conference of representatives of all the locals in the state of Massachusetts and told them I had three names on my list of people who had the necessary qualifications to fulfill the responsibilities of a district director for the state: Michael O'Keefe, Mike Donahue and Isador Pickman. I asked them to decide.

O'Keefe, the manager of the largest local in Boston, gave his opinion that Pickman had all the necessary qualifications for this responsible position. Organizer Mike Donahue explained that Pickman was capable and respected by the workers. Moreover, he said, by electing Pickman, a Jew, as district director, regardless of the fact that there were very few Jewish workers in the industry, it would be the best answer they could give to the disgusting anti-Semitic gang. And the assembled Catholic, mostly Irish, active union workers unanimously elected Isador Pickman as district director. As I am writing my memoirs, Pickman is still the district director for the state of Massachusetts.

The successes of the Fur and Leather Workers Union amazed and grieved our enemies. They were choking on their helplessness. And when America declared war on Japan and Nazi Germany, the anti-Semitic gang joined the "America First" organization which opposed the war against Nazism and Fascism. With the help of the AFL, they renewed their attacks against the union. They organized an AFL union, and the AFL's degenerate leadership gladly handed them a charter and took the Nazi gang under their wing.

For months, this Nazi gang strained every muscle to build up their AFL dual union. Angered and embittered by their lack of success, they declared a strike in the Peabody leather tanneries and used gangster tactics to force the workers to go out on strike. In one day, the workers organized "defense committees," but this time, a lucky coincidence saved the anti-Semitic AFL gang. Before the defense committees had a chance to protect the workers against these anti-Semites, the Federal Government intervened and demanded that its government order must be delivered on time because the leather was needed for the army. They insisted that the dispute between the two unions must be settled in a peaceful manner by the workers through a referendum.

The demagogue patriots of the AFL had to agree to this, and the workers of seventy shops participated in the balloting. The workers of 68 shops voted for the Fur and Leather Workers Union, and two small contracting shops voted for the anti-Semitic AFL union. Crushed and frightened by the enraged workers, the anti-Semitic union-busting gang vanished, and the AFL traitors were driven out of the leather industry, just as they had been driven out of the fur industry. Again the bosses lost their faithful servants.

The leather union bloomed. United in brotherhood and friendship, the leather worker organizers, with the help of the experienced fur organizers, fulfilled their objectives in an outstanding manner. The leather workers in every tannery, without exception, enthusiastically answered the call of the union. And when it was absolutely necessary to call a strike in any tannery, the united, militant strikers broke down the obstinacy of the bosses in a short time. The mass of workers were more than pleased with the gains they made. They won a 40-hour work week, their wages were more than doubled, they got time-and-a-half for overtime, paid holidays, job security, health insurance, and other important union conditions. Even in the states of the South, where unions were constantly being threatened and rarely able to function, all the leather workers were organized and won all the demands of the union.

It is no wonder that the leather workers praised the day that the Furriers Union merged with their weak and helpless union. The leather workers knew that Ben Gold, the president of the International Fur and Leather Workers Union, was a Communist, but the resounding applause of the leather workers for the leaders of the union drowned out the anti-Communist ravings of its enemies. In 1943, 50,000 leather workers were paying dues to the union. Fifty thousand!

Meanwhile, Back in the Fur Market...

The fur manufacturers were very much upset over the fact that the wages of the workers in all of the needle trades were being cut, while they had to raise the wages of the fur workers. The contractors hurt even more because one of the points in the agreement that resulted from the successful strike in 1938 was the prohibition of contracting.

The conscienceless leaders of the AFL were still smarting from their defeat in the ten-year struggle with the Furriers Union and from their defeat in the leather industry, where it was again the Communist Furriers Union that was the victor. The recent gains made by the united fur and leather workers under the Communist leadership angered them even more.

Helpless by themselves, our furious enemies now turned to the federal government for help. The reactionary leaders of the United States Justice Department were happy to do our foes a favor. After all, one hand washes the other, and so the Justice Department indicted the leaders of the Furriers Union for violation of the Sherman Anti-Trust Act. Ten union leaders — Potash, Schneider, Gold, Joseph Winogradsky, Sam Burt, Zanvil Wollin, Herman Paul, Maurice Cohen, Gus Hopman and Max Kochinsky — along with sixteen workers who were active in the union, were indicted. The charge was simple and clear: the union had entered into a conspiracy to unionize the fur dressing and dyeing plants in New Jersey. Naturally, the bosses were ready witnesses against the union leaders, as were some former workers who had been excluded from the union for their connections with its enemies. Some of them cooperated with the FBI and gave testimony against the accused union leaders.

A few scenes that were enacted in the courtroom deserve mention in my memoirs. A boss named Morgan testified that a large percentage of his finished products were sold in other states, and the union had called his workers out on strike because he did not want to sign an agreement with it. The judge asked the U.S. attorney what that had to do with the Anti-Trust Act, and he answered that a union that calls the workers out on strike against a manufacturer who sells his products in interstate commerce is guilty of violating the Anti-Trust Act!

Also, a fur manufacturer named Bader sat in the witness box and bemoaned his fate, telling about the troubles he had had with union business agent Jack Schneider. He finished his tale of woe by saying that every time Schneider came into his shop, it cost him money. The judge quickly asked Mr. Bader: "Mr. Bader, did you pay the business agent, Jack Schneider money?" "No," Mr. Bader answered, "Jack Schneider doesn't take any money, but whenever he comes into my shop, he demands higher wages for the workers, and I have to raise their wages." The judge just sat there as if he had just been slapped.

A fine comedy was enacted by William Karpouzas. This witness testified that he had belonged to a committee of active union members whose function was to beat up scabs, contractors and workers who dared to criticize the union officials, and that Gold, Potash and Schneider used to give them instructions on whom to beat up. When the witness finished telling these terrible stories, he asked the judge if he could make a statement.

With the judge's permission, Karpouzas then explained that everything he had just testified to was a lie, that he had never received any instructions from Gold, Potash or Schneider to commit any of these crimes, and that all the stories he had told were on orders from the U.S. attorney and from Soulounias, one of those who had been excluded from the union. He said that these two had instructed him not to forget to say that Ben Gold had given him orders to commit these acts. He said that on that very morning, Soulounias had reminded him again not to forget to say that Ben Gold was the one who had given him the instructions.

The U.S. attorney asked: "Mr. Karpouzas, when I spoke to you in my office, was there a stenographer present who wrote down my questions to you and your answers?" "Yes," the witness answered, "but the stenographer wrote down your questions and not my answers, because you, Mr. U.S. attorney, asked the questions, and you also dictated the answers. I didn't answer your questions because I didn't know what to answer."

How do you like these comedy scenes? How do you like the U.S. attorney who represented the Department of Justice of America, the land of the free and the home of the brave? In his *Fur and Leather Workers Union,* Philip Foner shows documentary proof that the bosses worked eagerly with the Department of Justice to spin the conspiracy web to ensnare the union leaders, and that the witness, Karpouzas, disclosed the criminal methods that the Department of Justice used to send the union leaders to prison on a trumped-up charge that they had violated the Anti-Trust Act when they were trying to unionize workers in the sweatshops that produced goods that went into other states.

The degenerate leaders of the AFL were overjoyed when seven union leaders were found guilty and sentenced to a year in jail and fined thousands of dollars. Finally they were victorious. Their baying about deporting the union leaders had not brought them the desired results. Their plan to murder the union leaders did not succeed because, as the Socialist *Forward* wrote the next day, "The gangsters were inexperienced." But finally, with the help of the Department of Justice and the assistance of false witnesses, they had succeeded in putting the main union leaders behind bars.

The Court of Appeals reversed the Anti-Trust convictions, but the Justice Department had indicted several union officials for obstruction of justice, and this second charge was not dropped. Corrupt witnesses were again instrumental in the resulting "guilty" verdicts and in sending several union leaders to prison — Potash, Winogradsky, Schneider, John Vafiades and Louis Hatchios.

Ten thousand fur workers sent a telegram to President Roosevelt, over three hundred feet long, demanding the release of their leaders. Many other unions sent telegrams to President Roosevelt demanding the release of the fur union leaders who were the "victims of persecution by the Justice Department." The CIO stormed its protests that the Anti-Trust Act was being used to break unions — but the beloved leaders of the furriers union remained sitting in jail.

In the Enemy Camp

The leaders of the bosses' association of New York and the AFL traitors were sure that their lucky day had finally arrived. The association of Greek fur manufacturers had built a company union and the AFL leaders were happy to hand this company union a charter.

And in 1941, just at the time when the union leaders were behind bars, the union's agreement with the bosses' association expired. At the first conference between the representatives of the union and the representatives of the association, the bosses let us know that they were now in the saddle and that they would dictate the working conditions in their shops. First, they rejected the union's demands. Secondly, they presented their own demands, and thirdly, they let us know that when the union was ready to accept their demands, we should inform the impartial chairman and he would call a conference of both sides.

I replied to the bosses that the union would never agree to conclude an agreement with their association unless they withdrew their unjust demands, and that when they were ready to acknowledge the justified demands of the union, they should let us know. On this note, the conference ended.

I moved out of my office in the International Union and moved into Manager Irving Potash's office in the building that belonged to the New York Furriers Union. Potash was in prison, and I knew that I had to cope with the serious problems with which the New York union was besieged. But I was certain that, with the help of the thousands of fur workers, the obstinacy of the fur manufacturers could and would be broken. I also had no doubt that with the help of the leather workers, we would break the resistance of the bosses of the leather tanneries and their company unions.

Nor was I mistaken. At the shop chairmen's meetings and at mass meetings, the fur workers raged with protests against the bosses and their demands to cut wages and rob the workers of all the gains they had made in the 1938 strike. Because of the war in Europe, the economic conditions in the United States were greatly improved, and things were much better in the fur industry, so the bosses were hardly in a position to threaten the workers with a lock-out. The union did not call a general strike. Instead, it dealt with each manufacturer individually, without the intervention of the representatives of the bosses' association. The vast majority of the bosses raised their workers' wages and instituted all the other demands of the union. Those bosses who refused to deal with the union settled after their workers had struck for only a few days. The Association was excluded from all of these negotiations and settlements.

And even though we were busy struggling against the Association, we were also successful in our fight with the AFL's Greek company union, which was effectively destroyed. The Greek fur manufacturers association signed an agreement with the union with healthy gains for the Greek workers. Then Mike Hollander renewed the agreement with the union without any problems or difficulties. The Hollander workers received wage increases totalling $450,000.

The organizing continued in the leather industry and brought encouraging results. In 1940 and 1941, thousands of leather workers joined the union. The leather-producing firms concluded agreements with the Fur and Leather Workers Union. The gains received by the workers strengthened their confidence in and their devotion to their

158

union.

In May, when the first signs of the fur season appeared, the leaders of the bosses' association invited the union to a conference for the purpose of renewing the agreement. On their way to this conference, the bosses lost their list of demands and their confidence in their invincibility that they had had just a short time earlier. Their arrogant obstinacy melted away like a pile of snow in the summer, and at the conference they assumed the roles of fine gentlemen, eager to live at peace with the union. At the second conference, the agreement was concluded. The gains achieved by the workers came to more than we had expected.

The union called a mass meeting in a large hall to report the gains of the new agreement to the workers, but on the same day on which the mass meeting was held, the bosses held a meeting of their own, at which they rejected the agreement that their conference committee had signed with the union. They argued that when they had had to deal with the union individually, without the help of the Association, they had had to raise the workers' wages, and now, according to the new agreement, they would have to raise their wages again. This, they claimed, was not fair, so they voted against ratifying the new agreement.

At the mass meeting, we reported all the gains for the workers that were included in the new agreement, and we also told them that just before coming to the mass meeting, we had received a report that the members of the Association had, at their meeting, rejected the agreement. This did not seem to worry the workers assembled at the mass meeting. They enthusiastically hailed the new agreement, and they refused to make much of a to-do about the internal feuding among the bosses.

A few days later, the leaders of the Association called a second meeting of their members, and there the renewed agreement, with all the gains for the workers, was ratified. We called another mass meeting, at which we read the letter from the president of the Association informing us that the renewed agreement with the union would remain the agreement for the next two years. The following week, the workers' pay envelopes contained the higher pay, in accordance with the renewed agreement.

In July, elections were held for the paid officials of the union, and the thousands of union members who participated in the balloting reelected their beloved union leaders who were in prison. Finally, when the glorious day came when the prisoners were given back their freedom, the workers carried their leaders into their offices on their shoulders. The workers told me to move right out of Potash's office and back to the International. I quickly obeyed.

The War Years

In his book, *The Fur and Leather Workers Union,* Dr. Philip Foner tells of the untiring activities of the fur and leather workers for the war effort and of their contributions in helping the nation in its bloody battles to save mankind from the bloodthirsty Nazi, Fascist and Japanese murderers. Dr. Foner has published copies of letters sent by the leaders of England, China and the Soviet Union, as well as letters from the United States government, all expressing gratitude to the fur and leather workers for their important contributions to the nation, the army and the navy in their fight against the Nazi murderers.

In my short memoirs, I cannot provide a complete report of all the activities and contributions the fur and leather workers made in the war effort. I only want to note a few outstanding contributions: 35,000 pints of blood for the wounded on the fields of battle, and 120,000 fur vests. The fur and leather workers bought bonds worth 43 million dollars. They sent contributions for hospitals in Leningrad and in China, for which they received warm thanks from Sun-Yat Sen of China. The members contributed 2 million dollars to the Red Cross for England, France, Russia, China, and the other nations that were fighting the Nazi beasts. And on the battlefields, many fur and leather workers distinguished themselves by bravery and were awarded medals. Some were raised in rank and became officers. They were devoted body and soul to their ideals of fighting for a world of freedom and justice. Among the fur workers who volunteered for the army when war was declared, there was a small number who had fought in Spain against the hated Nazis.

And the Manufacturers?

At home, far from the battlefields, were those avidly patriotic fur manufacturers who, like all industrialists in this golden land, enjoyed their gigantic profits, thanks to the wild war prosperity. They decided that this was the ideal time to curb the power of the Furriers Union. All the trade unions had agreed to assure the government that as long as the war lasted, the workers would not go on strike and would not in any way interfere with production. The fur manufacturers knew that the Furriers Union would not break this no-strike pledge made by the working class, so, at the beginning of 1944, when the two-year agreement expired, they rejected all the demands set forth by the union. The Association knew that they were not in a position to take on the union. Their one-time partners, the AFL, had long been driven out of the fur industry, and the gangster methods they had employed in the past would be of no use now.

They also knew that the strength of the Fur and Leather Workers Union had grown considerably. At the most recent union convention, the furrier delegates represented 50,000 members and the leather delegates represented over 50,000 members. But the bosses also knew that the most important objective of the union was to help the war effort — to use all its energy to insure victory over the Nazi armies — and that, because of this, they would never dare to violate the decision of the entire labor movement, and would never go on strike until victory was assured. Therefore, the bosses were convinced that the union would be forced to accept an agreement with the demands that they would dictate.

The union presented its problems to the War Labor Board. I want to relate a few of the things that happened at the Board meetings. Dr. Harry Bliss Carman, dean of Columbia University and a famous historian, was chairman of the Board. The fight between the union and the bosses went on for four weeks. The experts whom the bosses brought to the meetings tried to present the case that businesses would be ruined if the union's demands were met. The representatives of the union turned their arguments into dust. To save themselves from certain defeat, the worried bosses hired two important people to try to influence the Board members to oppose the demands of the union.

The union provided evidence that Dr. Paul Brissenden, an economics professor at Columbia University and an important member of the New York Labor Board, and Dr. Paul Abelson, the former impartial chairman of the industry, did everything they could to influence the Board to vote against the union's demands. After a thorough investigation, Professor Carman decided that it was not "advisable" that the Regional Board decide this case and he sent the matter to the National War Labor Board in Washington.

After several conferences in Washington, the chairman of the National Board told me in confidence that the Board was leaning toward a decision in favor of the union, but that the Board had no means of forcing the eight hundred fur manufacturers to comply with its ruling. I answered by telling him not to worry, that the union would see to it that the bosses complied with the decision of the Board. And when the Board rendered its decision that the union's demands were justified, sure enough, the bosses screamed that they would not follow the ruling of the Board.

For fifteen months, there was no agreement between the union and the bosses' association, but during that time, the union closely monitored the shops of the bosses who belonged to the association and settled all shop problems directly with the individual bosses, without the involvement of the association representatives. The Association of Retail Manufacturers and over three hundred independent manufacturers signed agreements with the union which included all the union's demands.

In May, 1945, the union called a mass meeting in Manhattan Center. It let the bosses' association know that if the workers, at the meeting, decided to declare a strike in the association shops, the bosses would have to pay the workers for every day they were forced to remain on strike.

One day before the mass meeting was scheduled to take place, the leaders of the association settled with the union. Without any difficulty and without any stubborn bargaining, the bosses agreed to accept the decision of the National War Labor Board, which included the long-sought security provision. It also included equal division of work, one week's paid vacation, and the payment by the bosses of $2\frac{1}{2}\%$ of their payrolls into a combined unemployment and sick benefit fund for the workers. The thousands of workers assembled at the mass meeting welcomed the new agreement with enthusiasm. The "no discharge" provision in the agreement, for which the union had fought for thirty years, meant that now each shop was a union bastion. The bosses no longer had the power to discharge workers from their shops in order to hire "needy unemployed workers" until the next season, when they would again discharge these workers in favor of other "needy unemployed workers," each time using this axe as a means of dictacting the workers' wages. This method of robbing the workers was eliminated in this new agreement. Job security — no discharge! Equal division of work! How these provisions swelled the pride of the fur workers! They were now assured improvements in their working and living conditions, and the union was finally freed of many of its chronic and painful problems.

Yes, that is why the leaders of the bosses' association had fought so stubbornly against this particular demand for thirty long years. And now they had finally lost! That is why the victory of the union inspired and exalted both the workers and the union leaders.

CHAPTER VI
Reaction in the Saddle

T he war was over. President Roosevelt had died. Harry Truman had taken his place. The New Deal died. Wild reaction swept the country. Millions of workers lost their jobs. The cost of living rose sharply. The wages of those lucky enough to have employment were cut. The employer class, which had reaped huge rewards from the horrible, bloody war in the form of huge profits amounting to hundreds of billions of dollars, was feeding its insatiable appetite at the expense of the living conditions of the workers. It also tried to involve the country in another war in order to swell its profits even more. Winston Churchill came from England and made a speech in Fulton, Missouri in which he called for a war against the Soviet Union, which had lost 20 million lives in the war to defeat the Nazi murderers.

But the workers did not want any more war. And they fought for higher wages so they could feed their wives and children.

The Fur and Leather Workers

As soon as the war was over, the bosses in the leather industry tried to cut the workers' wages. The union demanded higher wages because the cost of living kept rising. It became necessary to convince the bosses that the Leather Workers Union had the power not only to protect the gains already made, but also to carry on the fight for continued improvements until they were won. And for the first time in the history of the leather industry, the union declared a one-day general strike of the entire industry. The whole industry was paralyzed. Almost sixty thousand leather workers in eighteen states answered the union's strike call. The bosses were astounded. The reactionary wave that had swept the country, the growing anti-Semitism, the wild red-baiting, the brutal discrimination against the Negroes — none of these had any effect on the solidarity of the leather workers. The one-day general strike, the demonstration of the united, disciplined thousands of leather workers, did have an effect on the bosses. They agreed to the justified demands of the workers. The leather workers won wage increases and other improvements. Not all the bosses in the leather industry settled peacefully with the union. A small number of them remained adamant, but strikes in their tanneries broke their obstinacy, and they agreed to raise the wages of their workers and to accept the other demands of the union as well.

The New York fur workers won significant raises without any trouble. The fur workers in other parts of the United States and in Canada followed the example set by the New York furriers and also won raises in their wages.

In 1946, the cost of living rose even higher. The price of food alone rose 30%. The CIO unions fought for higher wages. Strikes broke out. The bosses mobilized their armies to protect their profits and their power against the aggressive onslaught of millions of workers. Attacks against the working class came like a hailstorm all over the country. The lackeys of the bosses in government and in the newspapers began a heated campaign against the Communists who "agitate and incite the workers to demand higher wages and who carry out strikes in order to ruin American industries." And the mighty, organized, reactionary agents of the bosses — the poisonous enemies of the workers — demanded that the CIO throw the Communists out of its ranks. Those dishonest reactionaries who occupied important positions within the CIO also began howling that the Communists must be excluded from the CIO in order to save the CIO.

The Special Committee

The atmosphere in and around the CIO became heated. President Philip Murray, who was elected when John L. Lewis resigned, appointed a special committee of six union presidents to deal with the serious problems within the CIO. The committee consisted of three right-wing union presidents — all well-known anti-Communists — and three left-wing union presidents. The right-wing presidents were Emil Rieve, president of the Textile Workers Union, Walter Reuther of the United Auto Workers and the representative of the Newspaper Guild. The left-wing presidents were Joseph Selly of the American Communications Association, Abram Flaxer of the United Public Workers, both intelligent, capable and progressive union leaders, and the Communist, Ben Gold.

As soon as the meeting of the committee started, Walter Reuther involved me in a sharp debate. President Murray said nothing, and the others did not take part in this war of words between Reuther and myself. Reuther opened the debate with a sharp attack on the Communists. He emphasized that they were a disaster in the unions, because they organized and led oppositions against the duly-elected officers of the unions, carried on vicious propaganda for the purpose of discrediting these union leaders, and hindered the constructive activities of the union. He also said that they agitated among the workers to vote against every settlement that the union leaders reached with their employers, and that they put forward fantastic demands which they knew were impossible to accomplish. Reuther heaped more and more such accusations on the Communists.

It was his opinion, he argued, that at this time, when the CIO was being attacked by the powerful enemies outside its ranks, the first thing it should do was to free itself from its internal enemies, the Communists. Reuther continued that this would enable the CIO leadership to show the entire world that the accusations made by the reactionaries that the CIO was dominated by Communists was untrue. Secondly, it would enable the union leaderships to unite the millions of union members, without hindrance, in their struggle for the interests of the workers.

As you can well understand, he did not get away without an answer from me. I told him that he should ask President Murray, and Murray would tell him that the Communists had distinguished themselves by their untiring devotion to the task of helping to organize the steel workers, the automobile workers, the mine, mill and smelter workers, the electrical workers, and other workers, when the CIO was first born.

Then I enlightened him by explaining that the reason the reactionary strikebreakers and union-busters were carrying on their propaganda all over the country that the CIO was flooded with Communists who were inciting the workers to strike for higher wages, was that the reactionary leaders would do anything to break the solidarity of the workers and cause splits in the CIO. I told him they would go to any extremes to insure that the bosses remained in a position to dominate the workers, and that this was the goal of the agents of the bosses. Then I said:

"And you, Walter Reuther, are demanding that the Communists be expelled from the unions! You know very well that the Communists in every union are connected with progressive workers, with workers who are left-wingers but who are not Communists, and that they have many followers among the workers who will fight bitterly against the 'exclusion' plan! Split the ranks of the workers! Cause bitter struggles within the unions! The bosses will bless you for your plan. Their well-paid reactionary servants who howl 'Communist unions' will bless you because your plan will help them accomplish their goal."

The debate between Reuther and myself got hotter and hotter, and President Murray found it necessary to close the meeting and to invite the committee to a second meeting on Sunday morning.

The Sunday Meeting

That Sunday meeting is so engraved in my memory and had such an astonishing effect on me that even now, so many years later, whenever I see the name, "Walter Reuther," that meeting looms up before my eyes.

President Murray opened the meeting and told the committee of the six union presidents that he had awakened that morning while it was still dark, and had gone to church in order to be one of the first worshipers there, to pray to Almighty God to lead him and those committed to him along the path of truth and justice for the millions of wronged workers. When he left the church, he said, he had a feeling of deep conviction that the committee, which was made up of devoted union leaders, would fulfill its duty to those who had elected them and who trusted them.

When Murray had finished his short speech, Reuther hastened to explain that, in his opinion, the absolute necessity of excluding the Communists from the unions in the CIO did not mean that they must be excluded from working in the factories. "No," he said, "such a punishment for workers who are the victims of false theories and philosophies is inhumane. They must be permitted to remain at their jobs in the factories. But in the interests of the workers, they must be excluded from the unions."

I wanted to avoid another heated debate with Reuther, so I asked a few questions: "Will the Communists who are excluded from the unions have to pay dues to the union? Will the business agents protect the excluded workers from unfair treatment by their foremen? If the excluded workers should be arrested during a strike while on the picket line, will the union defend them? If they should be beaten up by the police, would they be entitled to medical assistance from the union? Will they be entitled to strike benefits? What will Reuther do if these excluded workers quietly or secretly agitate the workers to demand higher wages or better working conditions? Will he be able to avoid fights in the factories between workers who have been poisoned by anti-Semitism and anti-Communism and the condemned Communists, who have lost their rights?" And other such questions.

Reuther tried to answer my questions, but he spoke in circles, using double-talk. He kept circumventing the questions by repeating that the excluded workers would keep their jobs, that they must avoid any dangers, that they would be given strict warnings, and that the unions would find means of disciplining those who were insubordinate. All my other questions about dues, arrests, lawyers, doctors, strike benefits and fights in the factories were only minor issues, he said, which the unions would deal with when it became necessary. Most of these questions, he said, would answer themselves in time, and then he unleashed a number of reasons which he claimed would erase all these minor problems I had mentioned. And he concluded with a statement that "for their own personal interests," the excluded workers would "discipline themselves and respect the union leaders."

In my answer, I said: "In many unions, there are probably often differences of opinion between the Communists and the anti-Communist leaders, but never with the kind of venom I hear from you. In many unions, in mine-mill, for example, and in the UE, the Communists are very active and hold important positions in the unions, and in some unions, the Communists are united with union leaders who are opposed to the Communists. Why has the united front between the Communists and the anti-Communist union leaders existed so long in the Fur and Leather Workers Union, and how has this united leadership managed to be quite successful in its achievements? Your friends, Walter, say that you are a capable leader, so I am asking you, can't you establish united fronts with the Communists that would serve the interests of the workers?"

Reuther got very angry and said that a united front with the Communists was a swindle tactic which the Communists used all the time for the purpose of eliminating the anti-Communist union leaders. In the shoe workers union, he said, the Communists had managed to fool the president into joining a united front, and then they had discredited him, besmirched his name, and chased him out of the union.

"No! No! That is not true!" President Murray shouted. "Walter, you don't know what you are talking about! Morgan was a thief! A thief! Do you hear me? Morgan was a thief!"

Reuther remained seated as if he had just been slapped in the face. He said nothing more after that. Murray's thundering words had destroyed his entire accusation against the Communists and had demolished his plan to exclude them from the unions.

I also remained silent. The debate had ended with a crash!

Then President Murray said that the CIO had been born during an unfortunate period when millions of hungry, jobless people had become beggars. Our enemies had hailed attacks upon us. David Dubinsky and his friends had betrayed us and had run into the enemy camp. But our struggle to organize the millions of workers, and our fight for justice for the millions of workers who enrich our land with their sweat and blood, had triumphed. In the present crisis, the CIO would fulfull its obligations and defeat the enemies of the workers, "and I have no doubt that our fight for justice will triumph again." And the meeting of the committee of the six union presidents ended.

The 1946 CIO convention, under President Murray's leadership, unanimously approved a resolution which raised the CIO to the level of one of the most progressive labor organizations in the world. The resolution mandated the CIO to fight against anti-Semitism, against anti-Negro discrimination, for higher wages, for peace and against war and war preparations, for unity between the United States, England and the Soviet Union, and against the reactionary anti-labor laws.

At the convention, Murray answered a speech made by Alexander Winter, the president of the Railroad Workers Union. "I tell you," Murray said, "no one will divide the mighty CIO organization. It was and will remain a united movement. We have our differences of opinion — that is good for the health. If we were to be ruled by only one opinion, we would get rusty."

At the 1946 Steel Workers convention, President Murray said: "We don't ask anyone what his nationality is, nor his color, his religion, or his beliefs. It is enough for us that he is a steel worker and he believes in trade unionism."

And at the Auto Workers convention in 1946, Murray made a speech in which he said basically the same thing. He spoke about solidarity in the CIO, about the rights of members, freedom of speech, the fight against our reactionary enemies, justice for the workers, higher wages, better conditions, peace and freedom.

At all these gatherings, President Murray's speeches were greeted with enthusiastic storms of applause from the workers. His prestige grew. His leadership was blessed by the millions of workers who were getting ready for the fight against the reactionary wave that was covering "the land of the free and the home of the brave."

But they were to suffer bitter disappointment.

The Taft-Hartley Plague

The CIO was in a position of power to save the working class from the strikebreaking, union-busting fascist law. An organized protest by the CIO would, without a doubt, have prevented many congressmen especially those in the Democratic Party, from voting for this law. But President Murray felt it sufficient to condemn the law as "the beginning of Fascism in the United States," and he did nothing to arouse the millions of workers to protest against this danger. I requested that the CIO call out the workers for one day, or even for a few hours, on a general work stoppage before Congress would be voting on the bill, but President Murray did not support my suggestion.

The 1947 CIO convention unanimously declared: "We will not recognize the Taft-Hartley Act, which considers free speech, free press and free assembly a crime. We would be betraying our fundamental heritage of political freedom if we permitted ourselves to shut our mouths about this law."

So — well and good! Yes? "A holy oath," the union presidents had shouted for the whole world to hear. They would never betray their "fundamental right to political freedom." But the very next day after the convention, the presidents of the CIO unions — Walter Reuther of the Auto Workers, Emil Rieve of the Textile Workers, and Jacob Potofsky of the Amalgamated Clothing Workers — were among the first to let the Taft-Hartley Labor Board know that they would obey the Taft-Hartley Act and would cooperate with the Board to the best of their abilities, and the majority of the CIO union leaders followed their example. Only a small number of progressive unions — including, of course, the Fur and Leather Workers Union among them — ignored the fascist law.

And President Philip Murray? He was also the president of the Steel Workers Union, and he struggled with the problem of whether to fight against the fascist law or bow to it. His former boss, John L. Lewis, condemned the law and condemned those AFL union leaders who were more than happy with the Taft-Hartley plague. But how could Murray compare himself with his mighty boss and teacher, John L. Lewis, to whom he was no more than an assistant? And President Murray also made peace with the fascist Taft-Hartley Act.

And in the Fur and Leather Industries?

There was a great deal of agitation and confusion in the fur and leather industries. Again I must emphasize that I am not writing a history of the union, only my recollections, stated briefly. Therefore, I want to briefly tell about the most important events that took place in the fur and leather industries during this tragic period of the cold war and reaction which began with the Taft-Hartley Act.

This fascist law certainly represented the greatest victory for the employer class over the working class in the history of democratic America. This law made the bosses in the fur and leather industries enormously happy. For fifty years, the owners of the leather tanneries had exploited their workers in the most brutal ways and had paid them literally starvation wages. Then, suddenly, a disaster! A union! And in a matter of a few years, the union forced them to raise the wages of the workers by 100%, made them pay for five holidays, two weeks' vacation, and health insurance. But now that was over with. Now they would no longer have to suffer because of the union. The Taft-Hartley Act put the union in chains!

And the fur manufacturers? They were jubilant. The Taft-Hartley Act raised their spirits and made them feel secure — that they were now invincible. When, at the conference in February, 1948, for the renewal of the agreement, the union asked for a raise in wages to offset the increased cost of living, the bosses gave the fine answer that according to their figures, during the past six years, they had raised wages every year, and the total of these raises came to three dollars an hour, and that the wages of the workers were now so high that the increased cost of living, which came only to a few dollars a week, meant nothing to the fur workers.

Secondly, they put forth a demand that from now on, they would set the wages for the workers at the beginning of the year, and how much they would give in raises for the season at the beginning of June, and that they would do this without the agreement of the union. If the workers didn't like it, they said, let them look for other jobs.

Clearly, this demand by the bosses was aimed not only at cutting wages, but also at robbing the workers of their important achievements of "no discharge" and equal division of work. Armed with the Taft-Hartley Act, the bosses let the union know that they would not conclude any agreement with the union unless their demands were accepted by the union.

Lockout and Strike

Both parties — the conference committees of the union and of the bosses — agreed that the bosses would not effect a lock-out, and the union would not call a strike. We would try to reach a peaceful settlement. But four weeks later, the gentlemen fur manufacturers went back on their word and declared a lock-out. The union then declared a strike in the industry. After five weeks of strike, the bosses withdrew their demands and signed an agreement with the union. But in the month of June, when the bosses were supposed to raise the workers' wages in accordance with their agreement with the union, the leaders of the bosses' association informed the union that they were not going to raise the workers' wages, and they warned us that they would invoke the Taft-Hartley Act.

The union informed each manufacturer that the agreement must be adhered to, and that they should give the workers the agreed-on wage increases. Those manufacturers who wanted to avoid another strike raised their workers' wages. Strikes were called against those manufacturers who ignored the agreement. These shop strikes did not last long. The bosses quickly settled with the union, and the workers got their raises.

The angered leaders of the bosses' association brought the union to court and demanded that we pay them five million dollars in damages, and that the workers pay back the raises that the union had unlawfully forced the employers to give them. And Taft-Hartley worked: the House Committee on Education and Labor decided to conduct a thorough investigation into the activities of the Fur and Leather Workers Union. The newspapers daily printed stories, for the whole world to know, of fur manufacturers who had come before the committee to tell of the terrible suffering the Communist union had caused them. Then there were the other tales: Ben Gold was the dictator in the union; Ben Gold controlled the election of union officials; the right-wing workers were being driven out of the union; the veterans who had returned from the war were not being taken back into the union and were prohibited from working in union shops, etc., etc.

Something interesting: a few somewhat decent fur manufacturers told the committee that they had no cause for complaint against the union leaders. True, they fought for the interests of the workers, but that was the duty of any honest union leader. These decent bosses told the committee that they had been able to settle their labor-management problems with these union leaders in a peaceful manner, without any difficulties. True, they were paying their workers higher wages, but the workers earned their wages honestly.

Over seven hundred war veterans sent a telegram to the congressional committee which stated that when they had returned from the war, the union had welcomed them back as heroes, had helped them find jobs, that they were active in the union, and a few of them had been elected to important rank-and-file union committees, and that the bosses were telling lies when they said that the union had not let the war veterans into the shops.

At the end, the congressional committee invited fifteen union leaders to testify. They questioned each one separately, and the answers they received to their questions baffled them. First, they called the older union officials in to be questioned — those who were on their list as well known right-wingers and anti-Communists. From them, the committee expected the necessary information they wished to get. But the committee questioners remained terribly disappointed. The right-wing union officials, members of the General Executive Board of the International Union, told the committee that the union was a democratic workers' organization in the fullest sense of the word. Right-wingers, left-wingers, Communists and anti-Communists led the union like a large, unified family. There was free speech, and the elections were honest, being carefully checked and supervised. No important decisions by the leadership was carried out without the affirmation of the union membership, etc., etc.

Then the congressional committee called the leaders who were on their list as left-wingers and Communists, for questioning. They asked pointed questions, and the answers they got from the officials did not provide them with any special pleasure. I remember one answer given by a business agent particularly clearly. I feel it deserves a place in my recollections. The young union official answered the questions put to him by the Congressmen clearly and to the point in his usual quiet and modest way. When the reactionary Congressman Lucas from Texas jumped on him with the question: "Are you a member of the Communist Party?" the union business agent took a packet of the medals he had earned in the war from his pocket and spread them out on the table near which the Congressmen were seated. "This, honorable Congressmen, is my answer to your question," he said. The Congressmen were struck dumb. They didn't ask him any more questions.

I was the last to be called. Lee Pressman, the lawyer for the CIO (a friend?!) was sitting next to me. I don't intend to write about all the questions or all my answers, nor about the discussions that took place during my questioning. But I will note a few of the important questions and answers, and that will suffice.

Congressman Schwabe, the chairman of the committee, asked me the first question: "Mr. Gold, why do you call so many general strikes in the fur industry? You know very well that frequent general strikes are harmful for an industry, that they ruin the businesses of many manufacturers and cause animosity between the bosses and the workers."

My answer: "Under my leadership, the union has never called a general strike in the fur industry."

"What? What did you say? You know you swore to tell the truth!" Congressman Lucas shouted at me.

My answer: "Thank you very much, Congressman, for reminding me that I am under oath, and I want to repeat that the union never called a general strike under my leadership. The bosses declared a lockout and forced the union to answer with a strike." And I placed a copy of the *Women's Wear Daily* on the table. "This newspaper will bear out what I have just told you."

"And why does your union collect large fines from manufacturers on the pretext that they are not following the agreement with the union?" Congressman Lucas asked.

My answer: "The union has no right to punish manufacturers who are found guilty of breaking important points of their agreement. The impartial chairman, Dr. Paul Abelson, decides on the guilt and the fines for any accused manufacturer. The biggest fines a manufacturer has to pay come when he is found guilty of falsifying his books about the earnings of his workers. The fines are not paid to the union. They are placed in a fund in the names of a committee of bosses and union representatives. The accumulated monies are then used for charitable institutions."

And finally, after many, many questions, the main question was asked: "Mr. Gold, are you a member of the Communist Party?"

"Yes," I answered. "I am a charter member of the Communist Party and I have been a member of the Communist Party for twenty-five years." And the interrogation was over.

And now read and be astounded. In the report that the special committee prepared for the Taft-Hartley Congress of the United States, these two reports were among all the other paragraphs: First, that "the wages of the fur workers are the highest in the entire country," and secondly, that the bosses "who used every possible means to break the union, including even violence, created the opportunity for the present leaders to become leaders of the union."

The Leather Workers

The situation in the leather industry was critical. The forces of reaction in the entire country had gone wild. President Truman used the fascist Taft-Hartley Act at every opportunity. The strike of the railroad workers was broken with the assistance of the president. The miners' union was fined 2 million dollars. The Cold War was getting hotter. In the newspapers and on the radio, propaganda against the Soviet Union and the Communist menace in America was glowing with an ever-burning flame. The warmongers agitated for war against the Soviet Union. President Truman was spending over fifteen billion dollars a year for armaments and threw in additional billions of dollars to rebuild the cartels and the millionaire-owned factories of France and Germany under the swindle that was called the Marshall Plan and that was supposedly set up to help the needy in these countries.

The army of unemployed Americans grew and the cost of living kept rising. The workers were hoping that their union leaders would fight against the bosses for higher wages, but President Philip Murray and Walter Reuther, along with the Rieves and the Potofskys, joined ranks with the reactionary groups and supported the Cold War, the squandering of billions of dollars on defense, and the preparations for a war against Russia. They joined in the organized propaganda campaign against the Communists and excluded Communists and left-wingers from important posts in their unions. They squelched every demand of the workers for higher wages. They tried to split and destroy, or to usurp power in the progressive unions. Reuther attacked the Farm Equipment Workers Union and tried to shut it down. The president of the Steel Workers Union tried using gangster methods to take over the progressive Mine, Mill & Smelter Workers Union. The fight against the Communists became the major objective of the leaders of the CIO.

But the leather workers and their leaders contemptuously separated themselves from the Murray-Reuther "family." They remained devoted and determined fighters for the union principles that they had accepted when they joined forces with the Furriers Union: freedom and justice in the struggle for the interests of the workers. In the United States and Canada, the tens of thousands of organized, united leather workers "convinced" the bosses that the Taft-Hartley Act and the war that the bosses and their reactionary friends were waging against the Communists was only a device to help them oppress and rob the leather workers. So the leather workers in 1948, like the fur workers in 1947, fought for and won significant raises in their wages. Strikes broke out, but the bosses were quickly convinced that they could not win against these determined and unified strikers, and they settled with the union.

But two long and bloody strikes were not won. The millionaire firm of Endicott-Johnson employed fifteen hundred leather workers and fifteen thousand shoe workers. The leather workers belonged to the union and won raises and other union conditions. The shoe workers remained unorganized. When the union demanded a raise for the leather workers, the bosses were afraid that the thousands of shoe workers would also demand raises, so they mobilized all their efforts and allies — the newspapers, the police, the judges and the Taft-Hartley Labor Board — in their fight against the "Communists." Oppressive police tactics, arrests, fines and jail terms for strikers followed, and finally, the workers were unable to rent a hall where they could assemble. The strike lasted a long time, and some of the workers lost their homes. The union had to call off the strike. The workers had won increases in wages, but the firm did not sign an agreement with the union.

The second strike that was lost was against the leather tanneries in Gloversville, New York. In that town, the leather workers had built up a united, powerful union which won every fight with the bosses, who were united into an association. In 1949, the union asked for a raise in wages. The bosses argued that business was such that they could not afford raises every year, and they also argued that in no other industry in the United States had workers received increases during the past few years because the union leaders of the other unions were "practical" and realized that the war prosperity years were over. The bosses demanded that the union withdraw its demands. For a few months, the union leaders held conferences with the leaders of the employer association, and when the union insisted on its demand for raises because the cost of living had gone up so much each year, the bosses declared a lock-out. The workers answered with a strike.

In his history, Dr. Philip Foner related what happened during that bitter and bloody strike which lasted for eight months. Here in my memoirs, I want to describe a few tragic facts which further prove that the traitorous leaders who dominate the trade unions constitute a tragedy for the American working class and the American people.

After two or three months of strike, the bosses already realized that they did not have the power to defeat the united, determined strikers, and they were ready to talk with the strike leaders about ending the strike. But suddenly, they got new hope. Organizers from the AFL came to Gloversville and began the job of organizing an AFL strike-breakers union.

Soon, organizers of the CIO showed up and strained to their limits to set up a CIO union with a charter which was prepared by none other than President Philip Murray himself. The bosses, the AFL strike-breakers and the CIO set off a propaganda campaign against the "Communists." An army of gangsters wearing deputy badges, carried clubs and kept "order." The picture of these deputies is in Dr. Foner's history of the union.

The heroic strikers had to fight the combined forces of the strike-breaking unions and the deputized gangsters, who readily used their clubs on the bodies of the strikers, men and women alike.

When the stage was all set, the Taft-Hartley Labor Board arrived. I don't intend to write about all of the Board's maneuvers and the strikers' countermaneuvers against their united enemies. It will be enough to note the end of the bitter, bloody eight-month struggle. When the Taft-Hartley Board conducted its election, the name of the Fur and Leather Workers did not appear on the ballot. The workers, having only the choice of the AFL scab union and the CIO rival union, decided to vote for no union at all! When the votes were counted, the CIO Textile Union had 180 votes, the AFL union had 144 votes, and 536 workers had voted for *no union*. The fight was not over.

It is interesting to note that a few days before the election, the bosses had circulated appeals to the workers by placing paid-for ads in the newspapers, headed: "To our leather workers. For your absolute security, vote for a union." (A copy of this document can be found in Dr. Foner's book).

After the elections in which the workers had voted down both scab unions, I received a letter from the workers who led the strike in which they informed me that "We didn't win, but we didn't lose. The bosses lost! The huge business losses caused by the strike, and the defeat of their scab unions, which the prostitute leaders of the AFL and CIO brought in, has hurt them badly and their wounds will not heal quickly. When our day will come, we will be ready. And when the bosses hear the word 'strike,' they will become paralyzed with fear. Our day is not far off!"

The CIO Convention

In the report that President Murray prepared for the 1949 CIO convention, which was distributed to all the delegates, it stated that only two unions had won wage increases in 1948: the Fur and Leather Workers Union and the International Longshoremen & Warehouse-men's Union under the leadership of Harry Bridges.

Only two unions! And why didn't the millions of workers in the other CIO unions win wage increases? The cost of living was rising and the profits of the bosses were rising, too. In all the unions, workers were protesting that their leaders were ignoring their demands for higher wages. There was not one word in Philip Murray's report about the inflation, about the army of unemployed, or about the need for organizing the open shops.

Instead, the report concerned itself with a venomous attack on those unions which were a minority in the CIO, "which carry on propaganda against the Marshall Plan, the aim of which is to help the hungry nations, and also against the NATO plan, whose aim is to defend the civilized nations against Communist despotism." These minority unions, the report continued, had carried on propaganda to try to elect Henry Wallace president of the United States, and the leaders of these minority unions were enemies of the labor movement.

The Discussion

It disgusts me even now, when I wrote about that discussion at the CIO convention on the report that President Murray had delivered to the convention. The venomous speeches against the Communists spring up in my memory. Walter Reuther really distinguished himself with his wild attack on the Communists — that they were the enemies of the labor movement, that every union must remove every Communist from positions of leadership, and that the minority unions which carried out "Communist policies" must be expelled from the CIO.

Isador Pickman, the district director of the Fur and Leather Union locals in the New England states, told the convention briefly that neither the AFL or the CIO had been able to organize the leather workers, but the Furriers Union, which had been condemned and persecuted by the AFL leaders on the excuse that they were a "Communist union," had managed to organize the thousands of leather workers, and had fought for and won higher wages, a shorter work week and other improvements in the working conditions. "I am amazed," he said "that the CIO leadership, instead of fighting for the interests of the workers, is using all of its talents and its strength in the unions to fight the Communists who helped to build the CIO and who are devoted members of the CIO."

The chairman of the Committee on the Officers' Report answered Pickman that the Fur and Leather Workers Union was not included in the list of "minority unions."

Pietro Lucchi, the secretary-treasurer of the International Fur and Leather Workers Union, bewildered the fire-and-brimstone speakers with his short speech in which he said: "For ten long years, I was one of the leaders who fought against the Communists in the Furriers Union. That was the most tragic chapter of my life. The workers paid very dearly and only the employers profited. These past ten years, since we have a united union, and Communists and Socialists, left and right are united, we have built a mighty, democratic union which has achieved

176

the best conditions for the workers in the history of the union. That is the best chapter in the history of my life." He then appealed for unity in the CIO.

I also appealed for unity when I spoke, and President Harry Bridges did the same in his speech. But the majority of the delegates had been selected as "reliable," and they applauded loudly when Emil Rieve of the Textile Workers Union screamed that he had waited a long time, and the day had finally arrived on which the CIO could no longer tolerate the unions which carried out "Communist policies." "From today on," he shouted, "The CIO will stick strictly to the decision: 'Carry out or get out!' "

The convention expelled the following unions from the CIO: the United Electrical, Radio & Machine Workers Union, the Mine, Mill & Smelter Workers Union, the United Office & Professional Workers Union, the Farm Equipment Workers Union, and the Food, Tobacco & Agricultural Workers Union. Two judges were selected to conduct trials against these unions that were accused of carrying out Communist propaganda. The two judges were Rieve and Jacob Potofsky of the Amalgamated Clothing Workers. It was a lucky day for the bosses and for all the reactionary union haters!

My Conversation With Philip Murray

I was no longer a member of the CIO Executive Board. It was no secret that I was a member of the Communist Party, and we had nominated, and the convention had accepted, Pietro Lucchi to represent the Fur and Leather Workers Union on the CIO Executive Board. Finally, the convention was over.

My friends demanded that I telephone President Murray and tell him that I wanted to speak to him about a very important matter. I did not agree with them because, first of all, I was sure that the friendship between Murray and myself was over and that he would not agree to talk to me. Secondly, even if he might agree to have a short conversation with me, "we won't accomplish anything, because Murray is no better than Reuther or Rieve these days," I told them.

But my friends pointed out that the chairman of the Committee on the Officers Report at the convention had stated that the Fur and Leather Workers Union was not on the list of the "minority unions," and that so far, our union had not been expelled from the CIO. Therefore, Murray wouldn't dare to refuse to have a talk with me about problems relating to our union.

The argument between my friends and myself was settled very quickly when the telephone rang. It was President Murray inviting me to come to discuss an important issue with him. He welcomed me in his comfortable hotel suite, cordially and politely, as if nothing out of the ordinary had taken place at the convention.

He began the meeting by making accusations against the Communist Party. He complained that the *Daily Worker,* the Communist newspaper, was calling him names, saying that he was serving the bosses, not the workers, and accusing him of being a "warmonger," because he supported the Marshall Plan, which was helping the hungry nations that had been devastated by the war, and because he supported NATO, whose goal was to unite the European nations so that they could protect their democracy and peace in the world. He continued to explain that the "minority unions" knew that this was the policy of the CIO and that they had no right to fight against his policy. He claimed that the leaders of the "minority unions" posed as idealists who were fighting against the reactionary leaders of the CIO. "President Gold," he said to me, "I will tell you what kind of idealists they are!" And he told me about a president of an important union who had gone to a conference to help his union settle with the employees in order to avoid a strike, but had stopped for a few days in Chicago, gotten drunk, had run around with women, and had forgotten about the union.

I knew all about this incident. I knew that union leader. He was an able, energetic and devoted leader, but such things do happen. He did sometimes get drunk and lose all sense of time.

"President Murray," I interrupted him, "the union president you are talking about is not a member of the Communist Party."

"Yes, yes, I know he is not a party member," Murray answered, "but he is a left-winger and carries out Communist policies."

He then told me a scandalous story about a second president of a union which was fighting against the CIO policies. Murray said he knew that this man was not a Communist Party member either, but "he is a sympathizer of the Communist Party and carries out Communist policies in his union. He —"

Again I interrupted: "President Murray, are you certain that what you are telling me about these union presidents is true? Are you sure your information comes from reliable sources?"

He answered me that the FBI sent him reports about the presidents of the left-wing "minority unions." I was surprised by his answer and I asked him if the FBI sent him reports about my activities.

President Murray's face broke into a smile. "About you? That's what I really want to talk to you about. Your life is similar to mine, President Gold. I was sixteen years old when I came to America, and I worked in a coal mine. I became active in the union. I became a union organizer and then later a vice-president of the miners' union. And I don't live in luxury! I still live in the same house I bought twenty years ago.

"You, Ben Gold, were also young when you came to America. You became a fur worker. You became active in the Furriers Union. The workers elected you as union manager, and later you were elected president of the International. And I know, I know what wages the union pays you. I know where you live — in a small, rented apartment. The union, the interests of the workers, are more important to you than a high salary and a life of luxury. Sooner or later, in the interests of the workers, you will have to resign from the Communist Party. You will have to, because of the Taft-Hartley Law. So why don't you resign from the party now and take your place on the CIO Executive Board, and the Fur and Leather Workers Union will, as before, have its honored place in the CIO?"

I answered that if I had to resign from the Communist Party because of the fascist Taft-Hartley Act, I would still not be resigning from my convictions. "And I am convinced," I said, "that the Marshall Plan is not aimed at helping the needy, but rather to rebuild the ruined industries of the capitalists. I am opposed to the United States sending billions of dollars to the Nazi capitalists in Germany to help them build their trusts and their monopolies. And I am convinced that this NATO, which President Truman and Churchill are organizing in Europe, is not for the purpose of defending democracy and peace in the world, but is a plan to fortify the capitalist dictatorships in these countries and to prepare for a war against the Soviet Union and the other countries which were liberated from the Nazi murderers. And President Murray, instead of fighting against Communists and left-wingers in the unions, the CIO should be fighting against Taft-Hartley, against the wild wave of reaction that is sweeping the country and for higher wages for the workers. That is the duty of the leaders of the CIO!"

In answer to my long speech, President Murray said that if the CIO would accept the program I had spelled out for him, it would bring the CIO into conflict with the government. "A revolution!" he emphasized.

"No," I answered. "Not a revolution! I want to tell you something about John L. Lewis." I knew that if I would mention Lewis's name, our conversation would calm down. I told Murray that at the Executive Board meeting held after one of the CIO conventions was over, several speakers, including Lewis among them, had condemned Communism and the Communists and had said that there was no room in the CIO for Communist leaders.

When the Executive Board meeting was over, I telephoned Lewis and asked him if I could have a short talk with him on an important matter. When I met with him, I told him that I and my friends from other unions were very much upset by the attacks on the Communists that had been made at the meeting. "And John didn't even let me finish my argument. He looked surprised and asked me: 'You didn't understand? You know that our enemies are ranting that the CIO is packed with Communist leaders, and that the Dies Committee will soon be calling us for a hearing. We have to be ready for that. We have to have the speeches of our major leaders down in black and white in order to wipe the floor with the Dies Committee when they dare to call us!'

" 'Do you remember what I said before I closed the meeting of the Board?' Lewis asked me. Then he reminded me that he had stressed that America is a democracy, and that the American people would never submit to a Communist or a Fascist dictator who hid behind a mask of patriotism.

" 'Our goal is the machine!' he explained to me. 'We must break the reactionary machine! We must have our representatives in Congress and in the Senate who will represent the millions of workers and curb the reactionaries, the enemies of the workers.' And I, President Murray, agree with John L. Lewis! He wasn't talking revolution with me! He was talking about democracy, about the CIO having a program that will safeguard democracy and protect the workers against the reactionary agents of the bosses."

With a smile and in a somewhat weak voice, Murray answered me: "John? Well, John — that was a different time — other problems — many, many changes — John! — well, John — John hasn't been the leader of the CIO for a long time now."

Our conversation was over.

In the Fascist Swamp

My conversation with Murray convinced me that he was no longer the leader of the CIO, that he received his orders from President Truman and his cabinet ministers, and that he was closely tied with the Reuthers and the Rieves and the other demagogues who openly declared that the only objective of the CIO was to fight the Communists. When he stated that opposition to Taft-Hartley meant opposition to the government, and that that meant revolution, it became clear to me that he was nothing more than a servant of the reactionary Truman administration.

But I found that I had grossly underestimated the traitorous role of the CIO leaders. In January, 1950, the American Legion called an anti-Communist conference, and James Carey, the secretary of the CIO, was an important speaker at the conference. In his speech, Carey ranted: "In the Second World War, we joined with the Communists to fight the Fascists; in another war, we will join with the Fascists to defeat the Communists."

The newspaper, the New York *Compass*, printed Carey's speech with an explanation that he was not speaking in his name alone. An important official of the CIO had assured the newspaper that Carey was speaking in the name of the CIO.

James Carey's fascist speech was printed and distributed to the delegates of the CIO Industrial Council in Philadelphia.

No Other Choice

Our enemies did not want to wait long. As soon as the convention was over, a committee of ten gentlemen was waiting at a leather tannery. At twelve noon, when the workers came out of the factory to go to the restaurant for lunch, the committee handed each worker a leaflet issued by the Textile Workers Union. The circular was an invitation to the leather workers to join the Textile Workers Union — "a truly American union." The leather workers surrounded the committee and warned them that if they ever showed up at the tannery again, they would be treated as strikebreakers. In North Carolina, the leather workers did not act as politely toward the committee that came to their tannery agitating the workers to withdraw from the "Communist" Fur and Leather Workers Union and join a "democratic" union.

I called a meeting of the main union leaders in order to work out a plan to prepare the leather workers to deal with these union-busting committees. Fights had to be avoided because any commotions around the tanneries would be used as an excuse by the bosses to seek assistance from other of our enemies.

The organizers argued that it was impossible to prevent fights in the leather tanneries. They could see how fights could be avoided in the fur shops because even the largest of the fur shops had only from fifty to sixty workers. But how could they keep those hundreds of angry leather workers from using their fists against the enemies of the union? The leaders also argued that we could expect the leaders of the CIO and the leaders of the AFL to join with the bosses in a fight to get rid of the "Communist" union which demanded higher wages for the workers every year.

It was the opinion of the main union leaders that in order to avoid strikes, bloody fights and arrests, I must resign from the Communist Party and register the International Union with the Taft-Hartley Labor Relations Board. Such a move would devastate our enemies with one blow, because they wouldn't dare to challenge our union in a referendum to decide to which union the leather workers wanted to belong. At most, our enemies might scrounge up 1½% of the votes for their unions. There was no other alternative, the union leaders argued. We had to bow to the Taft-Hartley Act.

I agreed with my friends and comrades, the union leaders. I explained that it might also be wise for me to resign as president of the International Union and that we elect a capable, experienced leader who had never belonged to the Communist Party as president.

My suggestion brought sharp criticism from the assembled union leaders. They argued that my resignation would confuse many of the workers; that many of the workers would accuse me of running away from the field of battle, and in such a serious moment, when the union needed to mobilize all its forces against its enemies. My resignation would be an encouragement for the bosses and would get us embroiled in strikes, and Reuther and Rieve and the whole Taft-Hartley family would consider my resignation a victory. There were other arguments against my resigning as president of the International. My answer to the leaders of the union was that I was not resigning yet, and that I would let them know my decision.

The thought that my resignation as president of the International would be taken as an attempt to "escape from the field of battle" really bothered me. I was almost certain that the Reuthers, Rieves and Careys, who were the rulers of the CIO, would persist in their efforts to split the Fur and Leather Workers Union and to organize a union without Communists — and the workers would suffer and the bosses would profit. I decided that I owed it to the workers. I resigned from the Communist Party and registered the International Union with the Taft-Hartley Labor Relations Board.

The witch hunts and the hysteria of the reactionary forces against the Soviet Union grew each day. The inquisition, led by the fascist Senator McCarthy against Communists, progressives and liberals as well, threw the unions and the cultural organizations of the country into a state of fear and panic. McCarthyism grew stronger and stronger. The leaders of the CIO carried out their duty. They split the progressive, militant UE and organized a "kosher" dual union under the leadership of James Carey, the advocate of joining forces with the Fascists against the Communists. Unions labeled "suspicious," meaning that they had leftist leanings, were expelled from the CIO. The workers who dared to ask their union leaders to demand higher wages were shouted down and condemned as Communist trouble-makers.

The Fur and Leather Workers Union continued its activities on behalf of the interests of the workers. The bosses and the union-busters knew that the fur and leather workers were prepared to meet their enemies. Our workers continued to fight against these union-haters, against the warmongers, and against those union leaders who had joined with the fascist groups against Communists and against progressive unions. In May Day demonstrations and in demonstrations for world peace and against war, the fur and leather workers played a prominent role. The Furriers Union was, it seems to me, the only union to call a mass meeting to protest and condemn the fascist McCarthyism that raged in the land.

The mass meeting at the St. Nicholas Arena demonstrated the unity of the union membership and their union leaders. This unity became even stronger and more fortified as the courageous struggles against the mortal enemies of the working class continued.

CHAPTER VII

Dismantling the Union

A Lost Treasure

This interesting event deserves a place in my memoirs. In short, this is what happened. At that time, in 1950, in the South, thousands of acres of land, woods and fields were unused. For the spring and summer months, the millionaire landholders rented the land to trappers, who, with the help of their wives and grown children, caught muskrat, raccoon, mink and other furbearing animals in their traps. Each trapper would lease a few hundred acres of land, and the trapper and his family lived there until the end of the summer.

The skins of the trapped animals would be sold to New York fur merchants through agents of the landholders. The largest share of the money received by the agents went to the landholders, and the trappers, who spent all summer working night and day to trap and skin the animals, got a very small share of the revenue.

From these meager earnings, the trappers did not have enough to feed their families, so those who lived near the Gulf or near the ocean went out in boats and caught shrimp and other fish, and the proceeds of their catch were divided in this manner: one-third belonged to the owner of the boat, one-third belonged to the boat itself, and the last third belonged to the fishermen who worked on the boat.

These oppressed and exploited trappers turned to the furriers and asked the union to help them. The call for the union rang out in Virginia, in North Carolina, in Louisiana, in Florida, in Alabama and in Tennessee! Thousands of black trappers welcomed the union's call. Bill Levner, who was not a fur worker, moved to Virginia among the black residents and proved his ability as an organizer. Julius Metz resigned his position as a high school teacher and moved to Louisiana, not far from New Orleans, and distinguished himself as an organizer. And Johnny Russell, the manager of the Leather Workers Union in North Carolina, organized tirelessly, non-stop, in North Carolina, in Florida, in Alabama and Tennessee. Very soon, the union appointed black organizers from among the trappers themselves.

The gratitude of these thousands of trappers toward the union — their devotion and dedication to the union and its leaders — cannot be described. Their pride grew. They felt their united, organized strength, which raised them spiritually and encouraged them in their determination to fight for a better way of life. They knew that the land owners would be full of anger and hate and would condemn the arrogance of "their Niggers," and would swear that they would never give in to their demands. But for the first time in their lives, the trappers understood that the anger of the landholders would be based on their fear of losing the millions of dollars in profits that "their Niggers" brought in every summer, and that they would give orders to their agents to settle with the trappers.

It is very important to note that the elected members of the executive boards and the members of the large organizational committees in the locals in these five states were intelligent, aware people who read the newspapers and were interested in the political and economic events in the country, and were particularly aware of the tragic condition of the black population. It was a pleasure for me to spend long hours at meetings with these people, discussing important problems.

Summers came and went and finally, one spring, the sun's rays were greeted by the thousands of trappers with joy and enthusiasm because that spring, the trappers decided that their leaders would let the landholders know that the trappers would not go out into the forests, fields and swamps to create huge revenues for the landowners, until their just demands were met.

Unfortunately, however, the decision was not carried out, because for weeks, I was busy in the courts in Washington, where I was accused of violating the fascistic Taft-Hartley Law. I was found guilty and sentenced to a five-year "vacation" in jail.

My immediate concern, before starting to serve my jail term, was to make sure that there was a responsible leader to take my place. I called a meeting of the General Executive Board and resigned from my office as president of the International Union; Abe Feinglass, the district director of the union locals in the Midwestern states, was elected as president of the International Union. I felt sure that under his leadership, the union would not veer from the paved road which had led it to its successful achievements and earned it a prominent place in the left-wing labor movement.

As soon as he was elected president, Feinglass had to go to Chicago to appoint a district director to take his place and work with him for a few weeks so he could become acquainted with all the problems of the individual locals.

In New York, the agreement with the bosses' association would expire in February, 1956, and it was necessary to utilize the few months

184

left in 1955 to mobilize the workers, secure the shops and prepare the shop committees to be ready for any contingencies that might arise when the agreement expired. It was no secret that the bosses hoped to take advantage of the McCarthyism that was rampant in the country for their own interests.

Potash was in jail with the other leaders of the Communist Party. Assistant Manager Joseph Winogradsky took over his position in the union. I had to accept the demands of the union to direct the mobilization of the workers and the preparation of the necessary apparatus so that the workers would be able to defend themselves when the agreement expired. I agreed to direct this important organizational work, but refused to take any wages. I would do my job as a rank-and-file activist. My office was not far from the manager's office.

As soon as I began my work, my office was besieged by workers, by shop chairmen, and by unemployed workers who brought their problems to me. And every day, the business agents consulted with me about their complicated problems.

Against my will, I actually became the manager of the union. It was impossible for me to tell workers or business agents or shop chairmen that I didn't want to know about their problems, and that I didn't want to help them when they were embroiled in important struggles with the bosses. That would have been a betrayal of the workers. So I had to continue my work. But I knew that my job would end very soon. I only had a few weeks more. That is why I carried out my work so patiently.

Before Feinglass left for Chicago, the union leaders called a mass meeting of the workers so that they could become acquainted with their newly-elected president. The large hall of Manhattan Center was packed. Feinglass made a marvelous speech. His powerful voice thundered. He heaped praises on the progressive, left-wing movement, and especially on the dedicated, class-conscious, courageous and determined fur workers and on the gifted, idealistic and devoted union leaders. The union and its wonderful leaders, he said, putting his whole soul into his words, had reared him and raised him to this high and holy level of leadership, had brought joy and glory to his life, and as long as he lived, he would fight against the mortal enemies of the workers. With all his might, he would serve the working class.

The workers responded to his speech with warm applause. Workers surrounded him after the meeting and expressed their pleasure that he had been elected president. I felt really good. My certainty that Feinglass would serve the workers sincerely and honestly was reinforced.

Under President Feinglass's Leadership

When Feinglass returned to New York from Chicago, he called a meeting of the main leaders of the New York union and told them that

Patrick Gorman, the leader of the powerful Amalgamated Meat Cutters and Butcher Workmen's Union had invited him to his office to discuss an important matter. Gorman told him that he had received reliable information that the Department of Justice intended, in the very near future, to indict Feinglass on the same charges on which Ben Gold had been indicted, and that they would certainly make use of their well-paid witnesses and Feinglass would also be sent to jail. The reactionary McCarthyites would use any despicable, underhanded means to smash the progressive Furriers Union.

Gorman had told him that the only way to outmaneuver the enemy would be for the Fur and Leather Workers Union to join the AFL-Butchers' Union and thus become a "kosher" AFL union. In that way, the Fur and Leather Workers Union could carry on its activities in the same democratic fashion as before, and its elected president would become a vice-president of the Amalgamated Meat Cutters and still remain the top leader of the fur and leather workers. Feinglass finished his report about his meeting with Gorman with an appeal to the union leaders present that they should accept Gorman's practical proposal and join with the AFL Butchers' Union in order to strengthen the Fur and Leather Workers Union against its reactionary enemies.

I remained silent. I knew that the right-wing union officers who were enthusiastic about the united front between the left-wingers and the right-wingers were now also enthusiastic about joining the AFL. I also knew that a few of the left-wing union leaders, who, like Feinglass, had not lived through the trials and pain of the long and bitter fight with the AFL, also leaned toward approving Gorman's recommendation about merging the two unions.

I knew that if I voiced my opinion right then at the meeting, it would have, without a doubt, caused a split in the ranks of the union leaders and would cause a fight among the workers while I sat in jail. So I did not say anything at the meeting, but decided to talk the matter over with Feinglass privately.

I remained silent, but not all the union leaders remained silent. Jack Schneider, the assistant manager of the New York union, opened the debate. He said that first of all, Gorman's information that Feinglass would soon be indicted like Ben Gold was not a certainty. And even if it were true, it would not happen the next day. It was also not a certainty that Feinglass would be found guilty because he had not been a member of the Communist Party for a very long time, and he could prove that with fifty witnesses if necessary. And even if Feinglass were found guilty, it would take a long time until the appeal would get to the Supreme Court. And if the union were to lose in the Supreme Court and Feinglass would be sent to jail, Potash would have already been freed from jail and back with us. "And it could happen," Schneider said, "that Gold will win his appeal in the Supreme Court."

"It is my opinion," Jack said, "that joining with the AFL would strengthen the reactionary forces. Our union must fight against the enemies of the workers. As a small and poor union of twelve thousand workers, we defeated all our united enemies. Now, when our union has over a hundred thousand members, we are strong enough to protect the union, defend the gains made by the workers, and, working together with all the progressive forces in the country, we can defeat the vile McCarthy reactionaries and not run away from the field of battle."

Feinglass was frightened by Jack's speech and by the absolute silence that enveloped the assembled leaders. He quickly said: "Jack, we are not running from the field of battle. Anyway, Gorman has to get the approval of his Board of Directors. When Gorman informs me that his directors agree to the merger, then we will have a broad and thorough discussion of the plan." He then adjourned the meeting.

It is painful for me to write this last chapter of my union memoirs. President Abe Feinglass agreed to carry out a McCarthyite program in the union so that the merger of the Fur and Leather Workers Union and the Butchers' Union would be consummated. President Abe Feinglass never told anyone about this. Months later, when he had to tell his "people" about his goal, it was too late even to protest.

The McCarthyite program: The leader of the Butchers' Union told his Board of Directors about his proposition to Feinglass to merge the two unions. The Board of Directors decided that, considering the fact that the Furriers Union had been expelled from the AFL, it was necessary to consult with Brother George Meany, the president of the AFL, before going any further. Meany insisted that until the Communist leadership was ousted from the union, and until the union guaranteed that it would sever all its connections with the Communist Party, the Furriers Union would not be reinstated into the AFL. He appointed David Dubinsky, the president of the International Ladies' Garment Workers' Union, to direct and supervise the program of cleansing the Furriers Union of its Communist leadership and freeing the union from the influence of the Communist Party.

Dubinsky's Ten Commandments

The conference in which Dubinsky, Pietro Lucchi, Gorman and Feinglass participated was a friendly one. In a friendly manner, Dubinsky explained that he would enumerate the points of his "clean-up program," which was to be carried out quietly, without publicity, so that the Communists would not be able to use it for their own propaganda purposes. Gorman and Abe Feinglass agreed.

1. Be it understood that when Irving Potash got out of jail, he was not to hold either a paid or an unpaid post in the union. Feinglass

agreed to this. Pietro Lucchi remained silent.

2. The same provision was to apply to Ben Gold. Even if Gold should win his appeal in court, he was to hold no office in the union. Pietro Lucchi, the secretary-treasurer of the International Fur and Leather Workers Union, protested. He said that if Ben Gold won his case in court, it would be proof that his resignation from the Communist Party was serious and sincere and that he —

Dubinsky broke in, almost pushing him aside, and said that if Ben Gold should win his case, it would be only because of legal tricks, because it was widely known that Gold was a Party leader and that the former leader of the Communist Party, Benjamin Gitlow, had sworn in court that Ben Gold was the "Babe Ruth" of the Party. "Ben Gold must not hold any office in the AFL — understood?" "Yes," Feinglass and Lucchi agreed.

3. All the paid officers of the New York union should be removed as quickly as possible, and for five years, none of them should be permitted to hold any office in the union. Feinglass almost begged Dubinsky that the manager of the union and two very able business agents, who had not been members of the Party for a long time, should be allowed to continue their work in the interest of the workers. Dubinsky answered that here they were not concerned with the interests of the fur workers — here, it was a question of the interests of the millions of workers of the AFL. Clear?

4. Workers who were members of the Communist Party or "sympathizers" should not hold any office in the union.

5. Party members should not be elected as shop chairmen.

6. The union would not participate in demonstrations and would not support any undertakings which were sponsored by the Communist Party.

7. The Communist newspapers, the *Freiheit* and the *Daily Worker,* would not be sold in the union buildings.

8. The history of the union which had been written by Dr. Philip Foner would not be sold to the workers.

9. The union would not support any opposition against the AFL unions.

10. The union would cut off all its connections with Communist-left-wing organizations.

"Well, that's enough for now," Dubinsky concluded. "Do we agree?" Feinglass and Lucchi agreed. Dubinsky shook hands with them and reminded them that this conference with him, and all the accepted decisions, were not for publication. Only Feinglass's trusted lieutenants could know about the conference.

Months later, a week before the elections for paid union officials was held, Feinglass called a meeting of the union leaders and told them that President Meany had issued an order to Gorman that the present union leaders who were Communists must be removed from office and their names must not appear on the ballot. "And," he added, "unfortunately, Meany's orders must be carried out in the interests of the union and the workers. There is no other alternative. And —"

"That's not news," Jack Schneider shouted out. "You, Feinglass, have known about this for several months, and I have already known this for a long time."

"How did you know? Who told you such a thing?" Feinglass asked Jack.

And Jack answered: "David Dubinsky told me about the conference with you and Lucchi and Gorman! Yes, and he also told me that as president of the International Fur and Leather Workers Union, your wages were $7,000 a year, and now as vice-president of the Butchers' Union, your wages are $47,000 a year. Forty thousand dollars is a lot more than thirty pieces of silver! Do you understand what I am saying, Brother Feinglass?" And Jack marched out of the meeting. That was the end of the meeting.

I was working in a fur shop. My hands, which for thirty years had not cut even a single fur coat, knew that I had to "make a living." They quickly regained their old skill. Thirty years before, I had worked 44 hours a week, eight hours a day, and four hours on Saturday. Now I worked seven hours a day, five days a week. The wages for 35 hours had been raised quite a bit. True, the workers now produced better and even a little more in the seven hours than in the eight hours before. But the profits of the manufacturers kept on growing.

Lost

I waited and I waited, and although I knew that the fascistic, reactionary wave was still sweeping the country and every corner of the government, I still hoped that the Court of Appeals would save me from having to go to jail. My lawyers were sure that they would win because the jury members had reported that FBI agents had visited them and demanded that they find Ben Gold "guilty." Moreover, the foreman of the jury had declared openly in court that the FBI agents had come to his home and demanded his promise that he would vote that Gold was guilty, and he therefore doubted whether he would be able to make a just and impartial decision in this case, and he had resigned from the jury.

But corrupt, reactionary judges have a way of becoming deaf, dumb and blind when it suits them, and they sometimes lose their understanding of justice and the law. And yes, the judges of the United States Court of Appeals were not ashamed to hand down the judgment that Ben Gold was guilty and should be put behind bars. So now I had to wait for the Supreme Court to hand down its verdict.

Where did I get money for the lawyers who were involved in all my appeals? The workers collected and set up a fund of a few tens of thousands of dollars for my defense. They brought their contributions to the union. The lawyers took only a few thousand dollars for their excellent work in my behalf. What happened to the other thousands of dollars that remained in that fund? I do not know.

And so I waited for the Supreme Court decision. But, as it seems, the Supreme Court was in no hurry. First of all, the court calendar was clogged with important work on complicated issues, and secondly, what was the rush? So I waited quietly and patiently. The seven hours a day of work in the shop was like a game compared to the long hours I had spent each day doing the highly responsible, difficult and intense work of the union.

It was so very difficult for me to wait for the situation in the union to get better. The experienced, dedicated and principled union leaders had all been removed, and I waited and hoped that the elected leaders who had taken their places would, under Feinglass's leadership, safeguard the gains that the workers had achieved. But, alas, under the new leadership, the union lost its vigilance, its brilliance, and its determination to serve the workers. Almost every day, after work, workers would surround me and heap their complaints against the union leaders on me. I thought that maybe the protests of the workers would have an effect on Feinglass and his lieutenants. But, unfortunately, the situation became even worse.

A Gift for the Bosses

One of the most important gains made under the left-wing leadership of the union was the point in the agreement with the bosses that prohibited "contracting." The conscienceless exploiters, the contractors, did not want to close their shops and the union had to carry on a continuous and determined struggle to get rid of the contracting plague. The bosses had to hire more workers, and the enlarged shops had become union fortresses. Why did Feinglass and his helpmates give the bosses such a juicy gift? How can such a daring crime be committed by union leaders against thousands of workers be explained? Stirred up, embittered workers shouted at me: "Ben, why are you keeping quiet? Call a mass meeting, Ben!" etc., etc.

I remained silent because I knew that if I called a mass meeting, the ranks of the workers would be split. Shop strikes and protest demonstrations would certainly be employed by the workers against the union leaders, and bloody fights would be unavoidable. The bosses would win. The workers would lose. I called a meeting of a group of workers who had distinguished themselves by their activities in all the struggles of the union. Not all of them agreed with me. Those opposed to my position argued that I should start a mass protest of the workers against the treasonous Feinglass leadership, and they would control the development of such a mass opposition and at the same time avoid splits in the ranks of the workers. But the majority voted with me to wait for further developments.

Victory!

My lawyers won! The Supreme Court threw out the trial and the verdict of the lower court and ordered that I was entitled to a new trial! This was certainly a great victory for the progressive movement, which was fighting against the forces of fascism and reaction.

And then, another victory! The desperate U.S. attorney told the judge in court that it was impossible for him to conduct a second trial against Ben Gold because none of the witnesses he had used in the first trial were any longer available! So I was freed! I had won one huge victory, and then a second one!

But my deep joy did not quiet my deep pain. The mighty Fur and Leather Workers Union which had, over the years, defeated all its conscienceless and brutal enemies and had won the first 40-hour week and then a 35-hour week for the workers — the union that had almost doubled the wages of the workers and won other improvements for them — the union with which I had been involved for almost my entire life — was being ruined and destroyed under the present bankrupt leadership and I could not escape from the accusations of the workers who yelled at me: "You, Ben, carry the responsibility. It is your fault. You helped elect that personage to be the president of our union!"

In Florida

For a whole series of reasons, and also because my health was not quite what it had been, I moved away from New York and settled in Florida. From the reports that I received from my New York friends, it was clear that the situation in the union was critical and was steadily getting worse. I began to question whether the reports I was getting were completely true, because I couldn't imagine that thousands of workers were slaving in the open shops of the contractors and that the union leaders acted as if this tragic problem did not exist.

Unbelievable?!!

Suddenly! For the first time in the history of the Furriers Union, the manager, the assistant manager, a business agent and the manager of the organization department were arrested and accused of selling out the workers over a long period of time for many thousands of dollars that they had received from the bosses.

Mr. Feinglass called meetings to calm the embittered, angry workers. At these meetings, he shouted that the union leaders were not guilty, that it was all a "frame-up"! He personally guaranteed that the accused union officials were loyal, devoted fighters for the interests of the workers. The accused union leaders swore at meetings with the workers "by all that was holy" that they were innocent and that they had served the workers to the best of their abilities.

But when the trial began, and as it unfolded, the union members who had built their progressive, militant, idealistic union which had been the pride of the progressive labor movement, were enshrouded in gloom and grief. Soon after the trial opened, Mr. Glasser, an important representative of the bosses' association, testified on the witness stand that he had, over a long period of time, collected tens of thousands of dollars from bosses and had given these thousands to the manager and assistant manager of the union.

Then other wealthy, respected bosses swore on the witness stand that they had paid thousands of dollars to a "collector" for the union leaders.

The U.S. attorney asked the gentlemen manufacturers how they knew that the money they paid to the "collector" was actually handed over to the union leaders. The bosses answered that since they had been paying, they were able to employ open-shop contractors without any interference from the union. They explained in court that in these contracting shops, the workers received much lower wages, and there were no union conditions, and that was why the contractors produced fur coats much more cheaply than did the union shops.

Then a business agent, one of Feinglass's "principled union leaders," confessed while on the witness stand that he had "taken." To the question posed by the U.S. attorney as to how much he used to take from a boss, the brave business agent answered: "From a hundred and up."

The union members were in mourning. On the corner of Seventh Avenue and 30th Street, where the furriers always gathered during their lunch hour and after work to discuss various problems, they now talked about the sad news of the trial. Now the workers understood why there had been a real epidemic of sweat-shop contracting firms, and why the union leaders had pretended to know nothing about this terrible plague. Now the workers understood why the contracting open-shop sweatshops were employing thousands of workers, while the union shops were now employing only two thousand workers. Many union members could not control their tears. Others could not control their anger and they cursed Feinglass and his corrupt helpmates.

An Opposition

When the union officials were found guilty of taking graft, the workers demanded that Feinglass throw the grafters out of their union offices. They also demanded that he call in an impartial committee from the labor movement to investigate all the facts in the graft accusations, and if the committee should find these gentlemen guilty, they should be expelled from the union. When Feinglass ignored these demands, the workers organized an opposition group which carried on an open battle against Feinglass's disastrous leadership. "At meetings with the workers," they said, "he shouts about his devoted service to the struggle of the workers, but in the union, he is deaf and blind and neither sees nor hears nor knows that his friends are selling out the workers, and he claims to know nothing about the open-shop contracting epidemic." And "poor Feinglass doesn't know that under his unfortunate leadership, the union has only two thousand members left and is in danger of going under completely," etc., etc.

Feinglass tried to act as if this opposition was powerless and would not last very long. The opposition group hired a progressive attorney, who informed Feinglass that he would bring charges against him of taking one hundred thousand dollars out of the union to pay for the lawyers who defended the grafters, without the knowledge or the approval of the union membership. Feinglass became frightened. When Feinglass's lawyer explained to him that the charges were of a serious nature, and that if they came to court, the opposition group would unquestionably win, Feinglass and his friends decided to use practical methods to disarm and quiet the opposition. He used all his intelligence and powers of persuasion until he succeeded in convincing the leaders of the opposition that paid union positions were much more practical than "playing with the opposition." And with the help of Feinglass and his colleagues, a few of the opposition leaders were elected to paid positions in the union. And that was the end of the opposition.

"Let's Make Amends"

For twenty years, I avoided Feinglass. For twenty years, I neither saw him nor spoke to him. He certainly knew that several times I had warned the workers that he would bring about the ruination of the union, but apparently it was no big deal to him what I and my friends thought of him. His extremely well-paying position in the union was, for him, the highest achievement.

But suddenly, twenty years later, in 1976, I received a letter from Mr. Feinglass in which he informed me that "the Fur & Leather Department of the Amalgamated Meat Cutters & Butcher Workmen of North America, AFL-CIO, is planning a conference in Washington in May, 1976, and the leadership of this department is inviting you to address the conference. What's past is past. Let us make up." He added that the president of the International Union, Joseph Belsky, and its international secretary-treasurer, Pat Gorman, would also be at the conference.

Why all of a sudden? Brother Feinglass knew that for many years I had judged him an enemy of the workers, and therefore my enemy. Why, then, did he dare to invite me, the condemned Communist, to a conference of an AFL-CIO union? The answer to both of these questions is that Gorman advised him — no, ordered him — to invite me to this conference.

I received several letters from my friends about the invitation to the conference. Some of them asked that I come to it and that in my speech, I should disclose the tragic conditions in the union. They asked for my help in trying to save the union from going under.

A second group — a small number of my old friends — let me know that they wanted to print and distribute a leaflet among the furriers before the conference in Washington began, and they asked my permission to have my name included as one of the signators of this leaflet. They also said that without my name, they would not put out the leaflet. The leaflet they wanted to put out took the form of a "conversation" with Feinglass about his leadership:

1. They asked Feinglass why he had gone back on his word about contracting in the new agreement. Why did the agreement read "contracting allowed" instead of "contracting forbidden"? Why did he hand the bosses such a golden egg?

2. Why did he, Feinglass, allow the bosses to employ open-shop contractors? Four thousand workers were slaving in the contracting shops for low wages and no union conditions, while in the union shops, there were only 2,500 workers. Why did he, Feinglass, hand over such a golden gift to the bosses and ruin our union?

3. "And when your friends, who led the union with your help and under your supervision, were arrested, brought to trial and found guilty of selling out the workers for thousands of dollars in graft that the bosses paid, you did not condemn the grafters, but shouted that they were innocent. Why? Were you afraid of these grafters? And, Brother Feinglass, you are not deaf and not blind, and you have enough experience in union leadership. How did you not know that there was something rotten in the union leadership?

4. "And Mr. Feinglass, how did you dare to take a hundred thousand dollars from the union to pay the lawyers who defended the grafters without the knowledge or approval of the union membership? That is theft! Did you think it would not be discovered that such a sum was missing from the union treasury? You knew that the grafters had

enough thousands to pay their own lawyers' fees. Why did *you* have to pay the lawyers to save the union grafters? And why with union money?

"Mr. Feinglass, you have distinguished yourself with your leadership. Your devoted friends, the grafters, amassed a considerable fortune from the thousands that the bosses paid them, and you, Abe Feinglass, from your wages — fifty thousand dollars a year, and maybe more. In all these years of your leadership, you have probably amassed quite a fortune yourself. And the bosses? Their profits have grown every year. But the workers have lost. The mighty, progressive furriers union stands at the brink of ruination.

"We are appealing to you, Mr. Feinglass, that at the conference in Washington, you explain that you have done enough already and resign from your post! Get out of the union! Get lost!

"And we appeal to Brother Gorman that he should remove all the close friends of the grafters, who are also Mr. Feinglass's lieutenants, from their posts, and that their positions should be filled by workers who built the union. They will mobilize the union members in the struggle to save the union from destruction."

My Answer

To those friends who asked me to accept Feinglass's invitation to the conference, I suggested that they speak to Gorman to see if he would agree that the conference should decide the following:

1. That the manufacturers who had paid graft to the union leaders so that the union would not interfere with their employing open-shop contractors, had broken the agreement with the union and should be punished. The impartial chairman and the conference committee, made up of representatives of the union and of the bosses, should decide what the punishment should be, and the bosses should present a list of the contractors they employed and should not employ open-shop contractors any more. If the manufacturers did not abide by the decision of the conference committee, they should be excluded from the bosses' association.

2. The union and the bosses' association should hire well-known and trustworthy accountants to examine the books of the hundreds of bosses who employed open-shop contractors. The union should present the facts about these bosses. The reports of the accountants should be presented to the conference committee, for them to decide.

3. Under Feinglass's leadership, the graft system operated and the epidemic of the open shops spread each year, unchecked. Now the union was on the brink of ruination. This showed that Feinglass was either incapable or dishonest and should be removed from leadership. A management committee of three able and principled individuals should take his place.

4. An organization committee of the best, most active union work-ers should begin the daily job of unionizing the workers in the open shops.

5. Mr. Feinglass should pay back the one hundred thousand dollars that he had taken from the union without the knowledge of the union membership to pay the lawyers who defended the grafters. This money should be used for organizing the open shops.

If Mr. Gorman would agree to all these points, I would come to the conference in Washington and would gladly help the union in its organizational work, without any pay.

Well? Well, my friends did not talk with Gorman, and I did not come to the conference.

To my other group of friends, about the matter of the leaflet, I answered that I lived in Florida and did not want to sign any leaflets about the situation or the conditions of the union in New York

Epilogue

In Florida

So what did I do in my later years in Florida? In the course of a few years, I wrote three books which were published. What prompted me to undertake such a delicate subject as writing books? I had never belonged to any literary organizations; I had never attended any lectures on literature. I had not even read many books, because I never had the time! Day and night, I was involved in the struggles of the exploited workers. But still I wanted to write books! Was it *chutzpah?* No — something else: When my dear comrades went to Spain to fight against the Fascist murderers, despite the fact that they knew that their lives were in danger, I had decided to write a book and dedicate it to these heroic, principled fighters. But where does one get the time? Each day, from morning until late at night, I was busy with the stormy union activities. Each week, I decided to set Sundays aside for my writing, but I could not carry out this decision of mine.

But it is a well-known fact that I have something that is called "luck." All the attempts of the powers-that-be to put me behind bars were unsuccessful. A few times I had been sentenced, but the Supreme Court had said "No — Ben Gold is a friend of mankind" — and I was free. All the attempts of the gangsters and the police to cripple me were unsuccessful, etc. Luck! Once more, my luck came along to help me. The influenza, which wrought such havoc in New York, hit me, too, and I lay in bed cooking with a very high fever.

I ran that high fever for two days, and on the third day, it went down a little, and the bed was brutally uncomfortable for my weakened body, so I dragged myself off the bed and sat down on a chair near my desk, on which there was always plenty of writing paper and a pen. And the idea hit me that at last I had the opportunity to begin to write the book dedicated to the heroic comrades who had gone to fight the Fascist murderers in Spain. I took the pen in hand and it went smoothly and without the slightest exertion.

When the doctor came to find out if I was still alive, he became angry with me and ordered me to get right back into bed and not to

197

dare to get out of bed again without his permission. But the bed pressed mercilessly against me, and the people who were waiting there, inside the book which I had begun to write, were asking me not to leave them in the middle of their story, and I obeyed. I crawled out of bed again and worked with my pen. When the doctor came again, I was back in bed, and he was pleased that I was following his orders.

Finally, the doctor permitted me to get out of bed and even to write when I wanted to. When the doctor came for his last visit, I had already finished my book titled "Avreml Brodie." Finished? Yes. But who knew if my effort was worth seeing the light of day? So I invited three of my comrades — my old friends and union leaders — Potash, Schneider and Winogradsky — to decide whether my pen work deserved to be published. I was sure that if my writing did not meet with their approval, they would not be shy and would let me know the truth in simple, clear and friendly words.

Well, we spent an interesting evening. I read them one chapter after another, and my friends sat quietly and listened as if I were reading an important document. When I finished reading, my friends' faces lit up. We had a lively discussion about everything and everybody about whom I had written. They all agreed that it should be published as soon as possible.

Encouraged by my friends' enthusiastic opinions, I telephoned Mr. Friedman, then the manager of the *Freiheit,* and asked him to come to the union to talk about an important matter with me. Our talk did not last long. I told him that I was giving my book to the *Freiheit.* It was possible that the book would bring in a little profit, but if there should be any losses incurred, we, the union leaders, would cover the losses.

Friedman gave the book to the talented *Freiheit* writer, Naphtoli Buchwald, so that he could decide, first, if my pen-work deserved to be published, and secondly, if he should like it, would he edit it? A few days later, Naphtoli telephoned me and invited me to his home to discuss my book. Of course, I was happy that he praised my writing efforts, although I understood that his songs of praise were a bit exaggerated, to encourage me to continue my writing. But to his demand that I write five more books, I answered: "I have no time and no desire to write books, but I will try."

The *Freiheit* published my book, and it sold over four thousand copies. At that time, many years ago, when there were tens of thousands of Jewish workers employed in the needle trades, there were many workers, especially among the left-wingers, who bought and read Yiddish books. But today? What once was, is no more.

I didn't even think about writing a second book. I was flooded with important union problems and busy with the complicated and strenuous tasks involved with organizing the thousands of fur workers who were slaving in the open shops in the United States and Canada. I was busy with strikes, conferences and obstinate bosses, from whom I had to wrest higher wages and better working conditions for the workers. In New York, thousands of fur workers were on strike for eighteen weeks before they won their demands. I didn't even think about writing. But when, finally, almost all the union battles were over and the results were successful, I was able to stop and catch my breath. Then, in the more or less quiet hours, I wrote a second book of short stories and called it "Mentschn" (Persons).

But no more! I wrote no more. World tragedy broke out! Hitler set a torch to the world. And when the terrible war was over, the American government launched the cursed cold war, and the wild, fascist reaction and McCarthyism came like a tidal wave over the country. The leaders of the Communist Party were locked up in prison, and the leaders of the CIO sank low to become the partners of the reactionary rulers and joined forces with Meany, the treacherous leader of the AFL. America, the giant land, which boasted about its freedoms and prided itself as the land of democracy, stood on the threshhold of Fascism. I forgot about the matter of writing books. The Fur and Leather Workers Union was embroiled in its struggle against the wild enemies of the working class — the enemies of mankind — the leaders of the cold war, who were expending all their energies to achieve their goal of a third world war. I did not have either the time or the desire to write.

Many years later, when I was no longer young and was settled in Florida, the days, the evenings and the nights were mine. So I busied myself with my pen, and with a minimum of effort, I wrote three books: "Lucky Jim," then "In Those Days" and "The Storm in Riverville."

And that was all. I didn't write any more because my dear friends in New York were working very hard to collect money to pay the printer, then were busy with the printer, and then involved in selling my books. How long could I allow myself to exploit my friends?

And the main reason my desire to write was dampened was that people were no longer buying Yiddish books. Despite the fact that the famous poet and essayist, Ben Green, praised all three of my books in the *Morning Freiheit,* and despite the fact that even that wonderful magazine, *Soviet Homeland,* which was filled with literary gems every month, praised my three books, they did not sell as well as was expected. Well, my pen and I got divorced.

So why did I suddenly, so many years after my last book, decide to write my sixth book — "My Memoirs"? First, because my comrades, with whom I grew up in the progressive labor movement, insisted that I "must" — that I have a debt to pay to the workers who fought all those years for their progressive union and who contributed so much to the progressive forces of the labor movement. Secondly, I have of late received letters from what seems to be well-meaning people who inform me that they want to write books about the left-wing labor movement. One letter writer let me know that he had graduated from a university and wanted to publish a monthly magazine about the left-wing labor movement, and that he was ready to come to Florida to speak with me about the Furriers Union.

In April, 1982, I received a letter from a lawyer in Brussels, Belgium who was writing a book about the Jewish labor movement in Europe and in the United States and who knew that I was president of the Furriers Union. He asked me to write a little about my involvement and send it to him. I sent him a copy of Philip Foner's book, "The Fur and Leather Workers Union."

So I decided to write briefly my recollections of all those years of union involvement. It satisfied my friends. And if I should receive any more letters asking me about my union activities, I will send the letter writers copies of my memoirs. I have omitted several somewhat important events because I did not intend to write a "fat" book. What was most important and most necessary, I have noted briefly.

It is possible that among the readers of my memoirs, there will be some individuals who will be unable or unwilling to believe that the highest elected, anointed and crowned leaders of the AFL and of the Socialist Party should join forces with bosses and hire gangsters to butcher strikers and to murder left-wing union leaders. And it is not impossible that someone of the right-wing school will rant and rave that everything I have written in my short memoirs is untrue, is Communist propaganda, etc.

I want to point out once more that in his history, "The Fur and Leather Workers Union," Philip Foner has reprinted many letters and other documents which show the traitorous and criminal acts committed by the AFL and the Socialist leaders. These letters were written and signed by the degenerate persons who held the high positions of leadership in the AFL and in the Socialist Party. Even the greatest magician cannot twist, interpret or minimize these incontrovertible proofs.

I find it necessary to answer an important question: "From what source did the small and financially poor Furriers Union get the strength to reward its murderous enemies, after a bloody fight of ten years' duration, with such a decisive defeat?"

Certainly, the thousands of fur workers distinguished themselves with their solidarity, their determined, courageous and heroic resistance, which amazed their enemies and paralyzed their bands of murderers.

But without the principled, devoted leaders of the left-wing union, the historic, victorious struggle of the workers would have been impossible.

The millions of workers in the American trade unions also have the

200

strength to defeat their enemies, and, like the fur workers, they also have the power to fight for and win a 35-hour week, higher wages, and better working conditions. But their union leaders don't even think about making such demands for their workers. Workers who would want to demand such improvements would be shouted down by their union leaders as "Communist trouble-makers," and might be risking their jobs.

Even worse: It is widely known and an established fact that in very many unions, the leaders receive high wages, but the bosses pay them more than they get from the unions. It is also widely known that some union leaders are connected with the underworld gangsters and racketeers who use the unions for their businesses, which bring in lots of money. These union leaders are the tragedy of the American working class.

When the lucky day will come, and the workers will free their unions from the demagogues, the gangsters and the thieves who serve the bosses, the American labor movement will take its deserved, honorable and important place in this country, and the millions of exploited, robbed and oppressed workers will bless the day of their liberation.